DIVERSIFIED
THEOLOGICAL EDUCATION
Equipping All God's People

ROSS KINSLER, EDITOR

WILLIAM CAREY INTERNATIONAL UNIVERSITY PRESS
PASADENA, CALIFORNIA

WILLIAM CAREY INTERNATIONAL UNIVERSITY PRESS

William Carey International University Press
publishes works that further the university's objective
to prepare men and women to discover and address
the roots of human problems around the world.

Published by
William Carey International University

1539 East Howard Street
Pasadena, California 91104

Ross Kinsler, Editor
Diversified Theological Education:
Equipping All God's People

Cover Illustration: Jonathan Pon

Library of Congress Control Number: 2007943660

ISBN: 978-0-86585-004-0

First Edition, January 2008

*Printed in the United States of America
on acid free paper*

CONTENTS

FOREWORD

$\mathbf{O}$ne of the most creative and widespread movements of theological education in our time has been called Theological Education by Extension, which is usually identified with a small experiment beginning in the 1960s in Guatemala, Central America. In 1973, when I was on staff of the Theological Education Fund of the World Council of Churches, we invited Ross Kinsler, who was deeply involved in the Guatemala experiment, to present a case study at our annual meeting, which carried the theme, *Learning in Context*. The case studies from that meeting were then published with a sub-title, *The Search for Innovative Patterns in Theological Education*. Two years later I invited Ross to a conference organized by the Theology Department of the South African Council of Churches and the Association of Southern African Theological Institutions, which was held in Johannesburg and which launched the Theological Education by Extension College in 1976. Shortly thereafter I returned to South Africa, and Ross took my place on staff of what was then called the Programme on Theological Education of the WCC. From that vantage point he was able to follow the TEE movement around the world. In 1983 he edited an anthology of case studies under the name, *Ministry by the People: Theological Education by Extension*.

Almost 25 years have gone by since then, and we are now invited by this publication, also edited by Ross, to consider recent developments and new possibilities of this remarkable movement. The fundamental concern and foundation of TEE remain the same: the biblical foundation that all God's people are called to ministry and mission and the concern to enable all to gain relevant skills for their mission. The case studies offered here demonstrate ongoing creativity, so much so that a new name is proposed in the title for this anthology: *Diversified Theological Education*. The current debate about theological education has moved beyond the earlier polarization, TEE vs. residential training, as all of us are encouraged to integrate diverse models and methods however best to provide access to and quip all God's people for their mission.

Readers will want to pay particular attention to the Preface and the opening chapter, which set the stage for consideration of the following case studies and reflection on their own experiences in theological education with a sense of urgency in the face of devastating threats to life in the twenty-first century.

Desmond Tutu
Archbishop Emeritus

Preface

book on theological education is unlikely to catch many readers'
attention, and it may seem improbable that this book can have any meaningful
connection with current debates about global justice, the destruction of the
environment, and the wellbeing of peoples everywhere. On the other hand,
relevant theological education today must surely make connections with these
urgent realities we all must face, and we might even expect these realities to
become the conscious context for all theological education.

This anthology of theological education case studies goes back to the
birth of a movement called Theological Education by Extension in the early
1960s and another anthology of reports co-published in 1983 by the WCC
and Orbis Books under the title, *Ministry by the People: Theological Education
by Extension*. Since that time TEE has continued to reach out to large numbers
of people in Africa, Asia, Latin America, the Caribbean, Australia, the South
Pacific, North America, and elsewhere, and the wider theological education
family has continued to diversify, often combining residential and extension
or distance education models. So we have felt the need to prepare this new
collection of case studies under a new title, *Diversified Theological Education:
Equipping All God's People*.

Our primary concern here is mission, that is, the mission of theological
education in terms of the churches' mission and, above all, God's mission
in today's world. More specifically we want to explore the reality and the
potential of emerging, diverse approaches to theological education in response
to the two great threats to life in the twenty-first century: economic injustice,

which lies behind the death by hunger and other poverty related causes of at least 30,000 people a day, and ecological destruction, which may well cause far greater death and destruction among future generations. The case studies of Diversified Theological Education presented in this volume demonstrate some of the ways that theological education is now reaching out widely among "the people of God" at all levels, but especially among the poor, the marginalized, the ones most in need of and responsive to the call for justice and ecological integrity and wholeness.

The central concern of Theological Education by Extension and Diversified Theological Education is **access**. TEE and DTE models of theological education have made enormous progress in the urgent task of opening access to and equipping all God's people for ministry and mission. This has many interrelated dimensions.

Geographical access

Traditional, centralized patterns of theological education have reached out primarily to those who could leave home, community, employment, and the local church for extended periods of full-time study. By decentralizing and diversifying its programs, theological education can reach out across regions and entire countries to growing numbers of local leaders, the very ones most capable of guiding their churches and communities in their struggles for spiritual and socio-economic life, without causing them to leave home, community, employment, and the local church.

Economic access

The cost of theological education drops considerably when the students remain within their local base of support. Institutional resources can serve many times the number served in centralized programs, and the students themselves, even those who are poor, instead of giving up their normal means of employment, are able not only to support themselves but also to contribute significantly to their academic expenses. And they do not enter into a process of economic dependence on the churches, as usually happens in traditional, centralized programs.

Cultural access

Decentralized programs can adapt to the cultural and linguistic diversity of their constituencies, as these students normally study at home and meet within their own local realities, though they may occasionally gather with wider constituencies for special activities. Centralized programs tend to homogenize their social and academic work, obscuring the cultural and linguistic diversity which the students and their churches represent.

Ecclesiastical access

Due to the high cost per candidate of centralized programs, many churches have traditionally selected for theological training only candidates for ordained ministry, and only those interested in becoming ordained ministers should apply. Decentralized programs open wide the door to theological education and ministry to any and all members of the churches, and this can play a significant role in challenging and overcoming elitism and professionalism in the churches.

Gender access

Women have traditionally been marginalized from theological education, and they have largely been limited to ministries with women and children, reinforcing sexism and patriarchy in the churches. Decentralized theological education can readily open the doors of theological education and ministry to women as well as men, though the full participation of women often requires a whole range of shifts in orientation, vision, and practice.

Race access

Many centralized theological education programs still marginalize "second class" minorities or majorities through educational standards and other requirements set by the dominant culture. Decentralized programs can adapt much more readily to the standards and leadership patterns and orientations of diverse racial-ethnic groups.

Class access

In many regions theological education and ministry are oriented toward high academic and professional standards that alienate the poor from leadership and tend to orient the churches to certain class expectations. Decentralized programs can operate at very diverse socio-economic levels simultaneously and work to overcome class biases.

Differing abilities access

Centralized institutions can make adjustments for greater physical access for those who can get there, but decentralization offers more comprehensive access to persons of differing physical, emotional, and mental abilities.

Pedagogical access

Traditional, centralized theological education tends to build its curricula on institutional tools—professors with advanced degrees, large library resources, heavy academic demands on the students, classes dominated by one way lectures, etc. Decentralized programs offer the entire learning process in the context of the living realities of family, church, community, and work, even while making use of basic academic tools, and they develop a pattern of lifelong learning within the vicissitudes of life in church and family and community.

Spiritual access

Centralized theological education tends to communicate the sense that God's Spirit is to be found there in the theological institution and its accouterments. Decentralized theological education is more likely to communicate the understanding that God's Spirit is to be found precisely in the struggles for full participation identified in the previous paragraphs, i.e., in the struggles of all God's people for fullness of life.

The case studies gathered for this anthology offer to readers, especially those who are involved in or concerned about theological education, an opportunity to explore widely diverse programs in widely diverse contexts. The opening chapter provides a socio-economic-ecological analysis of our global context, offers a biblical foundation for God's mission in this global context, and identifies some essential educational components for Theological Education by Extension and Diversified Theological Education. Subsequent chapters present the case studies, each one ending with some questions for reflection and discussion. Our hope is that each case will stimulate critical and creative thinking about the model presented and about the models experienced by the reader or readers. None of these cases should be considered ideal or universal, but all of them are capable of opening up important possibilities, basic issues, and ongoing concerns.

The writers of these case studies did not see the opening chapter before preparing their contributions, but their pioneer efforts have inspired the editor to articulate the challenges set forth in this chapter. These challenges are as much for them as for all of us. The case studies bring to our attention new possibilities for the mobilization of all God's people for God's mission.

We affirm that theological education is called to equip all God's people for God's mission in the world, which we now understand to be four-fold: personal, ecclesial, social, and ecological. We believe that TEE and DTE are given a special calling within that general calling, which is to engage and equip all God's people at all levels, but especially at the most basic levels, for the work of human and ecological transformation. That is why we have begun this conversation with reference to access. With our Latin American colleagues we have learned that the preferential subjects (protagonists) for the work of human transformation are the exploited and marginalized poor, the ever-oppressed women, the ignored and depreciated indigenous and "minority" peoples of many lands and languages, the differently abled, the disenfranchised and unemployed young and elderly, and so many others. These are all now present in our churches, and they are gaining access to extension or diversified theological education. The challenge we now face in the TEE/DTE movement is not simply to engage more people in theological education but to build among God's chosen, especially those who are despised and neglected, the movement for human transformation that began with Jesus among the poor, the sick, the possessed, the marginalized, and the oppressed of first-century Palestine.

Not all readers of these case studies and not all the writers of these case studies share these same priorities. Fair enough. But we feel the need to state at the outset our bias and invite all to join the debate and the movement. The urgency of life and death in today's world demands no less. And with God's Spirit the possibilities for creative theological education are unlimited.

- An ecumenical program in Zambia offers a very basic TEE program that has already reached some 10,000 local church leaders, and one of their priorities is to equip them to train others to confront the HIV & AIDS pandemic, which has devastated life for so many. What might be the impact of this work of grass roots theological education for the prevention and healing of HIV & AIDS, if it were extended all across Africa?

- The TEE College of Southern Africa, based in Johannesburg, is now the principal theological education program in that region. Almost 3000 students are studying for diplomas at high school, college, and degree levels. They have just gone through a transformation of their curriculum in conformity with the government's mandate for Outcomes Based Education. This case study lays out the new materials in some detail.

- The Organization of African Instituted Churches, founded in 1978, has given priority to the development of TEE programs in 22 countries and seven regions that respond to the cultural and religious realities of thousands of charismatic, indigenous church movements with almost 60 million members.

- The Senate of Serampore College, which accredits all theological education in India plus neighboring countries (over 50 institutions), has opened a new office in Calcutta under the name Senate Center for Extension and Pastoral Theological Research. SCEPTRE oversees several decentralized programs throughout Southern Asia: the Diploma in Christian Studies, the Bachelor's of Christian Studies, and the Doctor of Ministry.

- Nepal is predominantly Hindu (80%), Buddhist (10%), and Muslim (4%), but Christianity is growing rapidly (perhaps reaching 3% of the population). In response a TEE program with a primary focus on discipleship and leadership was launched in 1995 and by 2004 had enrolled 3600 students. This case study includes an extensive evaluation and testimonies.

- A theological center located in Canberra, Australia has joined ranks with a university with electronic capabilities, and this is enabling them to offer theological training at several academic levels, including doctoral studies, to local leaders all across that island continent.

- The Latin American Biblical University, based in San José, Costa Rica, has built up a network of 14 partners/centers in 10 countries to serve some 2000 students at degree levels with a contextual, diversified curriculum and another 2000 at a more popular level through its Pastoral Bible Institute and a larger number of partners throughout the region.

- A TEE program in Argentina, directed by a Pentecostal pastor, is providing theological training for hundreds of pastors in the major cities, most of whom have never been able to go to a seminary. They have found an opening to federal prisons, and right now 500 prison inmates are finalizing their theological training with the assignment for each student prisoner to disciple 10 others, which would include some 10% of the national prison population.

- The Women's Pastoral Program of the Central American Center for Pastoral Studies offers women throughout that region holistic training to confront the challenges of daily life, to contribute to the development of their families, churches, and communities, to eradicate violence, and to promote justice and live in equality. In 2005 a total of 3007 women participated in courses, workshops, celebrations, and other CEDEPCA events.

- The Latin American Doctoral Program offers a radical alternative to most Ph.D. programs through selection of outstanding faculty and students, intensive seminars and tutorials with extensive preparation and follow-up, institutional support and accompaniment by mentors, a focus on research method, and specialization in the field of ecclesiology or missiology, ending with a dissertation. This case study provides a summary of its first five years.

- The Native Ministries Consortium has brought together indigenous ("First Nations") leaders of various denominations in Canada and the U.S. to design and direct a unique combination of theological education resources (The TEE Center in Northern British Colombia, Vancouver School of Theology, Cook Theological School of Arizona, the SEAN materials from Latin America, and others) to offer contextual, decentralized training for ministry in Native communities.

- Fuller Theological Seminary is "the largest and most diverse theological seminary in North America" with well over 4000 students representing over 100 denominations and 67 countries. "Fuller produces more Ph.D.s than any other seminary in the world," and its Doctor of Ministry program, with 600 students in the U.S., Canada, Korea, and Australia, "is the largest program of its kind in the world." Less than half of all these students study or live on the Pasadena, California campus. Fuller's M.Div. program, which provides the basic training for ministry in most North American denominations, enrolls some 900 students each year at nearly 20 sites in 4 regions throughout the Western states. This case study focuses primarily on the new Master of Arts in Global Leadership, which makes extensive use of electronic media for distance education.

- The Open Russian Theological Academy has launched TEE for local leaders of small congregations scattered across the vast regions of the Far East of Russia, and these resources are now being shared with programs among the ex-Soviet states of Central Asia, where new churches require new leaders.

This is just a very small sampling of what is now going on in the movement we have called TEE and DTE. Our hope is that these reports and testimonies will inspire many others, those who are already in this movement and others who will take up the challenge to equip all God's people for God's mission in today's threatened world.

As we review the story of TEE and DTE, Gloria and I are personally overwhelmed by the opportunities and challenges we have been given, by the dedication and service of grass roots theological educators we have met in many places, and by the contributions of close friends throughout this journey.

At the very beginning, as neophytes at the Presbyterian Seminary of Guatemala, we had the great privilege of working with colleagues such as José Carrera and his wife Rosa, Baudilio and Alma Recinos, Nelly and Benjamín Jacobs, and Jim and Gennet Emery, and we recognize that it was the genius of Jim Emery and Ralph Winter that gave birth to Theological Education by Extension in the early 1960s and launched a global movement.

Then we were thrown into the ecumenical world of the World Council of Churches in Geneva, in particular its Program on Theological Education, and our closest colleagues were Aharon Sapsezian, Shoki Coe, Marjorie Sandle, Sam Amirtham, and John Pobee.

The next stop along the way was the Southern California Extension Center of San Francisco Theological Seminary, where we enjoyed the support of John Hadsell, Jo'Ann DeQuattro, Edmundo Vásquez, Don Smith, Eugenia Cloud, Dan Newhall, and Charles Marks.

Our next big assignment came from the Latin American Biblical Seminary in Costa Rica, which while we were there became the Latin American Biblical University with a network of centers and partners throughout the region and the vision of colleagues such as Elsa Tamez and José Duque, Rubén Lores, Irene and Dick Foulkes, Jaime Prieto and Silvia de Lima, Pablo Richard, Roy and Janet May, Arturo Piedra, José Enrique Ramírez, Elizabeth Cook, Mireya Baltodano and Nidia Fonseca.

We now find ourselves in Southern California among good friends whose contributions to the struggle for justice, peace, and life in fullness for all creation give us great hope in a world of privation and despair: Bob and Hedy Lodwick, Darrel Meyers, Ched Myers and Elaine Enns, Rick Kidd, Marty Coleman, Rosemary Guzmán, Merilie Robertson, Bob and Barbara Miller, Pat Krommer, Edie Gause, Ted Von der Ahe, and others.

The proposal to gather and publish case studies of programs of Diversified Theological Education was first articulated at an International Consultation on Theological Education by Extension and Technology at Vancouver School of Theology, June 2–6, 1997. It was again proposed at a similar meeting at VST, August 8–12, 2004. The challenge was taken up by the writers listed on p. 296, and through them it is now extended widely to all who are involved in and concerned about equipping all God's people for God's mission. For future contact with this movement see www.theteenet.net.

Ross Kinsler

Chapter 1

EQUIPPING ALL GOD'S PEOPLE FOR GOD'S MISSION

by Ross Kinsler

One of the extraordinary challenges of the twenty-first century is the rise of religion as a major player in the lives and movements of people everywhere. Each religious community separately and all of them together, insofar as is possible, are facing urgent questions about their understanding of and response to the great threats to life in our time. This chapter will focus on two global threats to life, economic injustice and ecological destruction, and a third comprehensive and urgent need, the need for healing and integral wellbeing throughout humankind and the biosphere. This analysis, from a socio-economic and biblical perspective, will provide a framework for our consideration of the growing potential of Theological Education by Extension (TEE) and/or Diversified Theological Education (DTE) for the equipping and mobilization of all God's people for human transformation and ecological restoration, i.e., to respond to the growing threats of economic injustice and ecological destruction and to build global and local communities for life.

This anthology is as much a challenge *to* as it is a challenge *from* the movement we have called TEE or DTE. Each author or team was simply asked to analyze their socio-economic and spiritual context, summarize their biblical-theological understanding of God's mission/the churches' mission/ the mission of their theological education program, and explain the main components of their educational model. There has been no meeting among the writers of these case studies, because they are widely scattered around the globe, but we hope that they will be the first to take up the challenges that arise out of this anthology. We can all see that the diversification and consolidation of the TEE/DTE movement offer enormous potential. Previous reports and anthologies have demonstrated the widespread growth of this movement, primarily in terms of the numbers and kinds of people who are gaining access to theological education and ministry. We believe it is now time to press upon those of us who are already in the movement, upon all who are in any way related to theological education, and upon the churches in general the challenge to take up massively the challenge to equip all God's people for God's mission in terms set forth here in this chapter.

Christianity is of course a massive movement. The question we must ask here is whether Christians are using their enormous potential to pursue today's struggles for life—human life and the life of the biosphere. This leads us to ask whether the churches' leaders are being equipped to lead their congregations and all their members and organizations in that struggle. At this point we then turn to decentralized, locally based theological education programs among those whom the churches and their communities have too often marginalized, to discover whether there is new hope for personal, ecclesial, social, and ecological transformation, not from the top down but from the margins to the center of the church's institutional life, to the church as movement. All forms of theological education hold major responsibility to incorporate and equip God's people for God's mission. The danger is that programs dedicated to "higher" academic "levels" of training and research may disqualify and marginalize local leaders. Our hope is rather that these "professional" pastors and theologians might play strategic roles in resourcing and equipping locally based, extension and diversified theological education networks.

GLOBAL CHALLENGES
From the Struggle against Apartheid in South Africa to a Worldwide Call for Justice

Thirty years ago the primary challenge for the churches of South Africa and one of the critical challenges to churches everywhere was Apartheid. The consultation that gave birth to the TEE College in Johannesburg was itself, I believe, "illegal," because it was inter-racial. Racial and socio-economic change has taken place in South Africa since then, with much to be grateful for and no doubt with deep, enduring problems. But today we face what has been called global Apartheid with many local and regional expressions of racial-economic-gender-ecological injustice.

I would like to focus briefly on this global challenge from the perspective of a recent experience within one of our church families, the World Alliance of Reformed Churches (WARC). That body, which embraces 218 Reformed,

Presbyterian, Congregational, and United denominations with 75 million members in 107 countries, chose for its 2004 General Council meeting in Accra, Ghana the text John 10:10: "...that all may have life in fullness." Something powerful happened at that meeting, which led the participants to call upon their own and other churches and ecumenical bodies to covenant for justice in the economy and the Earth. The Letter from Accra to the churches begins with these paragraphs.

> *Our most moving and memorable moments came from our visit to Elmina and Cape Coast, two "castles" on the Coast of Ghana that held those who had been captured into slavery, as they suffered in dungeons waiting for slave ships that would take them to unknown lands and destinies. Over brutal centuries, 15 million African slaves were transported to the Americas, and millions more were captured and died. On this trade in humans as commodities, wealth in Europe was built. Through their labor, sweat, suffering, intelligence and creativity, the wealth of the Americas was developed.*

> *At the Elmina Castle, the Dutch merchants, soldiers, and governor lived on the upper level, while the slaves were held in captivity one level below. We entered a room used as a church, with words from Psalm 132 on a sign still hanging above the door ("For the Lord has chosen Zion . . ."). And we imagined Reformed Christians worshipping their God while directly below them, right under their feet, those being sold into slavery languished in the chains and horror of those dungeons. For more than two centuries in that place this went on.*

> *In angry bewilderment we thought, "How could their faith be so divided from life? How could they separate their spiritual experience from the torturous physical suffering directly beneath their feet? How could their faith be so blind?" Some of us are descended from those slave traders and slave owners, and others of us are descendants of those who were enslaved. We shared responses of tears, silence, anger, and lamentation. Those who are Reformed Christians have always declared God's sovereignty over all life and all the Earth. So how could these forbears of Reformed faith deny so blatantly what they believed so clearly? Yet, as we listened to the voices today from our global fellowship, we discovered the mortal danger of repeating the same sin of those whose blindness we decried. For today's world is divided between those who worship in comfortable contentment and those enslaved by the world's economic injustice and ecological destruction who still suffer and die.*

The Letter from Accra goes on to affirm, "the world today lives under the shadow of an oppressive empire," i.e., "the gathered power of pervasive economic and political forces throughout the globe that reinforce the division between the rich and the poor." "This is not just another 'issue' to be 'addressed.' Rather, it goes to the heart of our confession of faith. . . . How can we say that we believe that Jesus Christ is the Lord over all life and not stand against all that denies the promise of fullness of life to the world?" (For other WARC documents, especially "Covenanting for Justice in the Economy and the Earth," see *www.warc.ch*.)

Those who participated in the Accra meetings and many others who have joined them to covenant for justice in the global economy and in the Earth believe that this calling is as urgent as was the call of the Confessing Church in Germany in the 1930s and 40s against National Socialism (Nazis) and the call to denounce the ideology of Apartheid in South Africa as heresy and its practice as sin in the 1970s and 80s. I believe that we must invite all theological education programs, beginning with those at the bottom through those at the top, in poor and wealthy countries, to clarify their vision and prioritize their curricula in these same terms. We hear that 30,000 people die every day of hunger, perhaps twice that number die unnecessarily every day if we include curable diseases, contaminated water, and other effects of extreme poverty, especially in Africa. (We have to remind our friends in the U.S. that the daily global toll of death by hunger is ten times the loss of life in the U.S. on that one fateful day, September 11th, 2001.)

From Ecological Destruction
to "the Great Work for This Generation"

Ecologist and poet Wendell Berry explains in his book, *The Art of the Commonplace*, that Christianity has been for over 500 years largely complicit with or indifferent to "the rape and plunder of the world." Another ecologist, Thomas Berry, expresses the extraordinary challenge faced by our generation in passionate terms in his book, *The Great Work: Our Way into the Future*.

> *We find ourselves ethically destitute just when, for the first time, we are faced with ultimacy, the irreversible closing down of the Earth's functioning in its major life systems. . . . with biocide, the extinction of the vulnerable life systems of the Earth, and geocide, the devastation of the Earth itself. (104)*

> *The labor and care expended over some billions of years and untold billions of experiments to bring forth such a gorgeous Earth is all being negated within less than a century for what we consider "progress" toward a better life in a better world. (164)*

> *The Great Work now . . . is to carry out the transition from a period of human devastation of the Earth to a period when humans would be present to the planet in a mutually beneficial manner. (3)*

To bring this eloquent, lofty challenge down to earth and to people like us, we turn to Kenyan Wangari Maathai, Nobel Peace Prize laureate for 2004. Her trajectory began in 1977 with a tree-planting campaign in response to devastating deforestation and widespread unemployment. Her work later became known around the world as the Green Belt Movement. She won a seat in Kenya's Parliament with an unprecedented 98% of the vote and also became Assistant Minister for the Environment. On receiving the Nobel Peace Prize she commented, "Protecting the global environment is directly related to securing peace." She articulates for all of us the integral relationship between peace, justice, and creation in a brief article for the September 2005 *National Geographic* magazine entitled "My Seven" concerns for Africa: Environment, Empowerment, Education, Good Government, Sustainable Development, Employment, and The Future—"to create a world that honors and rewards women."

Surely theological education, especially Theological Education by Extension and Diversified Theological Education, must carry major responsibility for taking up this challenge among and beyond the churches, which will require a paradigm shift for many, from an almost exclusively individualized concept of salvation to a personal and collective and ecological understanding of the Reign of God—before it is too late. Important resources come to us from the indigenous peoples of Africa, Latin America, and elsewhere, for their cultural and spiritual heritage values the integrity and integration of all life—person, family, community, the land, nature as a whole, and the world of the Spirit. Our churches and theological institutions will want to work, locally and regionally, with projects such as the Green Belt Movement, of which there are many, as we all struggle for justice, peace, and the integrity of creation.

From Individualized and Privatized Healing to Integral and Systemic Wholeness

No one can ignore the historic role of the Christian movement in the development of scientific medical resources with amazing achievements among those who have access to these resources. At the same time all of us must be astounded at the failure to provide basic, appropriate healthcare among the vast majority in Africa and other Three-Fourths World countries and even among significant poor populations in the so-called First World. Not too long ago it was said that a mere one billion dollars would have been sufficient to permanently eliminate the scourge of malaria, but it did not happen, and now it will take many times as much, if indeed it is now possible. Studies indicate that the great pharmaceutical companies have developed thousands of new medicines in recent years, but those related to tropical diseases, where the needs are most urgent, are just a handful. Retroviral drugs are still inaccessible for most AIDS patients in many countries.

The Prime Minister of Great Britain, Gordon Brown, has noted that thousands of African children die unnecessarily every day, that 25% of those deaths could be prevented by providing a $4 mosquito net for each child, and that half of all malaria deaths could be prevented by providing diagnosis and drugs costing $0.12 per person. The disease underlying all the others is, of course, poverty. So Brown calls on the rich countries to complete debt relief for the poorest countries, to increase development aid to achieve the Millennium Development Goals for health and education and gender equality, and to reduce global poverty by half by the year 2015. But he notes that these goals, adopted by the rich countries in 1999, have already fallen behind miserably.

> *On present progress in Sub Saharan Africa, primary education for all will, at best, be delivered not in 2015 but 2130, 115 years too late; poverty will be halved by 2150, 135 years too late; and avoidable infant deaths will be eliminated by 2165, 150 years too late. This is too long to wait for justice, too long to wait when infants are dying in Africa while the rest of the world has the medicines to heal them. ("What is Morally Unjust Cannot be Economically Correct," envío, March 2005, 50)*

> *What began as the greatest bond between rich and poor of our time is at risk of ending as the greatest betrayal of the poor by the rich of all time. As a global community we are at risk of being remembered not for what we promised to do but for what we failed to deliver, yet another set of broken hopes that break the trust of the world's people in the world's governments. (50)*

Top-down solutions, locally and globally, are most likely to fail. Among poor and wealthy countries unjust distribution of economic and healthcare resources prevails. So we must turn, sooner or later, to grassroots, community-based movements, where our churches can offer a mission and a message of integral wholeness, *shalom*, real human development. And we must ask our theological formation programs, especially TEE and DTE, what resources and models and curricula they can offer in response to these vital and urgent challenges of our time.

Good News for the Twenty-first Century

We turn now from critical analysis of today's world to the biblical roots of our faith in order to find Good News for our time and for our people, i.e., for all God's people. We have noted that the two great threats to life in the 21st century are economic injustice and ecological destruction, both of which are driven by the corporate-led, imperial, global economy, both of which bring immeasurable threats to the life of this and future generations. When we read the Bible with a concern for economics and ecology, we discover a vital thread for life running through the Hebrew and Christian Scriptures. It has been called Sabbath Economics or Jubilee Spirituality. Following is a brief introduction to this economic-spiritual paradigm, which offers Good News for the 21st century and which may provide a new vision for theological education in our time.

Jubilee and Justice

Let's begin by re-reading some biblical texts that have often been spiritualized so that their economic message is lost.

First, we observe that Jesus himself, after fasting for 40 days, is tempted (tested) to make stones into bread, and he responds to the devil, "One does not live by bread alone but by every word that comes from the mouth of God." (Mt. 4:4) It almost seems that he places "spiritual" matters or "spiritual" bread above "physical" bread and "physical" hunger. Then we find that Jesus is here quoting Dt. 8:3, which refers back to the manna story (Ex. 16), which is the first lesson for the former slaves, just delivered from Pharaoh's Egypt, about how to live in freedom. They must take only what is needed, no more, no less, and this is what the **Sabbath Day**, which is first introduced in this very passage, is meant to teach God's people. This is in direct rejection of "free enterprise," which encourages and enables some to take more than they need and forces many into poverty and even slavery. In Mt. 4:4 Jesus makes this connection in order to show us, not that bread is unimportant, but that we are to ensure that all have enough bread and none of us has more than enough. This is the critical word that comes from the mouth of God.

Next, we turn to the story of Jesus' anointing in preparation for his crucifixion and burial. The disciples complain that the ointment should have been sold and the money given to the poor, but Jesus challenges them with these enigmatic words, "You always have the poor with you." (Mt. 26:11) It seems as if Jesus discounts or minimizes their concern for the poor. But then we note that he is here quoting Dt. 15:11, which says that "there will never cease to be some in need on the earth," but it also says in v. 4 that "There will be no one in need among you" if you obey the **Sabbath Year** mandates to cancel debts and free slaves every seventh year. So in Mt. 26:11 Jesus affirms that beyond charity there is a more fundamental responsibility to break the chains of poverty by reversing the economic mechanisms that produce wealth for a few and increase poverty for many, most notably the debt/slavery system.

Lk. 4:16-21 is a key passage, located at the outset of Jesus' ministry. Here Jesus identifies himself and his mission with Is. 61:1-2a: Good News to the poor, release to the captives, sight to the blind, and liberation of the oppressed, ending with the proclamation of the year of the Lord's favor. This seems to be a reference to the **Jubilee Year** (Lv. 25), which called for not only the cancellation of debts and liberation of slaves but the return of mortgaged lands, i.e., the redistribution or restitution of lands and homes to all the families of Israel in the 50th Year, a "super Sabbath Year." It is remarkable that Luke's narration of Jesus' ministry begins not with a reference to the Kingdom of God, as do Matthew and Mark, but with this Nazareth synagogue story and its reference to "the year of the Lord's favor." Luke's Gospel does refer frequently to the Kingdom of God, but at this critical point in his narrative he chooses to identify that Kingdom with the Sabbath-Jubilee call to radical justice.

From this point we cannot but go on to the Book of Acts, which was also authored by Luke, for we find that the key passage in Acts, parallel to the Nazareth sermon in Luke, is the story of the coming of the Holy Spirit, which includes sharing in worship and table fellowship "day by day" and the distribution of the believers' possessions "as any had need" so that "there was not a needy person among them." (Ac. 2:43-47, 4:32-35) Empowered by the Spirit, they practiced the **Sabbath Day** mandate to share equitably, as in the manna story, "day by day," the **Sabbath Year** mandate to overcome the mechanisms of poverty by canceling debts and freeing slaves (no doubt the believers who were debt slaves were being released), and the **Jubilee** mandate to redistribute their possessions so all could have life in fullness. This is an essential clue to the mission of the early church throughout the Book of Acts, for Jesus' followers down through history, and for us today in our unprecedentedly unjust and unequal world.

Does social-economic justice, as set forth in the Sabbath and Jubilee texts, occupy a central place in our curricula, especially among our decentralized students, who can lead their congregations and communities in their struggles for justice, equality, and life in fullness?

Jubilee and Creation

If we were to trace the Torah passages (Covenant Code, Deuteronomic Code, Holiness Code) dealing with the Sabbath Day, the Sabbath Year, and the Jubilee Year, we would find that many of these passages include the mandate to give rest to the land and those who work the land, humans and laboring beasts, and even to provide for the landless poor, aliens, and wild animals in the fallow years.

For six years you shall sow your land and gather in its yield; but the seventh year you shall let it rest and lie fallow, so that the poor of your people may eat. You shall do the same with your vineyard and with your olive orchard. Six days you shall do your work, but on the seventh day you shall rest, so that your ox and your donkey may have relief, and your homeborn slave and the resident alien may be refreshed. Be attentive to all that I have said to you. Do not invoke the names of other gods, do not let them be heard on your lips. Ex. 23:10-13

Remember the Sabbath Day, and keep it holy. Six days you shall labor and do all your work. But the seventh day is a Sabbath to the Lord your God; you shall not do any work—you, your son or your daughter, your male or female slave, your livestock, or the alien resident in your towns. For in six days the Lord made heaven and earth, the sea, and all that is in them, but rested the seventh day; therefore the Lord blessed the Sabbath Day and consecrated it. Ex. 20:5-11

On the seventh day God finished the work that God had done, and God rested on the seventh day from all the work that God had done. So God blessed the seventh day and hallowed it, because on it God rested from all the work that God had done in creation. Gn. 2:2-3

God rested on the seventh day of creation, blessed it, and hallowed it. And the Sabbath Day became a permanent memorial and covenant for God's people, who are to regard that day and all of creation as a holy responsibility. We are to serve and worship God through the preservation of planet Earth for the life of all its inhabitants. What are the ways in which this challenge is taken up in our churches through the leadership of our theological education programs?

Jubilee and Shalom (Wholeness, Wellbeing, Peace)

In response to the devastating state of the poor in our world, we again turn to the Jubilee message of Jesus. What we find in Jesus' ministry is not only healing for individuals who are sick, paralyzed, blind, possessed of demons, even dead, but the formation of a healing, caring, sharing community. This dimension of Jubilee has not often been taught, even less practiced.

Consider first the man with paralysis in Mk. 2:1-12. He was disabled not only by the paralysis but also by the social marginalization that came with his physical limitations, by the prejudices of the Purity Code of the Pharisees that identified his disability as the result of sin, by the poverty and debts that came from his inability to work and from spending on ineffectual cures, and above all that came from the Temple monopoly on purification rites. So when Jesus told him (three times), "Your sins are forgiven," he revealed to this man and to all who were there that the coming of God's Reign meant that he and they could be released from the sins of popular prejudice, the Purity Code, family debts, and Temple rites. The term "release" (*afiemi*) which is used here appears in other Sabbath-Jubilee texts such as Lk. 4:18-19 (twice) to refer to the release from prison, debts, and oppression as well as illness and sin.

The story of the rich man, who apparently was very religious and who ran to Jesus in order to be sure of his eternal life, ends on a tragic note, for he rejects Jesus' call to sell his possessions, give the money to the poor, and follow him. (Mk. 10:17-22) But then Jesus tells his disciples two times, "How hard it will be for those who have wealth to enter God's Reign." Then he adds the analogy of the camel and the eye of a needle, and the disciples, utterly astounded, respond, "Then who can be saved?" Jesus says, "For mortals it is impossible, but not for God; for God all things are possible." The story then takes a surprising turn. Peter, no doubt out of desperation, cries out, "Look, we have left (released, *afiemi*) everything and followed you." And Jesus responds, "Truly I tell you, there is no one who has left (released, *afiemi*) house or brothers or sisters or mother or father or children or fields, for my sake and for the sake of the Good News, who will not receive a hundredfold now in this age . . . and in the age to come eternal life." For most of us this is a mystery, simply because we have never really understood or practiced Jubilee, for if we "release" into the community our possessions, as Jesus asked of the rich man, not just abandon them, we will in effect have access to a hundred times more family and possessions—as the disciples were just beginning to experience and as they understood more fully at Pentecost. (Mk. 10:23-31)

The problem of the rich man is explained in a series of Jesus' sayings in Mt. 6:19-34, which deal with economic-spiritual issues in Jubilee terms. Laying up treasure in heaven rather than on earth means to release them for the work of God's Reign, not literally "in heaven" but precisely here on earth. The healthy eye sees and desires God's Reign rather than selfish gain. The rich man thought he could have eternal life and keep his possessions (his god), but Jesus says, "You cannot serve God and wealth." Perhaps most difficult to imagine is the final, longer saying about living like the birds of the air or the lilies of the field with no concern for tomorrow. The only way that could happen amidst the awful poverty of Jesus' day—or in our time—was and is to become part of a community in which all care for all mutually, as Sabbath economics teaches us, i.e., to seek first God's Reign and God's Justice (Mt. 6:33).

Do our decentralized theological education programs contribute significantly to the formation of recognized leaders in the congregations who can lead their people into a deeper experience of community, sharing, caring, and healing?

MANDATES AND MODELS OF THEOLOGICAL EDUCATION
A Movement for Change

The Theological Education by Extension movement began in the 1960s with the primary purpose of giving access to a much wider circle of clergy, laity, and ministerial candidates, men and women, for theological education and ministry. More precisely, it affirmed that theological education should give priority to local leaders who demonstrate their calling and dedication through their service and should not require them to be uprooted from their diverse cultural contexts, extended families, economic base, and ecclesial communities and responsibilities. More fundamentally, it was founded upon the belief that ministry is commended to the people of God through baptism and discipleship, not to a professional or clerical class through schooling, credentials, and ordination. This movement soon demonstrated that large numbers of people, especially the natural leaders, women as well as men, older as well as younger, less and more highly schooled, poor as well as non poor, who had been largely excluded from formal theological studies, can and will respond to the TEE challenge and pursue serious theological studies, largely at their own expense and under often difficult circumstances. That story is told through another anthology, *Ministry by the People: Theological Education by Extension*, which was published in 1983 by the WCC and Orbis Books.

In July 2004 a small group of theological educators, the Steering Committee of TEENET, met at the Vancouver School of Theology in British Colombia and approved the proposal to gather a new collection of analytical reports of what we have been calling Diversified Theological Education. We believe that there has been a significant shift away from earlier polarization between TEE and residential programs and concepts of theological education toward an increasingly diverse use of methods, models, and concepts of theological education, often combining centralized and decentralized elements. The challenge is to build theological learning systems with diverse methods and models as needed and available. The case studies in this volume offer an enormous variety of possible elements and combinations.

This whole development of Diversified Theological Education takes on real meaning when we consider its potential, at all levels but especially at grass roots levels, for theological-biblical-ministerial formation with a Sabbath-Jubilee perspective. Can people of faith with minimal schooling and marginal economic and political power capture that vision and take up their calling as God's people to struggle for fullness of life for themselves and all God's children? What basic tools, skills, and concepts do they need to pursue this calling effectively?

It can be argued that the poor and marginalized are precisely the ones most apt to understand the global challenges and pursue the Good News as set forth above. The fundamental ingredients for this kind of theological education are socio-economic analysis of the local and global context, biblical-theological foundations for responding to that global and local context, and pastoral or missional action in keeping with this kind of socio-economic analysis and these biblical foundations. This has been called the hermeneutical circle, and it is often set within a framework of spirituality and discipleship. In their consideration of the case studies presented in this book and their own programs of theological education, readers will want to examine these basic ingredients over and over again. This should not be undertaken simplistically. In fact, some of us have chosen to add the notion of an "epistemological rupture" as essential for the authenticity of our socio-economic analysis, our biblical foundations, and our pastoral or missional action. This epistemological rupture or breakthrough does not exclude but goes far beyond the traditional pietistic and individualistic understanding of conversion. It is an integral conversion to the Reign of God in our lives and all of life in this world.

In recent years the peoples of Latin America have emerged from a period of deadly military oppression only to find themselves overwhelmed by the global and regional domination of corporate, "free trade" capitalism, otherwise known as re-colonization, the new imperialism. In this context the heritage of Catholic and Protestant missions has left their churches somewhat ill-equipped for critical social analysis, relevant biblical understanding, and effective missional guidance—with the notable exception of base communities, liberation theology, and some of the ecumenical and charismatic movements in the region. The contribution of programs such as those mentioned above must be measured in terms of their ability to mobilize hearts and minds and hands, throughout the ecclesial movements, for socio-economic, ecological, gender, and racial justice.

Educational Components

With the proliferation of TEE and DTE program designs, which can be a healthy response to our diversities of contexts, church traditions, and mission priorities, it will be important to hold onto some of the basic learnings that have emerged over the last 40 years. TEE began to develop a distinctive educational design out of pragmatic necessity and along the way discovered very important components for any effective learning system, theological or otherwise, but especially appropriate for grass roots ministerial formation among local church leaders. In Guatemala, since our students were local church leaders, heads of families, mostly employed in secular jobs or subsistence farming, scattered over large areas, we could only plan to meet with them once a week or twice a month at locations accessible for them, though some travel for them and more for our faculty was often necessary. Since those meetings could only last for two or three hours, we had to use that time for discussion and debate, not for lectures or monologue. This in turn meant that the students had to be able to get the basic course content (cognitive, affective, practical) on their own in preparation for each group meeting. So we devised basic self-study materials for the relevant "academic" levels and cultural contexts. The third component, in addition to daily individualized study and weekly or bi-monthly group discussion, was on-going, practical testing or application of the substance and issues of the course material in the students' local ecclesial and social contexts.

At an opportune moment Ted Ward, an educator at Michigan State University met with leaders of the TEE movement and articulated a basic curriculum design that matched our experience and facilitated the communication of the TEE concept. We call this design "the rail fence analogy." It refers to the three basic components mentioned above, and it focuses on the combination and balance of these three components. One rail represents on-going daily or weekly individual home study with appropriate materials and assignments. The other rail, parallel to the first rail, is the on-going practical application or testing or utilizing of the material being studied in the local church and/or community. The third element, represented by posts holding up, in parallel, the two rails, is the weekly or twice monthly group meeting, with a local or visiting facilitator, to review, clarify, and discuss the material studied and to share experiences with that material in their local context. There are two critical questions regarding this analogy. One is the purpose of the fence, which will determine its size and strength, whether it is meant to keep horses or dogs or chickens, etc. The other is how best to combine and balance the three elements. If the posts are widely separated or too frail, they will not be able to hold up the rails. If the rails are two heavy or too thin or wrongly spaced, they may be unable to fulfill their function.

TEE and DTE programs are generally designed to prepare local church leaders to guide their people into faithful discipleship and mission. They should be carefully designed with appropriate self-study materials, constant practice, and regular opportunities to integrate and confirm learnings from these two elements through meetings with peers and a facilitator. If the materials are confusing or abstract or simplistic, or if group meetings are too widely separated or irrelevant or boring, students will be discouraged, and many will drop out. When the three basic educational components are ideally combined and balanced, participants are constantly challenged to work effectively toward their mission, the church's mission, God's mission.

The rail fence analogy is just one way to identify the essential components—their combination and balance—for TEE and DTE programs. In some contexts audio or visual materials may be more effective than or in combination with written materials. Some programs are beginning to use the Internet and CDs, which offer extensive resource material and also can offer group contact over wide distances on a regular basis. In many contexts regular face to face encounters are considered to be essential. The possibilities for practical or missional action are almost unlimited, as are the possibilities for individual and group assignments emerging out of the study materials and the regular group meetings. As Ted Ward indicates, something almost magical happens when the three educational components come together and the mission of the rail fence is realized. This charismatic experience can take place—with the right ingredients—among old timers and/or new comers, among highly schooled and/or little schooled, among peasant farmers and/or urban professionals, among women and/or men. The case studies included in this volume provide a great variety of examples.

Mission Paradigm

Many Christians and many churches maintain, as we have suggested, a mission paradigm that is individualistic and pietistic, that gives priority to individual "salvation" and "spiritual" or religious practices, and that ultimately focuses upon eternal life after death. We have chosen in this chapter to follow a mission paradigm that focuses on the biblical mandates associated with the Sabbath Day, the Sabbath Year, and the Jubilee, because they deal with fundamental economic and ecological realities that are preeminent in our time, that are the primary threats to life in the twenty-first century, that are largely beyond the reach of traditional mission paradigms, and that are eminently biblical and spiritual matters. This paradigm does not minimize the personal relationship with God, but it may in fact call into question any understanding of salvation that ignores or minimizes these realities. The critical question for this paradigm is, What was Jesus' understanding of God's mission? And this leads to the question, What does it mean to follow Jesus in today's world? It leads us to what Jesus called "the greatest and first commandment," which is "'You shall love your God with all your heart, and with all your soul, and with all your mind' . . . and a second is like it, 'You shall love your neighbor as your self.'" (Mt. 22:38-39, Lk. 10:27, Mk.12:30-31)

It is interesting to note that Jesus very rarely mentioned eternal life, and in the most prominent case, the Parable of the Judgment of the Nations, Matthew 25:31-46, he gave priority not to correct theology but action on behalf of the hungry, the thirsty, the stranger, the naked, the sick, and the prisoner. His ministry on behalf of the "little ones"—the poor, women, the sick, and the possessed—was at the same time a denunciation of the powerful and the rich and the structures of oppression and marginalization, including the Temple in Jerusalem, which was a major institution for the support of the Roman Empire. As Walter Wink has explained so powerfully, when Jesus told Pilate, "My Kingdom is not from this world," he really meant, "My Kingdom is not of this domination system." (John 18:36) From the beginning of his ministry Jesus announced the coming of God's Kingdom precisely to bring Good News to the poor, the prisoners, the blind, the oppressed, the deaf, the lame, the lepers, and even the dead, and to challenge and transform the domination system of first-century Palestine. (Lk. 4:18-19, 7:22-23)

To follow Jesus in our time, which is our primary concern, we need to consider whether our programs of theological education are equipping local church leaders to defend and support the weak and also to practice non-violent resistance and begin to transform the structures and institutions of domination, locally and globally. This perspective raises many questions about our curricula, our biblical foundations, our mission vision, and our actions for justice in the economy and *shalom* in the Earth.

It is evident, for example, that professional, Western models of healthcare will not in the foreseeable future be able to provide adequate services among the expanding poor populations of **Africa**, where 15,000 children die daily for lack of clean water, basic nutrition, and preventive healthcare. Grassroots health education and community development combined with Theological Education by Extension might transform that situation, if in fact a new holistic vision of God's mission could bring together those three parallel movements that depend primarily on local leaders.

In **Latin America** Christian base communities have brought powerful renewal to the predominant Catholic Church, and some of the Pentecostal churches have done something similar among Protestants, but both are in danger of being eclipsed by other worldly movements and TV evangelism, recently linked with this worldly prosperity theology. There is an urgent need among all ecclesial sectors for holistic, critical biblical foundations for faith and life in the 21st century, especially at the local level, in the struggle for ecclesial and social and ecological as well as personal transformation. Formal and non-formal theological education at grassroots levels may be the key.

Europe and **North America** still invest enormous resources in formal theological education, but the contribution of these institutions in the formation of prophetic churches is questionable. The primary threats to life in this century, economic polarization and ecological destruction, seem to advance unimpeded by moral challenges in these two regions, which are the prime movers and chief beneficiaries of the global domination system.

Conditions vary widely in **Asia**, but ruling elites there as elsewhere seem to seek increasing access to and benefits from the global economic empire at the expense of their own people. Even China's socialism is said to be caught up in a feverish drive to compete in production and consumption along with the West, and India's skilled professionals are being bought up by the West. Meanwhile Asia's tigers emulate the best and worst of Western capitalism. What is the contribution of theological education in these contexts?

One of the most promising examples of poor people who are escaping from the most extreme forms of poverty was highlighted by the awarding of the 2006 Nobel Peace Prize to Bangladesh's "Banker of the Poor," Muhammed Yunus, and his Grameen Bank for their leadership in the microcredit revolution. When Yunus discovered that the very poor were trapped in a cycle of debt and poverty because they did not qualify for bank loans, he began to offer them loans as small as $27 to start a business with the oversight of five member peer groups and the bank's field workers. After three decades the Grameen Bank has 6.6 million borrowers, 97% of them women, with 2226 branches among Bangladesh's 71,371 villages. The standard interest is 16%, but the bank has recently offered Bangladesh's 50,000 beggars interest-free loans of about nine dollars to buy bread, candy, and other items they can sell to supplement their income from begging. The bank has made more than $5.7 billion in loans averaging $130 and claims a repayment rate of more than 98%. Perhaps most surprising is the fact that these borrowers make up about two-thirds of the bank's depositors. Could not this example be taken up by grass-roots theological education programs, especially in poor countries, with students who would study basic economics and work with microcredit agencies as part of their preparation for and leadership in mission as integral human development? (*Los Angeles Times*, October 14, 2006, A1)

Another example is the Heifer Project, now Heifer International (*www. heifer.org*), which for almost 60 years has offered a very attractive and very credible model of human development that is overcoming poverty even among the poorest of the poor in 50 countries. The basic concept is called "Passing on the Gift." Heifer provides a cow, a pair of goats, or a few chickens to one family; that family promises to give its first new female cow, goat, or other offspring to another family; and self-perpetuating chains of sustainable economic growth spread through communities as recipients become donors.

The idea is so attractive that Heifer has been growing almost 20% a year to a budget of more than $50 million, largely through small donations. Some faith communities in rich countries hold Christmas markets that challenge their members to make animal gifts through Heifer in lieu of presents on behalf of family and friends and in their names, which brings them, too, into the struggle against poverty around the world. Could not TEE and DTE students participate in Heifer and similar programs as part of their formation in ministry and mission?

Perhaps the most critical dimension of today's global economy is the increasing concentration of local, national, and global trade in the hands of corporations, whose sole motivation is to produce wealth for their investors at the expense of poverty for vast sectors of the population and ecological destruction for the planet. The "free trade" ideology underlying this reality simply negates the Sabbath and Jubilee mandates and foments greed and wealth concentration. The churches, other faith traditions, and many social movements need to work together to reverse this trend and build mechanisms of "fair trade" that give priority to social justice and ecological integrity and *shalom*. This too can be an essential part of the new mission paradigm of Theological Education by Extension and/or Diversified Theological Education.

Conclusion

This introductory chapter raises many, many possibilities and questions for theological education as a whole and TEE/DTE in particular. It sets forth a socio-economic analysis of fundamental, urgent needs that this generation must deal with; it offers a biblical foundation based on a Sabbath/Jubilee reading of the Bible; and it ends with a paradigm of missional theological education that responds to this socio-economic analysis and the biblical foundation. At each stage in this process we have noted that priority should be given to the theological formation of local leaders, especially those who have traditionally been marginalized, because they are the ones most apt to follow the way of Jesus and most able to understand and respond to the challenges and the needs of holistic salvation.

The case studies that make up the rest of this book invite readers to examine reports of a limited but significant number of programs of Diversified Theological Education, to learn from their experiences and reflections, and perhaps to consider new possibilities for their own vision and practice of theological education. The case studies may offer boards, faculty, and students of theological institutions material for discussion, debate, and planning. They may then broaden that discussion among church leaders who are or should be seriously engaged in the support and oversight of theological education among pastors, ministerial candidates, and/or lay people. At the very least they should raise critical questions and issues about the mission of theological education, the mission of the churches, God's mission in today's world.

Ross Kinsler
rgkinsler@sbcglobal.net

Chapter 2: Africa

Theological Education by Extension in Zambia

by Kangwa Mabuluki

Historical Background

In the middle of 1977, having heard and read much about Theological Education by Extension, I received the first copies of the Certificate Level Course "Introduction to the Bible" from the Theological Education by Extension College of Southern Africa. [T]his TEEC material immediately appealed to me as (a) material that can be produced relatively cheaply by us without requiring the use of a printing firm and (b) its content was very well prepared and very suitable for the kind of lay leadership training program that we need in the United Church of Zambia.

Thus reads part of the introduction to a progress report given by Rev. David Curtis, a British Methodist Church missionary working with the United Church of Zambia, who initiated the process of establishing TEE in Zambia.

Rev. Curtis first tested out the course material with a few students, having first adapted the Theological Education by Extension College of Southern Africa (TEEC) material where necessary to the Zambian context, and reproduced them locally with permission from TEEC.

In 1978 Rev. Curtis was working with 45 students in his local congregation. His experience was sufficient to bring the idea to the Synod of the United Church of Zambia, through the Committee responsible then for Ministerial Training. So in January 1978 the Synod of the United Church of Zambia gave backing to the idea of developing a TEE program using the TEEC material.

Rev. Curtis also had to assure the Zambian Church leaders that links with the South African based Theological Education by Extension College of

Southern Africa were not an endorsement of the apartheid system to which the United Church of Zambia, a relatively socially and politically engaged church, was opposed. So as part of his progress report he stated, "I should stress at this point that the TEE College of Southern Africa serves both black and white churches in South Africa and Malawi, and the thrust and form of their teaching is very suitable for us here—it is definitely non-sectarian and non-racial".

At the time of starting the initiative of using TEEC material to train lay leaders of his congregation, Rev. Curtis was a minister in a congregation in the small mining town of Luanshya in the Copperbelt Province of Zambia. He was later to be given an appointment as staff at the Ministerial College of the United Church of Zambia based on Mindolo Ecumenical Foundation campus. Here he had the support of the other members of staff who saw value in "this new extension of theological education to the "grass roots" of the Church.

Efforts within the United Church of Zambia were complemented by efforts in the Anglican Church. Rev. Nicholas Beddow, a member of the Anglican training team in Zambia, having established contact with his counterpart in the UCZ, Rev. Curtis, and being convinced of the potential of TEE methods in enhancing theological training, in September 1978 wrote a discussion paper for the Anglican bishops on "The Possibility of A Joint Anglican-United Church of Zambia project for further developing Theological Education by Extension in the two Churches".

The Anglican bishops accepted the idea of using TEE methods for training in their Church, but they were also convinced that the best way to undertake the TEE program was on an ecumenical basis, initially between the UCZ and Anglicans, with the hope of other churches joining in later.

So in January 1979 Theological Education by Extension in Zambia (TEEZ) formally came into existence as a training project of two churches, namely the United Church of Zambia and the Anglican Church in Zambia. The main aim of the project was "To prepare all God's people for the work of Christian service" (Ephesians 4:12).

The Rev. Nicholas Beddow's discussion paper spelled out three key areas where both the United Church of Zambia and the Anglican Church in Zambia felt the "extension method" of training would be most helpful. These were:

1. In-service training for full-time clergy;

2. Post-ordination training for supplementary and local clergy;

3. Lay leadership training and increasing theological awareness among interested laity.

It should be noted with that more than 25 years down the line only the third one of these key areas has been prominent, making TEEZ one of the few TEE programs in Africa whose main focus is lay training, while other sister TEE programs train ministers for ordination.

This project, that started with only two churches with about 100 students and only three tutors, was to grow to the current eight member churches with over 5,000 students and over 500 tutors all over the country, including the most remote areas, therefore going beyond just a lay training program as a tool for empowerment and a prime example of viable ecumenical cooperation.

Social and Political Context in Zambia

Zambia got her political independence from Britain in 1964. At that time Zambia was one of the rich countries in Africa and even in the world. The price of copper, which is the main export of Zambia, was high. At that time the Zambian currency had the same value as the British Pound.

At independence the new government faced political pressure to change the situation of people who had suffered under colonialism. It was partly this pressure that dictated economic decisions. The focus of improving infrastructure was mainly on urban areas along the line of rail. A process of "Zambianization" was also initiated, which involved putting the control of the economy in the hands of Zambians by ensuring that all the big (state controlled) industries and companies were headed and managed by Zambians. All social amenities, like education, health, housing and even basic food, were subsidised. The political and economic system was socialist, so all major economic aspects were strictly controlled by the state.

The 1970s drop in copper prices and increase in oil prices turned things around. The government did not have enough income to sustain the subsidised system, but it was politically expedient to maintain the system. So the government went into borrowing (at a time when the IMF and World bank were looking for borrowers they could lend to). Zambia's foreign debt rose to US$ 7 billion. (In a country of 10 million people that is almost $1000 per citizen.)

Liberation wars in the region took a toll on the infrastructure. Restrictions in trade with South Africa due to sanctions made the importation of essentials like medicines and raw material for various industries very expensive, since Zambia is a landlocked country and South Africa had the nearest and most reliable port. Tourism, which was an alternative foreign currency earner, was down due to insecurity. These and other factors contributed to the rapid drop in the economy.

During the late 80s and early 90s, under pressure from the IMF and WB, Zambia's government liberalised the economy and removed subsidies for health, education, and food. Discontent was high. The socio-economic situation of most people dropped drastically. There were constant shortages of essential commodities and food and a shortage of school places. Unemployment was high because most people had moved from rural areas to urban areas looking for a better life. (Zambia is one of the most urbanised countries.)

In 1991 a new government came into power and instituted an immediate and rapid shift from socialist policies to free market capitalist policies: removal of subsidies, privatization of the major industries, including the mines. This in turn led to reduction of the workforce, capital flight through privatised companies, failure to curb rising corruption, increased poverty, and the disappearance of the middle class.

Current Situation

Today, Zambia is one of poorest countries in the world. 80% of the population is poor, with 53% living in abject poverty (living on less than US$1 per day). A Catholic Church organization, CCJP, which produces statistics of a food basket each week, indicates that prices of basic commodities from the cheapest sources are beyond what the average wage is able to cater to— even for the very essential basics. As an official international confirmation of the extreme state of poverty, in March 2005 Zambia qualified as one of the Highly Indebted Poor Countries (HIPC). Almost US$5 billion of external debt has been written off as a result, but the tangible (on the ground) results of this debt write-off will still take several years to be seen.

HIV&AIDS has a great effect on the fight to improve the economy, because it has a heavy toll on health facilities and spending. It is killing the most productive and educated manpower and reducing production due to constant sickness of infected workers. While increased by poverty, HIV&AIDS also increases poverty, in that families affected by HIV&AIDS become poorer than their previous poor state because they have to focus their resources on the sick person who in many cases would also be the incapacitated bread winner.

The Role of the Church and TEEZ

Like many African countries, Zambia is a very religious country, with many Christian churches (Christianity accounts for over 90% of the population) and a number of other religions (about 10%). The Christian churches can roughly be divided into four categories, namely mainline churches, evangelical churches, Pentecostal churches, independent churches. Religion plays a key role in the lives of people in Zambia, evidenced by the rapid growth of almost all forms of churches.

The church in Zambia has always been involved in the economic and social life of the people. Starting with the early missionary era, church mission stations were centres of education, medical facilities, and even general political response (either for or against colonial domination). During this period and many years after independence church involvement in the socio-economic situation of the country was mainly in the form of charity towards the poor and vulnerable; in fact, this charity response increased when the economy started declining. The churches then also started providing skills training in the hope that with skills the people can be able to help themselves.

The fall of the Berlin wall in 1989 and the triumph of capitalism, reducing the world system from bi-polar to uni-polar, had a great impact on the social-political system of many countries in the world, especially those that had been socialist-inclined. The impact was not only on the economic system, which for Zambia made a drastic move from a socialist, state-controlled economy to a privatized open-market capitalist system. This shift also opened the way for more players from civil society, with the churches assuming a new role in mitigating social and economic hardships of the people.

So the increased visibility of the effects of the poor economic situation on the people (which includes church members), among other reasons, led to a shift in the churches' attitude towards economic issues from indifferent or casual to deep concern and urgency to do something. But this opportunity for the churches to play a key role in shaping the social political direction of the country was affected by lack of adequately trained ministers/pastors. Most of the churches are largely managed by lay people, who serve as volunteers, while having other jobs. In order for them to serve effectively these lay people needed to be trained and equipped. TEEZ became, and has indeed continued to be, one of the viable options to provide training for these lay leaders.

Focus, Mission, Aims and Structure of TEEZ

The main focus of TEEZ is theological training. This training happens at the local church. To facilitate this, TEEZ trains local tutors, and produces course materials for the various subjects. These subjects cover such key and critical areas as Preaching, Counselling, Teaching, Leading Church Meetings, Church Constitution, and Worship. The course material is translated into local languages to ensure that it reaches those who need it in the local churches. The training provided by TEEZ is critical for the churches in Zambia because of the need for lay people to know and understand the theological stand as well as the governance and polity of their churches. The courses are also provided in prisons.

The training is affordable and does not require the learners to leave their work and local situation to go to theological school or college. Because of the relevance and great demand for the training, there is need to ensure continuity and improvement through training of more tutors, providing refresher training for those already trained, as well as improving the course material.

The aim and mission of TEEZ is:

To equip and prepare Christians for effective service within the church and the world through relevant, contextual non-residential theological training.

To fulfill its vision and mission TEEZ pursues the following aims:

1. *To develop and produce relevant theological course materials.*

2. *To train tutors and encourage them to form TEEZ local study groups.*

3. *To encourage other churches to become members of TEEZ.*

4. *To carry out other services that will enhance the mission and/or vision of TEEZ.*

The TEEZ courses and programs are conducted in different churches in all the provinces where TEEZ member churches are present. There are also classes in four main prisons in Zambia.

Organizational Structure

At policy level, the highest policy body is the Annual General Meeting (AGM), which brings together six representatives from each member church as well as observer churches. In between the Annual General Meetings, the organization has a Management Committee, which is made up of four representatives from each member church. The Management Committee meets at least three times a year. A smaller group of ten people comprising six office bearers elected at the Annual General meeting: The Chairperson, Vice Chairperson, Secretary, Vice Secretary, Treasurer, Vice Treasurer. These plus two general Trustees and two TEEZ senior staff, the Director and Training Officer, constitute the Executive Committee. The Executive Committee acts in between meetings of the Management Committee.

The representatives are selected by the churches, normally from already existing church leaders. As such the gender balance is often very weak, because most leaders in the churches are men. Currently there is only one woman in the Executive Committee and about 12 in the wider Management Committee.

KEY PROGRAMS AND CHANGES IN THESE OVER THE YEARS

Regional Tutors' Seminars

In order to ensure that the TEEZ courses indeed respond to the needs of the communities, each year regional tutors meet and review the work and identify areas needing special attention. At the meeting of 2002, the issue of HIV&AIDS was identified as one needing increased involvement of TEEZ students and tutors. This annual event brings together regional and local tutors to evaluate the progress of TEE courses in the various provinces and to provide specialized training for the regional and active local tutors.

HIV & AIDS Program

It was resolved that engagement in breaking the silence and communicating the effects and severity of the AIDS scourge, without encouraging stigmatization, was critical. To this end it was proposed that, should resources be available, psychosocial counseling courses in HIV&AIDS should be conducted first for regional tutors and then for local tutors as well as active students. But with so many organizations already involved in the fight against HIV&AIDS, and the main focus of TEEZ being Theological Training for lay people in the Church, there was need to justify why TEEZ should also be involved.

The main and initial rationale and justification for involvement is the extent of the problem of HIV&AIDS, which requires involvement of as many people and organizations as possible at various levels:

- TEEZ involvement in HIV&AIDS work is in line with the efforts to increase church involvement in breaking the silence. TEEZ, as an ecumenical body engaged in training, has the possibility of engaging the churches in exploring effective ways of breaking the silence and discussing controversial issues in prevention, such as the use of the condom.

- TEEZ was already involved in training and in the process has built a reputation among a critical group, namely lay leaders, at almost every level of the churches.

- TEEZ has a wide and effective network reaching some of the remotest areas of the country. This network had to be utilized to disseminate educational information and material on HIV&AIDS and to utilize the same community educational methods to teach on HIV&AIDS.

Goal: To give regional and local tutors an opportunity to be better equipped to respond to the situation of HIV&AIDS in their churches and communities and to equip Regional and Local Tutors with information to correctly respond to questions regarding HIV&AIDS which they often encounter among their students and fellow tutors.

Other aims were:

1. *To initiate a process of engagement of TEEZ tutors and students in the issue of HIV&AIDS by training Regional and some Local Tutors in psychosocial counseling in HIV&AIDS.*

2. *To develop a pool of people within the network of TEEZ who are trained in HIV&AIDS counseling and are available to the use of the community.*

3. *To make available to the member churches and the community at large trained resources to respond to the issues of HIV&AIDS.*

4. *To effectively contribute to the efforts of the churches in breaking the silence, fighting stigma and carrying out education and counseling in the area of HIV&AIDS.*

5. *To contribute to the development of contextual theological response to HIV&AIDS.*

Through this program 50 people were trained in three courses over two years, 2003 and 2004. Those trained were drawn from all the nine provinces of Zambia and from all the TEEZ participating churches. The three courses were facilitated by the Zambia Counseling Service, which operates under the Ministry of Health. Each course took eight weeks and was in three phases. The first phase was a one-week residential session during which participants covered a broad range of topics. The second stage involved six weeks of practical work. During this period each participant was attached to a counseling center where he/she worked under the supervision of the person in charge or one of the key staff persons at that center. The third and final stage comprised another one-week residential period during which a review of the journals and reports compiled during the fieldwork were discussed, and further theory input was given.

At the end of each course the participants sat for an exam to complement the continuous assessment of their performance throughout the course. The participants received certificates validated by the Zambia Ministry of Health, UNAIDS, and WHO. With these certificates the participants could practice in any health institution and counseling center in the country and in any other country where the operations of UNAIDS and WHO are recognized. So this was an internationally recognized training and qualification.

The Unique Role of TEEZ in Equipping Churches to Respond to Issues of Society

ALL God's People—Ministry of the Laity

It has already been noted how, despite the commitment to seek to include clergy in the courses, TEEZ has been and continues to focus mainly on lay people. The need to strengthen lay people so as to enable them to play their role in the mission and ministry of the church is very critical. The focus on the formation and inclusion of the *Laos* in the work and ministry of the church has not only been a concern of the churches in Zambia but that of the wider ecumenical movement. With regard to the member churches of TEEZ, this has been taken care of by the lay training programs of the churches, which in most of the churches have not been as well funded, articulated, and regulated as the theological colleges belonging to these churches. The general courses of TEEZ address the areas where lay formation is necessary and are designed with the level of lay leaders in mind. The general aim is "formation" rather than academic achievement. But this intention has not always matched the content and format of the courses, necessitating review from time to time. The reviews are also of course necessitated by the change in context. The major changes have mostly been at key anniversaries, i.e., 10th Anniversary, 20th Anniversary, and 25th Anniversary. In the new syllabus are added two key courses on Ecumenism and Living in Community, which takes on board concerns of the environment.

ALL God's People—Beyond Prison Walls

TEEZ has added a feature to its ministry that emphasised the training of all God's people. This involved the extension of the training to prisons. Like most areas where TEEZ is involved, the initiative came as a response to a request from an organization, Prison Fellowship of Zambia, whose main focus is Christian witness in prisons. Prison Fellowship had constant requests from prisoners for substantive Bible study or Bible course material. Their effort to meet this need with Bible correspondence courses from Europe and America was not fully satisfactory. Their discovery of the availability of TEEZ courses proved a more adequate response to this need. So a request was made to TEEZ. TEEZ saw this as an opportunity not only to respond to a situation of evangelism and ministry but a social responsibility to contribute to making the prisons places of reform rather than just punitive punishment. With the willingness to respond positively came two immediate challenges, namely how to cover the cost of the course material (as it would be unrealistic to ask prisoners to pay even the subsidized cost), and how to train tutors to conduct the courses in prisons. This program was therefore designed as a special program and special funding was sought. With the support of Prison Fellowship, prison chaplains who were already part of the prison system, employed by the Prison Service, were trained as tutors to start the courses in prisons. Initially permission was granted for the start of work in three prisons in different cities (Kitwe, Kabwe and Lusaka). After only two years of starting prison classes, the prisons recorded the highest and most consistent number of students. The highest was the Mukobeko Maximum Prison, which is the biggest and main prison in the country, where a substantive number of students were on death row. The number declined between 2002 and 2004 with the work in the Lusaka prison completely stopping. This decline was due to the changed situation of the chaplains. In the case of Lusaka, the chaplain who was a volunteer outside the prison system could not devote sufficient time to follow up all programs including TEEZ, and additionally some other groups linked with Prison Fellowship felt that TEEZ program was not focused enough on "evangelism", which they felt was to be the main focus. In the case of Kitwe and Kabwe, the chaplains went for further training and the ones who were brought in to serve in the interim did not know much about or have sufficient interest in TEEZ. This situation raised the need to train tutors among the prisoners themselves, especially those that were to be in prison for more than one year. Permission to conduct the training and the process of raising additional resources were hard to come by, but in 2005 permission was granted and in 2006 Tutors were trained in Kamfinsa and Mukobeko Prisons. Among those trained in Kamfinsa was the Officer In Charge for the main prison and the Officer In Charge for the Female Section, as well as one staff member. This indicated the acceptance and appreciation of TEEZ in the prison system.

The philosophy behind the acceptance to extend TEEZ ministry to prison, namely to participate in making prisons places of reform and also lessening the stigma of prison, demanded that TEEZ go beyond just offering courses to help with other areas. Thus as part of the program supplies were provided at least once a year, and, more importantly, a significant contribution towards reforming and making prisoners more self-supporting was initiated. In Kamfinsa farming inputs were given each farming season to help the prisoners extend their farm to the level where it could produce sufficient income to sustain itself. After support for four years, the Officer in Charge reported that this target had been attained. In Mukobeko support was given for prisoners doing various skills training in carpentry, brick laying and tailoring to undergo trade tests so that they could obtain a trade certificate. The support involved paying their exam fee and buying the material required for them to sit for the exam.

The prison courses have had acknowledged impact on the life of the prisoners, the Officer in Charge of Kamfinsa Prison acknowledged that "The behavior of those taking TEEZ courses evidently became less aggressive than before their involvement in TEEZ".

The Prison Ministry also provided an opportunity for wider ecumenical involvement. While outside prison, TEEZ is confined to member churches; in the prisons any prisoners can take the course irrespective of which church they come from. When they come out of prison, they take the good news of

TEEZ to their churches, some of which are indigenous Zambian churches very much in need of the training provided by TEEZ.

A Unique Model of Ecumenical Cooperation—Increase in Church Participation and Joint Tutor Training and Committee

The ecumenical composition and potential of TEEZ makes us constantly declare that TEEZ is not just a training program; it is evidence that ecumenical cooperation among churches is possible. Ecumenical cooperation gives us the possibility to jointly address key issues such as HIV&AIDS, prisons, the maximum use of resources. Resources accessed by TEEZ may not be accessed by one single church but should benefit a wider constituency. Through TEEZ churches with no significant links to partners and little capacity to raise lay training resources are afforded a chance to have these resources in order to their people trained. As already noted through work in prisons, more churches are being reached and benefitting from the relevant training provided by TEEZ.

A Real Tool for Empowerment—Role and Participation of Women and Rural Churches (Rural Promotion)

Although the climax for many of the students is to receive their certificate of achievement at the end of each of their courses and eventually a Basic Certificate in Church Ministries or Advanced Certificate in Church Ministries for those that complete the five courses at basic level and six courses at advanced level, it is stressed that TEEZ courses are not just for academic advancement but are meant to train and impart skill that is of immediate and relevant use to the churches. In this regard the struggle has always been to ensure the courses in content and methodology are formational and outcome based. Because of this approach, the TEEZ courses have been a tool for empowerment, because the effect of those who go through the courses can be visibly seen and experienced. Increasingly in many of the member churches, TEEZ is mentioned as a possible solution in identified areas of lack, especially preaching, teaching and worship.

This empowerment is seen more among women. In most churches leadership and key functions of the church are not the domain of women, even in the case where such women are more able than the men. With TEEZ training such women have both the proof and the ability to be given the opportunity to exercise their particular ministries.

The other area where this empowerment element is valued most is in rural areas. In a country as poor as Zambia, resources in the form of literature are very scarce, even in urban areas. Many ministers have to struggle to get literature in the form of commentaries, etc., to help them in their work. This is worse for lay leaders, especially those in rural areas. TEEZ course material is of high quality and adapted to the use of lay leaders. So the members are not only empowered with actual course material but also with trained people among them to whom they can turn for support and consultation.

Towards Holistic Evangelism—Discovering Things that Unite Us

TEEZ has not had a course directly focused on evangelism, as such the evangelism need has been indirectly addressed through the courses that equip the members in the belief that once the church is effective it also of necessity reaches out and attracts those who would be converts to the Christian faith. But this indirect response to the need for evangelism has not fully satisfied the churches, who made constant requests for a course to be developed aimed at imparting skills on evangelism. The then director, in providing some form of assurance in this regard, mentioned in his report to the Annual General Meeting of 1995, "We dream dreams of victory in our evangelistic efforts to make the Gospel available to all. But then it is God's Mission, and we are to participate with him".

Although the need for an evangelism course was clear and the cry from the churches loud enough, delicate dangers were also visible. One area of sensitivity was the view of evangelism as proselytism which posed a danger to the smaller churches and a source of friction between the mainline churches and the more evangelical churches with the former often suspicious and blaming the later of "sheep stealing".

But efforts continued, and in 2005 a definite move was made with an agreement to initiate a process to lead to a course in evangelism. The process was to include extensive consultations among churches on the nature of evangelism … the project was also to provide links with African Independent Churches, as it was felt the nature of the course required going beyond just TEEZ members in order to avoid suspicion.

Challenges:

- Potential conflicting roles with church theological colleges and lay training programs

- Financial sustainability

- Staying focused on growing needs

Looking to the Future:

- The continued need for lay formation

- Catering for churches with gifted ministers who do not fall within the academic bracket of theological colleges and seminaries

- The challenge of financing theological training—an ever present challenge that can not be ignored

APPENDIX (TAKEN FROM THE TEEZ PROSPECTUS)
Equipping the Body of Christ

TEEZ provides a means of training leaders in the churches which is relevant to the situation in Zambia, meets the needs of the churches, and is available at a price the people can afford. It helps the churches train leaders (elders, lay leaders, lay preachers, ministers, priests, pastors, Sunday School teachers, Bible group leaders) and any other interested persons. TEEZ courses involve home study, group learning discussions, and practical work. Each course trains the student in skills needed for the ministry as he or she studies the Bible. Most TEEZ courses are studied in groups led by TEEZ trained tutors. The study groups meet every week for learning and discussion. Students learn to study the Bible, gain experience, and reflect on their experiences.

Basic Certificate in Church Ministries

The Basic Certificate in Church Ministries courses are planned to help church leaders gain skills in Ministry and an introduction to Biblical studies. A BCCM Certificate is awarded on the successful completion of all five subjects. Each course has 24 weekly lessons. They are conducted in groups led by a tutor. Only the tutor needs to have a set of workbooks. He/she facilitates study in the group. These courses are suitable for people of all educational backgrounds. They are available in six different languages: Bemba, English, Chinyanja, Tonga, Lozi, Swahili.

Preaching

Counseling

Teaching

Worship

Leading Church Meetings

Advanced Certificate in Church Ministries

The ACCM courses are planned for students with a stronger education background. They give a solid groundwork in Bible knowledge together with training in the skills of the Basic Certificate Series. Each course has 24 weekly lessons. The courses are for individuals or groups. Each student needs a set of workbooks so that he/she can prepare for the group meetings. The ACCM certificate is awarded on the successful completion of six advanced subjects. These courses are available only in English.

Synoptic Gospels & Acts

Old Testament Introduction

Pauline Epistles

Biblical Doctrine

Psalms and Selected Texts

Church Administration

Kangwa Mabuluki
kampash2002@yahoo.com

QUESTIONS FOR REFLECTION AND DISCUSSION

1. *How has Zambia, a rich country, become one of the world's poorest countries? What challenge does this context pose for TEE?*

2. *Why has TEEZ given priority to lay leadership training? How does this compare with theological education in other countries?*

3. *How has TEEZ been able to provide access to theological education to thousands of local leaders throughout Zambia, even remote areas? Could this model of theological education be emulated in other countries?*

4. *TEEZ is currently giving priority to HIV & AIDS, potentially mobilizing and equipping tens of thousands of local leaders for this mission. What are the theological and pastoral, social and economic dimensions of this mission? What other urgent needs can TEE programs respond to in a similar way?*

5. *What does "holistic evangelism" mean in countries like Zambia? What are the biblical grounds for ministry with prisoners? Why does TEEZ work ecumenically?*

Chapter 3: Africa

TEE College of Southern Africa

by Tony Moodie

In the first section of this review, *TEE in a Changed South Africa*, the altered political and economic context of the TEE College of Southern Africa (TEECSA) is outlined. The focus is on post-1994 developments in South Africa and how these relate to the churches and therefore also TEE. Only brief reference is made to other countries in Southern Africa, but many of the same issues of the shift between the struggle against the old colonialism and the new conflict between neo-liberalism and socialism or social democracy are as relevant in the rest of the region as they are in South Africa, even though their manifestations may differ. South Africa is of course also of particular importance to TEECSA since not only do the majority of its students reside in this country but, as will be described in the following sections, TEECSA is significantly affected by South African legislation. This discussion in Section I leads on to a consideration of the relation of TEE to the churches in the new economic and political situation in South Africa.

In Section II, *How Should TEE College Relate to the Churches—Problems and Opportunities*, the question of the nature and status of TEE College in its ecclesial context is considered further specifically with regard to the educational functioning of the College. This is related also to the impact of statutory requirements on TEECSA as an educational institution—a factor of increased importance in recent years—as well as to the organization of the TEE tutoring system.

In Section III, *TEE in a New Educational Dispensation*, the relationship between legislation and theological education in the new South Africa is discussed in more depth with reference to TEECSA's adoption of an outcomes-based curriculum, which has been occasioned by national education policy initiatives in South Africa. The focus here is on issues of pedagogy and the relation of theology, knowledge and experience.

But, in the midst of socio-economic, political and legislative, and ecclesial issues that impact on the work of TEE, it is vital that we do not lose our focus on the "bottom line" of our endeavors. Therefore, before considering TEE in Southern Africa in relation to society, church and education in Southern Africa, as well as the new outcomes-based TEE curriculum, the essential outcome of TEE, in the lives of students, will be illustrated with a few personal stories.

SOME TEE STUDENTS' STORIES

Dr. Shashi Ledwaba—from Tailor to Theologian

Dr. Ledwaba began his education in the unpromising conditions of the schooling system provided for indigenous African people under the apartheid system. He initially qualified as a tailor through a vocational training school and thereafter completed his high school studies part-time. In 1993 he completed the TEE Certificate in Theology *cum laude* and then the TEE Diploma in Theology in 1995. He then proceeded to postgraduate degree studies at university, graduating with an MA (Theology) in 2000 and with a PhD in 2005. His MA research focused on the exodus from the mainline churches to African Initiated Churches, and his doctoral research focused on the development of indigenous leadership in the Anglican Church.

Martin Otto—Finding Meaning in Mission-oriented Theological Education

Mr. Otto entered TEE studies at Certificate level as one step in triumphing over difficult circumstances. He is now studying for the Diploma in Theology and Ministry while serving as the lay mission-coordinator in his local church. He speaks enthusiastically about the new core course, *Doing Ministry for a Change*, which he has completed in 2005. This course in the new diploma/degree program, which seeks to realize a missional approach to theological education, has provided an educational experience which has connected directly with his ministry. In his opinion it is "the best thing" that he has yet done in his studies.

The TEE program of the Centre for Constructive Theology— Making Religion Relevant to Ordinary South Africans

Lindiwe Mkasi works for the CCT in Durban and tutors their TEE program, which aims to serve members of African Initiated Churches (AICs). The AICs' membership comprises an increasing number of indigenous African Christians, who are largely drawn from the poorest and least educated sections of the population. Ms. Mkasi studied for a theology degree while working at the CCT. She says that theology is a "study about God, but also a study about you as a human being, as a person created in the image of God … you get to know yourself better." She adds, about the students, "They enjoy my class very much. They take it seriously. They love it. I feel the same way about them." She has taken over a class started by a young American missionary from the Congregational Board of Mission and now tutors them in the Zulu language. The TEE program of the CCT is based on TEECSA's "Award in Theology" course which is offered at a level equivalent to Grade 10 in the school system. The median educational level of the group is Grade 9. The program has impacted deeply on the lives of the students. The students tell their tutor, "We are better than before. We are not the same. We are proud to stand in front of our people and speak as academics would." Before undertaking their studies, 28-year old Vuyani Mbadu and 61-year old Mathews Khumalo both thought that Jerusalem and Israel were purely spiritual concepts. Now they understand that they can "take a bus" to Jerusalem. Bongekile Zuma and Vuyani Mbadu say how they really wish to do something for their communities as a result of the convictions they have developed by applying their reading of the Bible to their communities' needs.

Julian de Wette—Working with Dispossessed Agricultural Laborers

With two other TEE students Mr. de Wette conducted a project in fulfillment of their TEE core-course studies, in which they worked in the rural Western Cape region with dispossessed and demoralized farm workers. These people now struggle to exist in squatter camps after losing their homes and livelihood after being evicted by farm owners. In a situation bereft of hope the TEE students have facilitated a program in which they worked with members of the community of *Kleinbegin* (an Afrikaans name which can be translated as "small beginnings") to establish priority areas for action in working with the people to re-establish a sense of purpose. The project, titled *Modest Beginnings at Kleinbegin*, initially had to deal with a crisis of severe flooding of the squatter camp but has developed as an ongoing ecumenical effort.

Responding to Community-Trauma in Zimbabwe

As his project for *Doing Ministry for a Change*, Justice Ncube planned to work in an informal settlement with a group of widows who had lost their husbands to the HIV/AIDS pandemic, and who were themselves mostly infected with the virus. Before the project could get underway, the people's lives were devastated as a consequence of the Zimbabwean government's

"Operation Clean-up" in which homes were destroyed and people left homeless and destitute during winter. As part of an ecumenical effort, Mr. Ncube's project-report documents intervention to deal with the immediate trauma and enable people to make a new start.

TEE IN A CHANGED SOUTH AFRICA
The New Socio-economic Context in South Africa

The establishment of the Theological Education by Extension College of Southern Africa (TEECSA) took place within the context of Apartheid South Africa and was explicitly intended to address that situation. With the advent of the post-1994 dispensation many struggle-era organizations faced something in the nature of an identity crisis. What was needed now, it seemed clear, was not opposition but co-operation in achieving the goals of the Reconstruction and Development Program (RDP), as it was named by the new government, which went as far as to appoint a cabinet minister to oversee the RDP.

Within a few years, though, the RDP was scrapped and a new program, GEAR, the Growth, Employment and Redistribution strategy, was instituted by the government. Socialist-inclined RDP policies were exchanged for a new approach which sought to place South Africa in a position to meet the challenges of the new economic world order. GEAR has been consistently attacked as a neo-liberal initiative by the partners of the African National Congress in the ruling alliance (COSATU and the SACP, the Congress of South African Trade Unions and the South African Communist Party).

As this report is being written, these political tensions are manifesting themselves in what is often portrayed simplistically as a clash between President Thabo Mbeki and ex-Vice President Jacob Zuma that centers on corruption charges against the latter, which are currently before the courts. But the ill-concealed clash between these two leading political figures has served as a lightning-rod that has attracted and given expression to much more fundamental divisions in the ruling alliance. Commentators have been at pains to point out that Jacob Zuma has not distinguished himself as a representative of socialism, but dissatisfaction with the perceived neo-liberal trend of government has crystallized around Zuma in a situation in which he is seen as the most visible opponent of the Mbeki-establishment.

The complaint from the opposition within the now-troubled alliance is that redistribution of wealth through the BEE (Black Economic Empowerment) policy has produced a small but very wealthy black elite while the situation of the general population has remained untouched. It is widely recognized that Mbeki has sought to foster the development of a well-established and influential black middle class as a counter to the legacy of white domination, but the protagonists of socialism are not satisfied by success in establishing a new petit-bourgeoisie, which they see as supporting the grand bourgeoisie created by BEE. This is the vexed situation of 21st century South Africa within which TEECSA finds itself as it moves into its fourth decade of service within the churches of Southern Africa.

A Response from TEECSA and the Churches?

It would be rash on the part of the College to jump into this debate. On the one hand, there is clearly a desire on the part of some who are driving the GEAR initiative that South Africa should not drift into the economic doldrums suffered by countries to the north who committed themselves to socialist programs after independence. Opposition parties to the right of the ANC government have had to give grudging acknowledgement to the success that has been experienced by the South African economy after years of mismanagement by the previous government. But, on the other hand, the contrast between wealth and deprivation that marked the old South Africa has not diminished noticeably, despite the redistribution that has occurred between different sectors of the population.

TEECSA is not alone amongst church organizations and secular NGOs in finding itself in an ambivalent or at least an ill-defined situation. Most would express firm opposition to the "new world order", with its disparities of power and economic distribution between developed and developing world. But there is also appreciation of the difficulty of the task of keeping Southern Africa afloat in the treacherous waters of the 21st century world while simultaneously addressing the imperative of transforming the complexion of the social and economic structures inherited from the old South Africa.

There are, too, other complicating factors. For example, Rev. Frank Chikane, previously General Secretary of the South African Council of Churches (SACC) and a leading figure in the anti-Apartheid struggle, is now director-general in the Office of the State President, and this serves to highlight the complexities of the relationship between state and church in which many Christian leaders who led the struggle against Apartheid moved into influential positions in government after 1994. What course lies open to TEECSA as it faces this new situation? If an adequate answer is to be provided to this question, it is necessary to understand the nature and role of TEECSA.

TEECSA in the South African Ecclesial Context

TEECSA came into existence as the creation of the mainline churches of South Africa, and it remains responsible to them, most directly through the College Council, in which, apart from the principal, administrator and staff representative, they form the majority in the persons of their representatives. The churches which participate in TEECSA have recognized the need to continue to exercise a prophetic role in the changed South African situation. This has necessitated a shift which the churches have understandably sometimes been a little slow in making but which has nevertheless been unmistakably evident in opposition by individual church leaders and the churches collectively to policies of the new government. A case in point is the intervention of the SACC in the worsening Zimbabwean situation, in contradiction of the government policy of 'quiet diplomacy' which has been seen as increasingly ineffectual, while the previous SACC General Secretary, Rev. Chikane, has had to serve as the representative of that policy.

More generally, the churches have not seen fit to intervene directly in the debate within the ruling alliance, although through the SACC they have identified themselves with the Basic Income Grant proposal (BIG), which proposes a monthly R100 per-person-allowance across the whole South African population. BIG proponents argue that, in a country where many people have no source of income, there is a moral imperative to provide this kind of minimal relief. They have also argued that BIG could be implemented without undue strain on the national economy. The government has, however, rejected the proposal as impracticable and in conflict with GEAR policy.

In this situation, TEECSA, as the child and servant of the churches of Southern Africa, continues to take its stand in contributing to theological education that upholds a liberation vision. TEECSA courses promote an anthropology and a view of creation which opposes exploitation and dehumanization, in the hope that TEE will foster the concern for the promotion of critically aware and humane attitudes and action within the wider church community of Southern Africa. This approach of TEECSA can be seen especially in the courses of its new diploma and degree curriculum, such as *Engaging with People Pastorally and Ethically* and *Doing Ministry for a Change*. In the latter course, for example, students are required to participate in a project of social transformation in which they identify key injustices and link these with the *missio Dei* and their own action as agents of transformative mission.

How Should TEE College Relate to the Churches?—Problems and Opportunities

The Changing Context of TEE in South Africa

In 2006 the Theological Education by Extension College of Southern Africa (TEECSA) celebrates thirty years of service with the churches of Southern Africa. After some initial exploratory work with TEE had been carried out, TEE College SA came into being in 1976 as a joint project of the mainline churches, Catholic and Protestant, as one element in the churches' opposition to the Apartheid system. The establishment of the College took place at a crucial juncture in the history of South Africa, as dissatisfaction with the inferior education provided to the bulk of the population sparked open resistance in the Soweto demonstrations, which in turn sparked massive counter-repression.

In the course of the previous two decades the government had extended its grip over the educational services of the churches, which had until then been the primary educational provider for African and "Coloured" people in South Africa. The divisive policies of the Apartheid government had impacted also on theological education and, in this context, TEECSA's work represented an attempt to maintain a unified and inclusive approach to theological education. Now, thirty years later, TEECSA is in a stronger position than ever before in its history. For the first time the College will be offering a degree qualification of its own after new legislation has opened the way for TEE programmes to be extended beyond the diploma level. (Previously the authority to award degrees was statutorily vested in universities alone.)

TEECSA's total student number for 2005 is 2769, registered for 5729 courses. Corresponding figures for previous years are 1074 and 2655 in 1998, 1510 and 3067 in 2001, and 2688 and 5360 in 2004. In 2005 the student population is distributed over a range of programmes:

- the Award in Theology, at Grade 10 level (581 students registered for 1054 courses);

- the Certificate in Theology, at Grade 12 level (1112 students registered for 2270 courses);

- the Diploma in Theology (old curriculum), now being phased out (193 students registered for 374 courses);

- the new Diploma in Theology and Ministry (674 students registered for 1427 courses);

- the Bachelor of Theology (209 students registered for 604 courses).

Students do not necessarily register with the intention of completing a whole qualification but may elect to do particular courses that suit their needs. This option was exercised relatively rarely until recently when the Methodist Church brought its lay-preachers' theological education programme under TEECSA (see further comments below).

The 2005 denominational distribution of students is as follows:

Methodist	469
Methodist lay-preacher programme	1140
(Total Methodist	1609)
Anglican	679
Catholic	173
Lutheran	64
Congregationalist	47
Presbyterian	38
Moravian	22
Baptist	16
Salvation Army	14
Other	51

Amongst the challenging realities faced by TEECSA under the new political dispensation are stringent requirements and increased control by the state over non-educational education-providers. A major motivation behind these developments has been government's concern to protect the population from exploitation by private providers, something that has unfortunately not been an isolated phenomenon. For ideological and "security" reasons the Apartheid government had severely restricted the provision of education outside of state structures. With the demise of the old regime, the situation opened up dramatically but with this came abuses by some who took the opportunity to profit from the new situation.

Therefore, legislation by the new government has on the one hand created new opportunities, as in the freedom of institutions like TEECSA to offer degrees, but, on the other hand, it has imposed stringent requirements on providers outside the state system. These have included compliance with curriculum parameters laid down in the new national education policy as well as structural and institutional requirements relating to governance and quality assurance. Non-compliance carries the real threat of the refusal of registration and enforced closure. As a direct consequence there has been a heightening of the formalisation of the institutional aspects of TEECSA in a way that has put pressure on its education-by-extension role.

For example, the participating churches of TEECSA, through their representatives on the College Council, found it necessary to direct the College to obtain registration under the Companies Act as a so-called "Section 21 Company", which allows for non-profit service organisations. "Section 21" status has helped secure the position of the College in the new educational dispensation, but with it have come additional requirements, and these have incurred considerable financial expenditure on the part of the College in order to meet infrastructural and other legal requirements. In addition, the shift from what was in effect a voluntary association to autonomous company status has reinforced a distinction between the College and those whom it serves, which has to some extent been evident as a trend in the development of the College's situation over the years. This sense of difference has not necessarily been to the advantage of the College and its mission. (It should be noted that in terms of legislation control of TEECSA is now vested solely in the company directors, the principal in the role of CEO, and the administrative and financial director. Legally the College Council's governing role has now been rendered superfluous although the reality is that the lifeblood of the College is drawn from its participating Churches, and this is something to be maintained at all costs.)

TEECSA is not the only institution offering theological education outside of traditional seminary arrangements. The University of South Africa (UNISA) has a world-wide reputation as a premier distance-learning institution and has for many years offered theological qualifications of high standard. TEECSA's vocation is not to compete with UNISA as another distance education provider. Rather, it is to provide theological education that is rooted in the life of local Christian communities. But the pressures of the new situation in which the College has found itself have exacerbated the tension between the role of TEECSA as a facilitator of church-based education-by-extension and TEECSA's status as an autonomous institution. It is not possible for TEECSA to retreat from this latter status if it is to be permitted to continue to operate as it has in the past, but the challenge is simultaneously to maintain the grassroots church-involvement that is the lifeblood of theological education by extension. This report will highlight ways in which this challenge is being met, or may be met more effectively, but the increased institutional requirements that have had to be borne by the College have contributed to the tendency for TEECSA to be perceived like other theological institutions, as "them", in contrast with "we" in the churches. The question is how TEECSA will remain true to its extension function while it simultaneously upholds its right to operate under increased statutory requirements.

TEECSA's growing importance in church life in Southern Africa

Formal theological education in Southern Africa has come under severe pressure as a consequence of increased costs of residential training in relation to the financial capacity of the churches. This is part of a wider crisis that has seen the closure of theological departments and theological schools within universities. In this context the advantages of TEE are obvious, but the TEE approach has meshed with other needs in the Churches. For a number of years the Anglican Church provided over half of the TEECSA student population. But since 2005 the Methodist Church has had the largest number of students, although the prominence of these two churches has occurred within a situation of growth in the overall numbers of TEE students, and it has been paralleled by new understandings of ministerial formation.

The Anglican Church in South Africa has for a while pursued a reconceptualized programme of Training for Ministry (TFM) in which TEE has played a vital part. This reconceptualization has taken place alongside a commitment to the maintenance of traditional seminary-based training. But together with this has occurred the development of ordained "community ministry". The community priests and deacons who have emerged from the TFM/TEE programme are ordained to ministry in the same way as those who have followed the traditionally recognised route, although they generally continue in their ordinary employment within the community. The TEE component in the TFM is crucial and is very largely provided for by TEECSA. In the Anglican TFM programme the extension element is supported by local Fellowship-of-Vocation co-ordinators. The TFM programme has been accompanied by the most effective contribution of some FOV coordinators to the TEE programme by serving as regional coordinators for TEECSA.

It must be noted that other churches such as the Presbyterians have instituted a system of FOVs allied with TEE but in terms of student numbers the major increase in reliance on TEECSA recently has come from the Methodist Church of Southern Africa (MCSA). The MCSA education unit has devolved responsibility for the theological education of its lay preachers to TEECSA, where they now form a numerically significant component of the College's student population. The MCSA has an intern support system for those who are preparing for ordination, although this does not include the bulk of the Methodists who register for TEE studies as part of their training as lay preachers. But the involvement of TEECSA in the Methodist lay preacher development programme is of great importance because all those aspiring to ordination in the MCSA are required to begin their journey in the lay preacher programme. Because of this, increasing numbers of MCSA ordinands begin their theological education through TEECSA. For those lay preachers who do not intend to go on to ordination it is not necessary to complete a qualification, but all Methodist lay preachers in training are required to register for courses in Old and New Testament studies, doctrine or theology, and preaching, at one of the levels offered by TEECSA.

The trend begun by the Anglicans has been continued by the Methodists. In addition to these churches TEE students have, amongst others, included Presbyterian ordinands and Catholics preparing for the permanent diaconate. Thus in one respect TEECSA's work is becoming increasingly important in the life of the participating churches and their members who are studying to equip themselves for ministry—as well as some students from other church backgrounds. But how is the tension to be resolved between the two trends that have been described—the institutionalisation of TEECSA as an autonomous college with statutory recognition, seen by most in the churches as an entity that stands somehow separately from them, and the increasingly vital role of theological education by extension in the life of the churches?

Organization of Tutoring

The resolution of this tension must be sought in the tutor system, which has since its inception been regarded by TEECSA as key to its educational operation. The tutor system was rooted originally in the ecumenical nature of the establishment of the College thirty years ago. The ideal has been a fully functioning network of regional centres across Southern Africa led by regional coordinators serving students in their own localities. That network has remained a feature of TEECSA, but given the vicissitudes of life the actuality has fluctuated even while the ideal has been maintained. The large, sometimes vast dimensions of many of the regions constitute one problem facing regional coordinators as they seek to organise tutorial support. It is not uncommon for students to travel for two hours to reach a tutorial venue, and some travel even further—others choose not to make the trip and work individually or in small local groups formed on their own initiative. There is also an inherent dilemma which has not always been apparent when regional centres have been functioning optimally. In this regard it is perhaps significant that most of the really successful work at regional level has been carried out by coordinators in the Anglican TFM system who have served in a dual role as ecumenical coordinators of TEE work in their regions.

This dual arrangement has not been without its difficulties at times, as there can be tension between the goals of a denominationally oriented Training for Ministry organisation and ecumenically oriented education by extension. Despite this some of the best local TEE work has been done by people whose primary responsibilities have lain with Anglican TFM. The Methodist system of circuit and district study-facilitators functioned previously on the basis of separate study materials—generally not in as well-established a manner as in the case of the Anglicans. This was at least partly the motivation for the shift towards making use of TEECSA as the prime agent for educational provision for the MCSA (aside from the relatively small number of full-time students at the John Wesley College). The massive increase in TEECSA student numbers that has been occasioned by the Methodist move has created a concomitant need for expansion of local provision of extension services for students. The Methodist case should, however, be seen merely as the most dramatic manifestation of a wider need. It highlights the question of where TEECSA should be heading in respect of the maintenance and further development of tutoring at the local level.

As has been suggested already in this report, the tendency to view TEECSA as enjoying an autonomous existence, apart from its participating churches, is not in the interests of TEE in Southern Africa despite the considerable pressures moving the College in that direction. With regard to tutoring, what this kind of autonomy would mean, if it were taken to its logical conclusion, would be an independent network of regional tutors that would overlay separate tutoring or mentoring systems operated by the Churches as part of their TFM/FOV organisation. Unless some kind of "division of labour" were to be worked out, and probably even then, this cannot be an effective or desirable approach.

While Anglicans formed the largest proportion of TEECSA's student body, it was understandable that TEE tutoring relied largely, although not exclusively, on the Anglican TFM system. With the change in the denominational balance, along with the development of FOV/Intern Support systems of other churches, it seems that the time is right for a more deliberately ecumenical approach. But this cannot be effected by TEECSA in isolation—if for no other reason, because of the very small size of the College's academic and administrative staff. At present this amounts in total to only thirteen full-time staff—including a receptionist and housekeeper. Of this number only the principal and a subject-adviser are theologically educated academics, although there are also three part-time subject advisers. The College relies on the services of a large number of markers whose fulltime employment is elsewhere but who are integral to the life of the College, along with regional coordinators and tutors. (Because of TEECSA's organisational and geographical situation the roles of marker and tutor are seldom combined in a single person—contrary to usual TEE philosophy—and this is another factor to be brought into the consideration of the tutoring system.

Therefore, if TEECSA is to avoid the superimposition of TEE tutoring on top of denominational mentoring systems, a focused and well-coordinated ecumenical effort is required. It must be borne in mind that some students of participating Churches study through other institutions—primarily the University of South Africa (UNISA)—although the bulk of the Churches' populations of theological students outside of residential seminaries study through TEECSA. An obvious approach to establishing an inclusive and effective system would be to develop a shared tutoring system across denominations, centering on TEE studies, allied with denominational Fellowships of Vocation. The shared tutoring system and the separate FOV systems could mesh and complement each other in a very constructive manner. In the meanwhile TEECSA rejoices in its largest number of students in thirty years as well as an increased role in theological education in the Churches. It continues to operate a network of eighteen regional centres across Southern Africa with their associated tutoring arrangements.

TEE in a New Educational Dispensation
The New Political Context of Theological Education in South Africa

Over the last few years the Theological Education by Extension College of Southern Africa (TEECSA) has been engaged in a major curriculum transformation project, tying in with the post-1994 national education transformation programme in South Africa. The national move towards educational transformation in South Africa has challenged TEECSA to reconsider its curriculum approach, although the educational challenge that TEECSA has responded to in the last few years is broader in its scope than an attempt to adjust to national education policy. Before going on to consider curriculum issues it is necessary to examine the wider policy context of the new curriculum approach.

One element within the overall new national policy is the compulsory registration of non-state educational institutions. This process and its attendant requirements has impacted strongly on the theological education institutions of the Churches. Authorities within national education have made it clear that the previous arrangement, under which TEECSA operated the tertiary component of its education programme, is no longer acceptable. Under this system TEECSA was a member of the Joint Board for the Theology Diploma which included representation from across mainline denominations in Southern Africa. A common diploma was awarded to students of colleges that operated under the Joint Board, with quality assurance being provided by the Board.

TEECSA has, from 2005, withdrawn from the Joint Board, having pursued registration independently —the only course now open to it under legislation. It seems that the Joint Board system, originally instituted in order to counter the divisive policies of Apartheid, will not survive in the new dispensation. The extension of a degree of state control over at least this aspect of church life has not occurred without some expression of concern in Christian quarters. But in the main the issue has not been construed, on either side, as a church-state confrontation. It is widely recognized that the institutional registration policy has been motivated by a real concern to prevent abuses and to protect the interests of students. Abuses by fly-by-night operations have occurred in the wider education sector, and theological education cannot be regarded as being immune to such problems.

TEECSA has been expected to maintain a financial reserve to cover potential losses by students in the event of sudden closure or collapse of the College. This is one amongst many other requirements of an organisational, financial, health-and-safety, or educational nature, which the College has had to meet. Together they have imposed a burden which is beyond the capacity of small denominational colleges to bear—some with less than a dozen students. Already there have been colleges which operated under the aegis of the Joint Board that have now approached TEECSA with a view to registering their students as TEECSA students. As long as aspects such as registration, financial payments, and educational evaluation and quality control reside with TEECSA, as a registered college, these other colleges may continue their operations —although clearly with a radical reduction in their status, compared with the situation in the Joint Board, where they sat as equal partners.

The pros and cons of these developments cannot be seen in isolation from broader issues that have begun to emerge more insistently in national political debate within South Africa. The attempt to establish strong central political control has been seen within the government as a necessary means to the development of a transformed society, but it has evoked contrary opinions, and this has extended into broad differences within the African National Congress as the governing party. This wider political debate relates at most indirectly to the question of state registration of theological colleges, but there are wider issues relating to social democracy versus neo-liberalism which are more directly significant to theological education. These are dealt with elsewhere in this account of the work of TEECSA.

Curriculum Change

With regard to the process of education itself, the outcomes-based approach, which serves as the curriculum foundation of the new National Qualifications Framework (NQF), has much to commend it in the view of TEE College. Indeed, there is much common ground between the concerns driving the new outcomes-based education (OBE) in South Africa and wider trends in theological education over the past few decades, which have also been reflected in the broad theological education-by-extension movement (e.g. Fraser, 1988; Banks, 1999).

Amongst the issues that South African OBE was designed to address (RSA Dept of Education, undated, c. 1996) there are two essential concerns that can be identified: education should be rooted and applicable within its social context; and, as a consequence of the educational process, learners should possess usable knowledge. These concerns stand in contrast to an approach to education in which the idea of "knowledge for its own sake" is expressed in an exaggerated form, so that textbooks and the information that they contain are elevated to the status of sacred text, to be transmitted, memorized, and perhaps contemplated but not used.

Freire (2000) highlights the way in which this dovetails with the maintenance of the hegemony of oppressive governments, but the tendency to slide into this kind of educational mindset appears to be more pervasive than can be explained by political motives alone. Perhaps, to look on the more positive side, it has much to do with traditional respect for knowledge, of the kind that Peat (1995) attributes to Native American culture but which is characteristic of other cultures also. But the knowledge of traditional cultures was dynamically integrated within those cultures and was available to their members as a living reality. With the exception, perhaps, of the sacred texts of some of those cultures, it was not like the static, inert bodies of codified information that have been the currency of much Western education, since at least the Renaissance.

Experience, Knowledge and Theology

Theology serves as a particularly illuminating instance of these issues concerning knowledge. It is instructive to note the emphasis placed by Vladimir Lossky, from a perspective outside that of the modern West, on the dynamic basis of theological knowledge, in his *Mystical Theology of the Eastern Church* (Lossky, 1969). Lossky describes how "dogmatic theology" is dependent for its life and its reality on "mystical theology" or, as modern Western Christians would put it, on spirituality. Lossky, in opposition to the notion that mystics are a rare and unusual class, insists that the experience of the divine mystery is available to Christians in general. But the common mystical experience of Christians is crystallized and codified in the statements of dogmatic theology, to serve as a map, and a norm, to guide Christians on the spiritual path.

In the history of the West, though, as Hans Urs von Balthasar shows, dogmatic or systematic theology tended to become detached from experience (von Balthasar, 1997). And so "theology", now categorized and functioning separately from spirituality, was open to being taught and learned as a "subject" that was more-or-less divorced from the experience it was intended to represent.

It would be unjust to apply the term "arid intellectualism" to theology and the study of theology in general. Thomas Aquinas, who did most to establish theology as an arena for the operation of the rational intellect, and from whom von Balthasar dates the divorce of theology and spirituality in the West, certainly treated theology as a dynamic enterprise. The *Summa Theologica*, which embodies Aquinas's teaching and learning approach, does not proceed as a series of propositions, but instead deals with topics through successive steps of argumentation. Modern theology has certainly done much to maintain the tradition of argument and debate, as any review of theology over the last two centuries will show. But, whether it was presented as a set of propositions to be memorized or as a process of disputation, the heavily intellectual nature of the theological enterprise has been common cause. In this regard, TEECSA course writers have endeavored to take students beyond the merely intellectual, by attempting to engage students at other levels also. This is particularly evident in the treatment of "systematic theology", which now is incorporated in the new diploma/degree core course, "Growing Spiritually, Thinking Theologically", and the follow-up elective course, "Wrestling with our Faith". The workbooks and assignments in these courses demand that students relate theological concepts to their context and get them to engage affectively as well as intellectually.

Apart from systematic theology, an illustration of the intellectual emphasis in theological education in general can be found in the Christian Spirituality course of the old TEECSA/Joint Board curriculum. TEECSA course materials have always been written in such a way as to engage students intellectually and provoke them to debate issues. In the case of Christian Spirituality this approach was applied to the development of different forms of spirituality in the Christian tradition. What the course did not do was to require students to *practice* the spirituality of the *Cloud of Unknowing* or the exercises of Ignatius Loyola—which might rate high amongst the kinds of outcomes that could be expected from an outcomes-based version of such a course. By contrast, the TEECSA Certificate course, "Spirituality—Walking Closer with Jesus", has always, in the words of our Year Book, aimed to "introduce you to a variety of ways of praying and help you grow your own prayer experience", as well as helping students to "discover what a rule of life is and how to experience spiritual growth as a journey".

To a significant degree the Certificate and, at a lower academic level, the Award courses have consistently over the years maintained this kind of broad "outcomes-based" approach, long before OBE became an explicit educational policy. The old Joint Board diploma courses were not entirely lacking in this regard either, although they were presented far more in the traditional academic style of university courses—which was recognized positively, for example, in the direct admission of TEE diploma-graduates to postgraduate university studies. On the other hand, neither the Award nor the Certificate courses have lacked intellectual rigor at the level appropriate to those qualifications. For example, in the Certificate, currently equated to Grade 12 although to a large degree it goes beyond that level, students are required to engage with textual, source, redaction and form criticism. And in the Award program, students are introduced to the historical-critical understanding of the Bible. OBE is intended as holistic education, and one aspect of a whole education must obviously be a concern with intellectual development. But good educational intentions, including approaches that aim to be holistic, must be measured against the degree of success that they achieve in their implementation.

Looking Critically at OBE

Less than a decade ago, when OBE was still news in South Africa, the outspoken black educationist, Professor Jonathan Jansen complained sarcastically about a headline in an educational newspaper, which read, "OBE saves children". (Jansen, 1998) His comment was, "It sounds like a Methodist". Perhaps he might instead have said Baptist or Pentecostal—Methodists have not always maintained their evangelistic enthusiasm—but the point he made needed to be recognized. There was an initial widespread and uncritical enthusiasm for the "new education" that had some of the flavor of religious fervor. The old was bad, and the new was good, and therefore it was foreordained that its promise would be inevitably and triumphantly fulfilled.

Jansen's position was more realistic. At the time of the introduction of the OBE school curriculum he presented a paper titled "Why OBE will fail" (Jansen, undated c. 1997). One of his concerns related to the issue of complexity, which will be referred to below. More generally, Jansen's perspective was that of a political and educational radical—very different from that of a conservative TEECSA student who characterized OBE in an assignment in the Christian Education course as "humanistic and relativistic."

There are indeed major educational approaches that do proceed from that kind of ideological base, but a stronger case could be made for the assertion that the outcomes-based approach has stronger roots in neo-conservative concerns with accountability and means-ends thinking. This is not to damn OBE which, at least in the original South African version, is a complex amalgam of various educational approaches including a strong infusion of radical educational theory.

Apart from ideological concerns and the complex features of the school curriculum, some of Jansen's objections were at a more practical level. With large numbers of schools lacking electricity and even water, and quite often without glass in their windows, in his opinion it was poor prioritization, as well as irrational, to expend scarce resources on a complex approach, which was beyond the capacity of a poorly trained teaching work-force.

Problems with OBE at the school level, which had been predicted by Jansen, led to the appointment of a ministerial review committee early in 2000. The new education minister's forthright public criticisms of the complexity of the transformed school curriculum, which he had inherited from his predecessor, were addressed in the implementation of the review committee's recommendations (RSA Dept of Education 2000). But this was achieved by the introduction in the school system of a revised form of OBE curriculum that was, perhaps, somewhat closer to the older, content-based, 'aims and objectives' type of curriculum, than to the radical form of OBE which it replaced.

Where does this leave the new TEECSA curriculum? Along with the rest of post-school education in South Africa we have retained the original OBE-curriculum features of specific outcomes and the assessment criteria and range statements which specify how those outcomes should be achieved. But the aborted school curriculum had incorporated far more than these essential features. It had required the coordination of these features with two complexly intersecting sets of 'organizers' (themes): one set prescribed according to the phase of schooling and the other to be negotiated by schools in consultation with local communities. The school curriculum was therefore intended to be strongly contextual—an aspect which had been brought into the post-1994 curriculum process from the radical *peoples' education* of the anti-Apartheid struggle era, inspired largely by the work of Paulo Freire.

The intention in the initial curriculum transformation had been to produce an education system that would be sensitive to the need for contextualization, while remaining grounded in sets of specific outcomes that were determined by committees of educationists for each learning area. In practice the system as a whole was an over-complex synthesis of too many unfamiliar curriculum features, which was imposed on a teaching profession and parent communities who were very largely unprepared for what it required of them.

OBE in the TEEC Curriculum

TEECSA's new curriculum has not been without its teething problems—no new curriculum ever is—but it has not had to deal with the crippling complexities of the first attempt at an outcomes-based school curriculum. TEECSA's curriculum transformation has been built around the three curriculum features of specific outcomes, assessment criteria and range statements, instead of the multiplicity of features in the initial OBE curriculum for the school system.

In each course it is first of all the specific outcomes that are essential for the course: they describe what it is that students will be able *to do* when they have completed that course. This emphasis on performance originates in a strongly contested period of recent educational history. It goes back to the dominance of behaviorist psychology in the field of learning theory. This led to the emergence in the 1960s and 1970s of the "objectives movement", which had a powerful influence on education. Behaviorism modeled principles for human learning on research that dealt with the training of animal behaviors. The result was a very restricted notion of learning, as well as an emphasis on 'performance' as the only valid outcome of learning.

As is shown later in this article, the outcomes around which the new TEEC courses have been constructed are very different from the kind of 'educational outcomes' advocated by the behavioral objectives movement of a few decades ago. But the notion of 'performance', with some critical reappraisal, continues to be a vital one in the form of OBE espoused by TEECSA. To behaviorists, terms like "understanding", "insight" or "appreciation", are anathema. Only a directly observable performance could be accepted as a legitimate learning outcome, and this often tended to restrict educational outcomes to activities like naming or listing facts.

When OBE was introduced into South Africa, some of the initial explanatory publications seemed to indicate a behaviorist interpretation of the nature of outcomes and of performance. But this soon gave way to the much broader, and more educationally justifiable understanding of outcomes that is to be seen also in the new TEEC courses.

In view of criticism of the ideological basis of OBE, which has come from some conservative Christian quarters in South Africa, it is interesting to consider approaches that have been introduced from the USA into schools set up by conservative-evangelical and charismatic Christian groups in South Africa. It seems that the desire for a sound "scientific" footing (as opposed to an ideological base) for education has delivered some Christians into the hands of behaviorist psychological science, as they attempt to develop alternative curricula. Their curricula appear to owe much to rigidly structured approaches such as 'programmed learning' which were the educational expression of behaviorism. The questionable concept of education that is associated with the behavioral objectives approach seems to have escaped the notice of some who have tried to develop explicitly Christian curricula.

Neither the ideological argument against OBE, nor the problems in curriculum design that undermined the initial introduction of OBE within the school curriculum, are relevant to the process of curriculum transformation in which TEECSA has been engaged. Indeed, still further differences may be noted between the implementation of OBE by TEECSA and the implementation of the new curriculum ('Curriculum 2005') in the school system in the second half of the 1990s. 'Curriculum 2005' was heavily criticized by the review committee for its failure to address learners' needs for systematic progression and the development of a strong knowledge base. Laudable educational aims such as critical thinking and contextualization can only come to nothing in the absence of an extensive and systematic foundation of knowledge. This was a trap which TEECSA avoided in its own curriculum redevelopment.

The flawed and under-resourced implementation of the new school curriculum had seen ordinary teachers in the classroom grasping at whatever elements they could make sense of in the new curriculum. The most common, noted critically in the report of the review committee, was a reliance on group-work that grew out of the vague hope that this was somehow "doing OBE". As long as learners were placed in groups with some kind of task—any kind of task—teachers felt that they were demonstrating their progress in adapting to the new system. This kind of response, along with the shift from a "content" to a "process" emphasis, as well as the focus on "themes" or "organizers" led to a situation in which the committee found that there was too little attention given to the development of a knowledge base.

In the TEECSA curriculum process there has been a very firm commitment to the understanding of outcomes as more than a mere list of content-topics to master. But knowledge remains foundational to the new approach even though the emphasis is placed on performance-processes. The new curriculum has as its building blocks what have been called "Unit Standards", which are very different from the old notion of a syllabus, but a review of the outcomes and their associated assessment criteria in any TEECSA course demonstrates how process and performance are integrated with knowledge.

In order to clarify how the outcomes-based, Unit Standard approach operates, refer to the appendices relating to the course, "Growing Spiritually, Thinking Theologically"—which is based on two Unit Standards, one with a focus on spirituality and the other on theology, and the follow-up course, "Wrestling with our Faith":

Appendix 1: Extracts from the introduction to the workbook for Course 6/7003.

Appendix 2: Outcomes and assessment criteria for the Unit Standard: Analyse and apply key Christian teachings in context.

Appendix 3: TEE College Assessment Record and Feedback on Assignment.

Appendix 4: "Growing Spiritually, Thinking Theologically" examination paper, 2005.

Appendix 5: Markers' guide for "Growing Spiritually, Thinking Theologically" examination paper, 2005.

Appendix 6: Assignment 2 for Course 6/7243 "Wrestling with our Faith".

Appendix 7: Commentary on materials relating to Unit Standards and assessment.

References

Banks, R.
> 1999 *Reenvisioning Theological Education: Exploring a Missional Alternative to Current Models.* Grand Rapids, Michigan: W.B. Eerdmans.

Fraser, I.M.
> 1988 *Reinventing Theology As the People's Work,* 3rd edition. Glasgow: Wild Goose Publications.

Freire, P.
> 2000 *Pedagogy of the Oppressed (30th anniversary edition).* London: Continuum.

Jansen, J.
> undated, circa 1997 "Why OBE Will Fail." Occasional paper, Faculty of Education, University of Durban-Westville.

> 1998 Personal communication.

Lossky, V.
> 1969 *The Mystical Theology of the Eastern Church.* New York: St Vladimir's Seminary Press.

Peat, F. D.
>   1995 *Blackfoot Physics: A Journey into the Native American Universe.* London: Fourth Estate.

RSA Department of Education
>   circa 1996 "An Outcomes-based Approach to Educational and Curriculum Development in South Africa." Occasional paper. Pretoria: Department of Education.

>   2000 Report of the Curriculum 2005 Review Committee. Pretoria: Department of Education.

Von Balthasar, H. U.
>   1997 "Retrieving the Tradition: The Fathers, the Scholastics and Ourselves." *Communio 24.* 370-384.

APPENDIX 1: EXTRACTS FROM THE INTRODUCTION TO COURSE 6/7003

We welcome you to this course on Growing Spiritually, Thinking Theologically. It is a core course for the TEE Diploma in Theology and Ministry and for the Degree in Theology.

This course is made up of two Unit Standards—that is two educational building blocks. A Unit Standard describes a single *educational process with its outcomes.* It tells you that when you have completed it, you *will be able to do or achieve or perform this or that.* It also tells you what the **assessment criteria are.** These assessment criteria tell you how we can know *whether you have achieved the outcomes.*

The two Unit Standards that comprise this course are:

- Describe and assess key Christian spiritualities in historical and contemporary context

- Analyse and apply key Christian teachings in context

This means that you have two sets of outcomes to fulfil in order to complete this course. You will achieve competence in this part of your training in theology and ministry when you are able to do the things that these outcomes describe.

In order to simplify your reading of these outcomes they are listed firstly without their assessment criteria. Thereafter, the assessment criteria for the outcomes of this course are listed. In addition, there is an explanation of how to understand assessment criteria.

Here are the outcomes for the two Unit Standards that make up this course:

Outcomes for 'Describe and assess key Christian spiritualities in historical and contemporary context': **When you have completed the work required by this Unit Standard, you will be able to:**

- Outline and evaluate classical and contemporary models of Christian spirituality

- Demonstrate the relevance and applicability of various models to the Southern African context

- Identify and address key personal aspects of spiritual formation.

Outcomes for 'Analyse and apply key Christian teachings in context: **When you have completed the work required by this Unit Standard, you will be able to:**

- Describe and critique key Christian doctrines in a range of contexts.

- Outline and analyse a range of ways of constructing theology.

- Compare and contrast interpretations of key doctrines.

- Apply key Christian doctrines to contemporary contexts.

On the following pages you will find these outcomes repeated, but with the assessment criteria for each outcome shown next to it. But first, on the next page after this one, there is an explanation of how to understand and use these assessment criteria.

Assessment Criteria

Before you start Chapter 1, we need to introduce you to the assessment criteria that relate to the outcomes of this course, and to explain to you how they work.

For example, the first outcome of the first Unit Standard states that: "When you have completed the work required by this Unit Standard, you will be able to *outline and evaluate classical and contemporary models of Christian spirituality.*"

Can you do this? And how will you, and the marker, know when you are able to do it? If you look at the assessment criteria for this outcome you will see that the first assessment criterion says that, "*Models of Christian spirituality are outlined with reference to their specific social, cultural and religious contexts.*"

What this assessment criterion means is that somewhere in your assignments, and/or the examination, you must prove to the marker that you know and understand a range of different models of Christian spirituality. You will have to describe them and you will have to show how they are related to the social, cultural and religious contexts within which they have been developed and used. How will you be able to prove this to the marker? You will need to complete a task in an assignment (or the examination) in which you are required to do this.

But, as you will see, this is not the only assessment criterion for the first outcome: there are another two as well. So, in order to be competent in that outcome, you also have to be able to do what the second and third assessment criteria for that outcome describe.

[For the sake of brevity only the assessment criteria for the second unit standard are provided in Appendix 2.]

Appendix 2: Assessment Criteria for the Outcomes of the Unit Standard: Analyse and Apply Key Christian Teachings in Context

Outcome 1: Describe and critique key Christian doctrines in a range of contexts.

Assessment Criteria for Outcome 1:

a) The description locates the doctrines in their biblical setting.

b) The description is consistent with the historical development of key Christian teachings.

c) The critique shows an awareness of issues, conflicts and contemporary understandings of these teachings.

Outcome 2: Outline and analyse a range of ways of constructing theology.

Assessment Criteria for Outcome 2:

a) The outlines identify the key processes used by each theological model.

b) The outlines identify the key doctrines, issues and foci of each theological model.

c) The analyses show the strengths and weaknesses of the chosen models in contemporary context.

Outcome 3: Compare and contrast interpretations of key doctrines.

Assessment Criteria for Outcome 3:

a) The interpretations of the chosen key Christian doctrines show key contrasting perspectives and a sensitive outlook to difference.

b) The comparisons include an awareness of the positionality of the learner's faith community.

Outcome 4: Apply key Christian doctrines to contemporary contexts.

Assessment Criteria for Outcome 4:

a) The contemporary contexts chosen must be significant for the learner's faith and wider communities.

b) The applications are in keeping with the learner's understanding of the *Missio Dei*.

c) The application shows potential for transformation of the context.

Appendix 3: TEE College Assessment Record and Feedback on Assignment ______ of Course Number ___

Learner's Name__________Registration Number__________Marker_________

Resubmission results for Assignment number__		Was a resubmission required?	Was it submitted?	Result of resubmission
Outcomes	Outcome achieved? (Y/N)	Marker's comment (see script for fuller description)		Repeat and resubmit the parts listed below
Task 1 to achieve outcome no ______				
Task 2 to achieve outcome no ______				
Task 3 to achieve outcome no ______				
Task 4 to achieve outcome no ______				
<u>Source References</u>		Reference List	Word limit	Presentation

Marker's signature:_______Date of marking:______Overall result:___

Key: C—Competent, no need for further work. D—Resubmit the parts indicated. E—Resubmit all. B—Excellent work. A—Outstanding work.

APPENDIX 4: TASKS FROM THE 2005 COURSE 6/7003 'GROWING SPIRITUALLY, THINKING THEOLOGICALLY' EXAMINATION PAPER

Note: All three tasks had to be attempted in the 3 hours allocated.

Task 1

a) Choose *one* of the following spiritualities, with which you will work in this task in b), c) and d).

New Testament, Franciscan, Methodist, Pentecostal

b) You have been asked to give a talk to a group in your church about the most important features of the spirituality you chose in Task (a) above. Write brief notes on each of the important features of this spirituality on which you would base your talk.

c) Choose **one** of these features, and explain its underlying biblical and theological principles.

d) Give a Rule of Life based on this spirituality, for a minister working with a group of churches in *either* rural *or* township Southern Africa. Explain how this Rule of Life would be appropriate to the context and lifestyle of such a minister, and what the benefits would be.

Task 2

Write notes for a sermon entitled "There are many ways of knowing God." In these notes, include reference to knowing God through each of the following:

a) Jesus Christ

b) The witness of scripture

c) Personal experience

d) Conscience

Task 3

a) Choose *one* of the following doctrines, with which you will work in this task:

Christology—Soteriology—Christian Anthropology

b) A non-Christian friend has asked you to explain what Christians believe about this doctrine. **Write a letter** in which you list what

Christians believe about the doctrine, point by point, giving a simple explanation for each point.

c) After you have finished the letter, choose **two of the points** that you discussed, and outline their biblical foundations.

d) Discuss the importance of these same two points in relation to worship in your church and pastoral care in your community. In other words, what difference does believing those two things make to the way you worship and the way you care?

Appendix 5: Markers' Guide for 2005 Examination of Course 6/7003: 'Growing Spiritually, Thinking Theologically'

General Comments	• This is a summative assessment: therefore students should be competent in ALL outcomes in as far as they are questioned in this examination. A caveat, however, would be that if one of the Tasks is not finished (usually due to time constraints), the student may be declared competent provided the other two Tasks are well done and completed • There is no opportunity for a resubmission. • Source references and a Reference List (or Bibliography) are not required, although in certain questions students are required to make reference to biblical or other sources.
TASK 1 **To achieve the overall Outcomes for "Spiritualities"**	a) The choice of spirituality should be clearly stated. b) This should be in the format of a talk (but if it isn't, reserve judgement about 'competence' until you've gone through the whole script). It should cover the basic points of the chosen spirituality and give a brief description of them in lay people's terms. (A description of the group is not required in the question, but be ready to reward if the description is there and the language is appropriate to the described group). c) The chosen feature must be clearly stated. The student MUST give support from the Bible and give theological explanations of the spirituality's feature (in principle the workbooks should be referred to). d) The question wants to see a Rule of Life as being appropriate to a CONTEXT, so that must be shown. So there must be at least a basic Rule of Life, a brief explanation of the Rule and a list of benefits for the minister which shows at least some reference TO THE CHOSEN CONTEXT.

TASK 2 **To achieve the overall Outcomes for "Teachings"**	This should be in sermon format (building up a judgement, as said in 1(a) above). So there should be (in 'note form') an introduction, several 'points' and a conclusion (hopefully with an invitation or challenge to some action step). And it should use words which lay people will relate to and understand. It is not necessary that the four 'modes' are separated into four headings (although it's easier to assess if it is!) Look for relevance to the 'modes' and to 'knowing God'. (Reward awareness that 'knowing God' is itself quite a slippery notion!)
TASK 3 **To achieve Outcome "Teachings" 2**	a) Their choice of doctrine should be clearly stated. b) This must be presented in letter format (here's where a cumulative 'competence' judgement about 'form' and 'responding to requirements might come to a head). The question asks for a 'point by point' format, so look for that. Christian technical words must be explained simply. Reward attempts to relate to the friend's actual beliefs (e.g. if Jewish, the student might explain how the Blood of Jesus the Lamb washes our sins away.) c) This must (obviously!) not be a part of the letter. There must be biblical references (or at least allusions to biblical passages). Theological references would also be acceptable. d) There must be clear links between parts (c) and (d). The question asks for application to Worship AND Pastoral Care. This answer may be in point form. Reward awareness that the whole course has sought to integrate 'theology' and 'spirituality'.

C=Competent; B=Better than minimum performance, A=Advanced competence. D=not yet competent in some of the required outcomes. E=not yet competent in any of the outcomes. *(For borderline cases, take the year's record into account!)*

Appendix 6: Course 6/7243 Assignment 2
Task 1
This task is designed to achieve Outcome 2.1:

Describe and compare a range of key New Testament understandings of the death of Jesus and the symbol of the Cross.

The relevant assessment criteria are:

> *2.1.1—Texts dealing with the redemptive significance of the cross are identified and exegeted.*

> *2.1.2—A simple typology of New Testament perspectives on redemption is constructed.*

Part 1 (Assessment criterion 2.1.1)

Prepare notes on which you can base a series of sermons on 'The death of Jesus and the symbol of the Cross'. Your notes must be related to appropriate passages from the New Testament.

Note: You do *not* have to prepare full sermons. You only need to provide summary notes. These notes should be based on exegesis of at least four New Testament passages that you have chosen. These must include at least one from each of the Synoptic Gospels, John's Gospel and the Epistles.

Part 2 (Assessment criterion 2.1.2)

From your conversations with members of your local church you have realised that many Christians have a very limited understanding of the meaning of redemption through Christ.

Produce a simple table that you can make available as a resource for Bible study groups, to help them explore the topic: 'Different perspectives on redemption in the New Testament'. In your table provide an outline, in summary form, of major New Testament perspectives on redemption.

Task 2

This task is designed to achieve Outcome 2.2:

Describe and compare a range of key Christian understandings of the death of Jesus and the symbol of the Cross.

The relevant assessment criteria are:

2.2.1—A simple typology of Christian perspectives on redemption is constructed.

2.2.2—The impact on Christian life and preaching of different perspectives is outlined.

You have been asked to lead a seminar for lay preachers in which you will deal with the topic of the death of Jesus and the symbol of the Cross.

Prepare notes for a short talk in which you focus on different perspectives on redemption that developed in the history of Christianity after the New Testament period.

Note: In your preparation you should cover a wide range of major perspectives on redemption. You must identify each clearly and indicate the significance of these different perspectives for the Christian life.

Task 3

This task is designed to achieve Outcome 2.3:

Outline a personal faith perspective on the cross.

The relevant assessment criteria are:

> *2.3.1—The learner's own understanding of the cross is described in terms of the typology required in Assessment Criterion 2.2.1.*

> *2.3.2—The personal perspective is critiqued in the light of a broader and more inclusive range.*

A Christian friend has heard that you are studying theology. He/she is suspicious about academic theology, and thinks that it confuses ordinary Christians. Your friend also insists that there is only one acceptable way of explaining what the death of Jesus is about. You want to explain to him/her that there is no simple explanation of the meaning of the Cross of Christ. *Write a letter to your friend in which you:*

- *Describe the view of the death of Jesus and the Cross that you held before you began your theological studies.*

- *Show where your original view fits in the range of perspective(s) on redemption that have been put forward in the history of Christian theology.*

- *Explain how that view of yours is open to criticism from other perspectives.*

- *Identify your present view and explain either why it has not changed or why it has changed, since you began studying theology.*

Note: You should *not* divide your letter according to the four points listed in the task. These points are listed as guidelines for writing your letter.

Task 4

This task is designed to achieve Outcome 2.4:

Apply the doctrine of redemption in personal and community situations.

The relevant assessment criteria are:

> *2.4.1—The redemptive need is clearly and concretely defined (e.g. HIV affected orphans in the community; an enquirer into the Christian faith; a land restitution claim)*

> *2.4.2—The theological and practical elements of the process are explained (including how the Christian doctrine of redemption impacts on the situation and how practically the doctrine could be used to alter the situation).*

Reflect on the full meaning and the extent of redemption, as it has been dealt with in the workbooks of his course. Identify a redemptive need in your situation (see the assessment criterion 2.4.1 for examples, but do not limit yourself to these). Then proceed with the following task.

Analyse a situation, with which you are familiar, in which there is a clearly identifiable need for redemption. In your analysis you should do the following:

- *Define the redemptive need clearly and concretely.*

- *Survey different perspectives on redemption and identify one or more that are relevant to the situation which you have identified.*

- *Explain how the perspective(s) relate to the situation or impacts on it.*

- *Outline how the perspective(s) on the Christian doctrine of redemption might be applied in practice, to bring about a change in situation.*

Note: You are not required to provide evidence of the implementation of your plan for the application of the doctrine of redemption.

APPENDIX 7: COMMENTARY ON APPENDICIES RELATING TO UNIT STANDARDS AND ASSESSMENT

Appendices 1 and 2: Note that the new TEECSA diploma/degree course are most often composed of two Unit Standards although a few comprise one unit Standard, and it is also possible to build a course from three. Functionally it is the specific outcomes that are essential to the new courses. The assessment criteria are crucial to the setting of assignment and examination tasks, as they are the parameters which define what the outcomes entail in practice. Obviously, though, they are important to both course-writers and learners, and they are therefore included prominently in both the assignment booklets and in the workbooks of each course.

Appendix 3: This generic sheet for assessment and feedback replaces marks, percentages etc. As a consequence of the shift away from a syllabus/content approach, the nature of assessment has to change radically. It is not possible to assess work by counting ticks corresponding to either items of information or ideas. The 'marker' must instead assess the competence of learners in relation to the outcomes of the course, by referring to the relevant assessment criteria. In place of a numerical value, the assessor must make a judgement regarding competence in the performance of outcomes.

The assignment tasks (see **Appendix 6** for examples) provide learners with the opportunity to demonstrate their competence in the outcomes related to those tasks. Similarly, examinations present tasks that are related to the course's outcomes (see **Appendices 4 and 5**) although it should be noted that only a minority of TEECSA course now include an examination.

A major difference in the way that the new approach to assessment operates is that it is not possible to 'pass' a course unless all its outcomes have been successfully achieved. It is not possible for a student to rely on a summation of marks from good and bad answers to pull him or her through. But, on the other hand, this has necessitated a system of resubmission in order for students, who have not achieved competence in one or other aspect, to proceed. Where there is an examination the situation is perhaps more tricky but, because an examination is intended to provide an overall assessment of a course, failure to achieve competence in one or even a few aspects can be condoned in the light of performance in assignments.

With regard to the grades that are reflected in the sheet in **Appendix 3** some issues need to be pointed out. A strict OBE approach to assessment would provide grades of 'competent' or 'not competent' only. But, in common with other tertiary institutions, TEECS has continued to recognise the need to acknowledge superlative performance by students. Hence the inclusion of 'A' and 'B' grades. This can be problematic in that 'C' betokens *competence*, not a quantitative/numerical evaluation. This has led to the decision to replace at least the 'D' and 'E' grades with NYC (not yet competent) and NC (not competent) respectively. Note that D/NYC requires only certain tasks in an assignment to be redone, while E/NC requires students to redo a whole assignment.

With regard to resubmissions, these are limited, for example, to no more than two assignments in a course with four assignments. Also, student retain credit for assignments even if they do not achieve competence in a course as a whole. They can then reregister to complete the outstanding assignments in a further year of study. This is in line with a philosophy of assisting students to achieve competence, rather than seeking to identify certain students as failures.

Tony Moodie

tony@tee.co.za

Questions for Reflection and Discussion

1. *What was the role of the TEEC vis a vis the pre-1994 Apartheid regime? What is the role of the TEEC post-1994?*

2. *How does the TEEC relate to the churches of South Africa? What are the responsibilities of the churches in this model of theological education?*

3. *What is "Outcomes Based Education"? How does it differ from traditional curricula? How does the TEEC curriculum incorporate this educational philosophy?*

4. *What is your evaluation of TEEC's new curriculum as it is explained in the appendices of this case study? How does this curriculum design compare with your own program? Does your curriculum provide clear standards and assessment criteria for each unit?*

5. *What do the students' stories at the beginning of this case study reveal about its impact? What stories from your own program best reveal its impact?*

Chapter 4: Africa

TEE among African Instituted Churches

by Helena Hooper

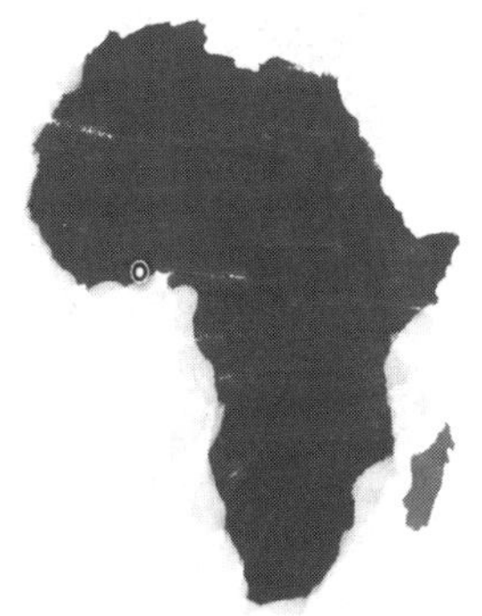

INTRODUCTION

The African Instituted Churches have been in existence since the early 19th century. Noted among the early churches or movements are the Mosama Disco Christo Churches, Nkansah, Cherubim and Seraphim, Aladura and Apostolic churches and the Church of Brotherhood, to name a few. Whatever the motives are, the indigenous or native people felt very much at home and identified with the traditional flavour and the way of worship, especially in liturgies, reading and hearing the Word of God in the vernacular, traditional ways of dressing, songs and welcoming as would be done traditionally, with not too many restrictions. It is also the church for the poor, semi-literates, or illiterates, marginalised and people on the fringes of society, even though this has slightly changed with time and trends.

The Organization of African Instituted Churches (OAIC), which was founded in 1978, is an association of African Independent churches (AICs) with membership in 22 African countries. It was formed as a response to the lack of unity among AICs, inadequate theological trained leadership, non-recognition by other churches, especially the mission churches, sidelining by national governments, thus not being able to contribute to development; and poverty in these churches. The OAIC was to create a common platform for the member churches to address some of these issues and more. This will also lead to a better future for member churches to be self-governing, self-propagating and self-sustaining.

The OAIC is organised into seven regional blocks, which are East Africa, Nigeria, Southern Africa, Anglophone West Africa, Francophone West Africa, the Democratic Republic of Congo, and Madagascar. The Mission Statement of OAIC states that:

The OAIC seeks to bring African Instituted Churches together in fellowship and to equip and enable them to preach the Good News of Jesus Christ in word and deed.

This vision and this mission are realized through its programmes in the various regions and chapters across the continent of Africa.

The OAIC has since come a long way. The belief was that once a sound theological education was attained, other churches, society and governments would embrace them, and they could hold their own and add to the on-going debate in society in their various contexts.

OAIC groups its members into three categories: **Nationalist churches** (also known as Ethiopian and African churches). These are churches that seceded from the mission churches during the colonial era (beginning in 1844 in South Africa and in 1891 in Nigeria) over issues of leadership and a desire that Africans should control the church and its teachings on cultural practices. **Spiritual churches** (also known as Zionist, Apostolic, and Aladura churches). These churches (dating from 1910 onwards in Southern Africa and 1920 onwards in West and Eastern Africa) are sometimes referred to as "prophet-healing" churches, because of the centrality of the charismatic gifts in their worship and ministry (prophecy, interpretation of dreams, healing, and prayer for protection against evil).

African Pentecostal churches. These are African-founded Pentecostal style churches that have arisen since the mid-1960s. Though the stimulus to their foundation has frequently been the evangelistic missions and training conventions associated with Western Pentecostals, and as a result, there is some dispute whether these churches are fully African, a number of them (those that give a positive value to African culture) have found a home in the OAIC. (Information from OAIC-Reformed Kigali Dialogue).

The case study will look at the OAIC TEE and Ghana Association of TEE programmes and how they have shaped TEE to suit the context, learners and enablers alike. They have trained different people at various levels in the church.

After the OAIC was begun in Cairo in 1978, it was realized that there was this need for training, and so a theological education advisory committee was formed, and they worked with the Programme on Theological Education of the World Council of Churches to send a couple who were Presbyterians (expatriates) to Kenya, to begin the TEE programme.

OAIC/TEE was a response to:

- the pastors' situation of poverty, the main reason why they are not educated, and the programme's potential for widespread learning,

- their lack of formal basic education and study skills, which prevents them from entering the seminaries, but which appropriate TEE materials can adapt to,

- the impracticality of abandoning their churches, family and employment in order to study,

- the need to learn what is relevant to their own context through new texts, which deal with contextual matters. Texts were created and written with a focus on needs as seen by the learners,

- the objective of learning through the facilitation of group discussion by trained enablers in the learners' own language and in homogenous groups where discussions are more relevant to the groups' contexts and strategies are planned to meet these needs,

- practical ministerial field experience in their local cultures and getting immediate feed back on their learning and training,

- the need to learn about participatory educational models like the dialogical method,

- the objective of serving the needs of a higher number of rural and poorer leaders in a given geographical area and rewarding the more mature leaders.

With the need assessment analysed they formulated general and specific objectives which would guide them in meeting the needs as enumerated above.

General Objectives of the programme were as follows:

- To provide biblical, theological, pastoral and spiritual studies and training for pastors and lay leaders of the member churches of the OAIC.

- To increase pastoral and administrative skills of church leaders.

- To provide the congregations in general with the opportunity for theological studies in order to develop a spiritually mature body of Christ, which affects positively the relationship between its members.

- To increase understanding of biblical truths through reflection upon the text and its relevance to the learners' existential content and context.

- To improve relations between the different independent churches in certain areas.

Specific objectives:

- To write and provide TEE texts with the relevant subjects in order to increase the learners' biblical knowledge and leadership skills.

- To use the Dialogical Method to help learners to reflect on the new knowledge and learn to apply it to their own situations.

- To increase opportunities for ecumenical relationships.

- To train the group leaders to use the Dialogical Method in the study centres as the way to help the learners reflect upon the subject matter in the TEE texts.

- To train Africans to write the Learning Through Discussion texts. (Batlle)

TEE done in a given context should be experiential as well as transformational. Learners should be mature at the end of the day and share what they have learned in the studies with the church. "Transformation in the learner takes place in three areas: personal faith development, cognitive, analytical and evaluative abilities for understanding Scriptures, personal experience and coping with the changing context, and acquiring skills that will supplement and or complement the gifts given by the Spirit, such as preaching, evangelising, teaching, administrating, communicating, meeting social concerns, for the situation where the believer lives and works." (Batlle)

The TEE director and the personnel realized that a number of needs had to be met, if OAIC/TEE was to educate and fulfil the vision and mission of the organization, that is, to train leaders and their churches theologically. They had to use the Dialogical Method. This method is an *educational technique to achieve the theological, philosophical and educational criteria* of the programme. It encourages sharing of ideas and experiences in a group. TEE is for adult learners, thus not only are the Bible and current issues to be shared, but there should be a process that will equip and empower the AIC member churches to realize and respond to the needs in their contexts. This will upgrade knowledge from one another and among the group. It will also build relationships and support, therefore fostering unity. The team decided to use the Learning Through Discussion (LTD) Method of writing of TEE manuals, which was most effective. To this end they began a process of producing manuals which were educative, interactive and friendly and uniquely OAIC.

Process of Training and Writing
Participants in the Programme

The programme was for all the member churches of the OAIC and a smaller percentage from other mainline churches. They realised that they had to create different levels for different categories or groups in the church. There were three levels: the basic, middle, and higher levels. They also took into consideration that a vast majority of AIC members were illiterates or semi-illiterates, that is, the number of educated people was not commensurate with the uneducated. They realized that most of the AICs were in the rural areas, and some could not study as a result of their occupation, family, and financial constraints. The main target groups were bishops and administrative staff, who were put at Level III; pastors and lay leaders were in the Level II category; other women and men were at Level I. All these were taken into consideration as they planned the writing of the manuals and training of facilitators.

The materials written concern the current needs, so they are relevant to the context of the learners and address situational needs. They are practical, as the learners make use of this education directly in their contexts. They are experiential because of the immediate application. As open sharing, study through the Dialogical Method, the giving and sharing with others in the groups helps the learners to minister to the church in a better way. The materials are written in such a way that they can study them on their own and at a point in time, depending on what the students decide, they meet together. This was being done as a distance education course, but it was popularly called a correspondence course. Study centres were created where trained enablers would meet with the group to study together.

Programme Personnel

There were the two Presbyterian ministers, two local pastors, one full time pastor and another part-time person also a pastor. They were responsible for planning and scheduling as well as coordinating the study centres, contacting persons, providing materials, etc. There was also a Coptic brother who was in charge of the accounts, and he helped to write a TEE text on Accounting. Among them they were able to write texts, which were tested as they were used in the field.

Some of the initial books written were *The Pastor as an Evangelist, What is the Bible? (OT), What Is the Bible? (NT), The Bible and Healing, Women and Evangelism (I&II), Understanding Youth, Guidance for Youth, Spiritual Leadership, Accounting, Amos, OT 1 and 2, Giving, Stewardship, Becoming a Christian (I &II)*, etc. Eventually thousands of books were produced in a year, as writers' workshops are held, and the programme spread to other parts of the continent. The numbers of enablers and facilitators have increased with time, with some trained particularly for their churches.

Profile of Facilitators/Enablers

The directors came up with a list of qualities an enabler or facilitator should have. Among these is for them to be humble, have some theological training in a Bible school or seminary, be respectful, interesting, punctual for studies, etc. This is because one meets different categories of people and an enabler should be an all round accommodating person.

The TEE Training Programme

Over the years, one of the major requirements of people from around the continent who have come to the centre to be trained was to write at least one TEE textbook, though some have written more than one. This is done over a three-month period, in which countries send trainees to be taught the principles of TEE. This begins with the study and analysis of the format and content of the TEE texts. The three weeks of exposure, participation or practical work in different study centres in West Kenya, further field work at two study centres in Nairobi writing two manuscripts based on issues in the trainee's contexts, and preparation of a TEE programme that will be used in the trainees' work in their context.

Format of the TEE Text

The book is always made up of four units with a fifth one on review. It has an introduction to the whole book with a general objective and aim. The units are divided into sessions with sub-titles. After each session there are multiple-choice questions, of which the correct answers are at the end of the book, but learners are not supposed to look at these answers until they have finished the whole unit or book. And they are faithful to that. The second part of the assignment is the discussion and sharing part. There are a number of open-ended questions for group discussion, and there is an additional question to clear any further misunderstanding on the session. The final part is the practical suggestion part, and this is what they do on their own and then share the results with the class when they meet.

Mini Libraries

The programme created mini libraries for some of the centres so as to equip the enablers with resource materials and also to supplement and complement the texts being used.

Methodology of Teaching

As already mentioned, the group meetings use the Dialogical Method, which complements the LTD format of the writing. "It was felt that this method would most likely encourage learning in the sense of discovering, exerting one's own intellectual effort, enquiring, comprehending the relationships among experiences, and questioning." (Batlle).

The enablers encourage everybody to participate in the discussion, as the principle is "Everybody deserves to be heard, and there is no wrong or right answer." Thus no one is sidelined as the questions are tackled. There is a last bit for practical suggestions that the learners are encouraged to do. The manuals were written in a way that it is very informative and educative and at the same time simple enough for all the different groups in the churches to be reached.

At the end of a series of courses learners are graduated with certificates. In order for people to be encouraged to study, the enablers would find an easy to be reached centre, which is usually an OAIC member church, and decide with the learners the most convenient time for them to meet. Based on this they meet once every week with the enabler. However, in no time contact people were being selected to be the conduit between the church and the organization so that information could be easily disseminated.

The manuals were given free of charge, so as to enable everybody in the churches who was prepared to learn to do so without hindrance. As it was donor supported and written and printed by the OAIC, the cost of production was not high, but huge numbers of the books were being produced. The number of centres increased over the years, and not only were they training the leadership, but classes were being held for the different groups in the churches as well. However, in Ghana, after some years, it was decided that learners should contribute a token fee of about fifty cents for the study. This was to enable them to defray some of the logistical cost. Of course the learners and churches understood this, and it has become an established norm. As time went on, especially in the North and Ashanti regions, they decided that fifty cents was not enough, and they made it eighty cents. This also meant ownership and contribution to their education.

The programme has served the evangelistic need of the churches as members have been equipped to fulfil not only the mandate of the Great Commission but have learned to study the Bible as a discipline. This has not only fulfilled part of the vision and mission of OAIC but has also brought them closer to God. Thousands of OAIC members have been taught and equipped through the TEE programme. The contexts, no matter where they are have been a hindrance to enablers, once enablers are prepared to go so deep into their rural settings to facilitate, the participants are also prepared to meet and learn.

Testimony One

Madam, so you want to tell us that we could also study the Bible like this? Fi! This study is good even for people like me who can't read!"

This was a remark made by one of the participants at Tamale, a city in the Northern Region of Ghana that is predominantly Moslem. We began the TEE programme there in 1998. Initially the participants did not understand what the whole thing was about, but the studies progressed, and they became excited. This lady, 'Maggie', confessed that most of the time she had to skip church activities to sell in the evening and on Sundays, especially, in front of peoples' shops, because she did not have her own shop.

However, with the introduction of the TEE class, things have turned around. Now she comes to class not only when we are there but when we are not there and the class is taken care of by an Enabler. Even though she had to contribute a token fee to defray the use of the facilities and also to pay part of the TEE material, it didn't deter her. We were studying 'How Jesus Sees Women' after studying 'Bringing People to Jesus', and these two courses had renewed and encouraged her to evangelise even though the community is male dominated and an Islamic community by far and large.

True to her words, the next time we went to Tamale, she had been able to convert two people from the Islamic faith to Christianity!

Testimony Two

In 2004, during my research study on the issue of whether skills training should be incorporated into the TEE program of the African Independent Churches in Ghana, I interviewed a number of TEE students in three different regions of the country. From one of the churches, I had this conversation:

"When the announcement was made in church about the TEE programme, a lot of us became very excited, but when they said it was only for leaders, and if any body wants to take the other class, they will have to sponsor themselves. A lot of people lost interest, but I decided to join the class. And I didn't regret it. I have learned a lot, and now it has changed my life, especially my spiritual life. I am more mature now, take my quiet time more seriously, and am able to reach out to others to talk 'Jesus'. But I think TEE has got to a point where skills should be incorporated, because people will not need to think about what to eat after the class or how to pay for their books, if they have an income-generating venture. But if I want to polish up to help in the church, this foundation I have gained in the three courses will help me to do a year's course at Good News Theological Seminary and College".

GHANA ASSOCIATION OF TEE

In addition to the OAIC materials and method of teaching or facilitating, the Ghana chapter also uses the Evangel Publishing House materials. This is because of its joint work with the Ghana Association of Theological Education by Extension (GATEE). This is a TEE Association, which works alongside OAIC and vice-versa. As its name indicates, it is a TEE association, which has as its members the AICs, Methodist, Presbyterian, Charismatic, Good News Theological Seminary and College, Maranatha Bible College, Pentecost, Sudan Interior Mission, World Evangelical Church, etc. GATEE began in 1988 and, with some of the leadership's involvement with OAIC, decided that it would be a supplier and resource provider and a coordinator of TEE programmes in Ghana. It also relates to other associations and creates a common platform for dialogue. It also coordinates the meetings and shares current initiatives in the world of theological education with its members.

GATEE uses the Theological Education by Extension College (TEEC) materials from South Africa, Evangel Publishing House, and the OAIC books. Thus people can pick and choose what suits them most. The Evangel textbooks were the most popular, and various associations patronise that material. They are programmed instruction books with no guiding resource. As the OAIC/TEE directors realised, people are not programmed to learn by rote, and any theological training must be adapted to suit the context and make it appealing and informative. It must be able to educate and relate and remain pertinent and relevant to the leaders or congregations. Hence the members of GATEE have decided to add other resources to make the dialogue interactive and stimulating as well as friendly, like the OAIC manuals.

They then looked through the books and picked the layout. With this they created three different resources to guide or accompany the use of the book. These were the step-by-step resource guides for the facilitator; weekly class quizzes based on the day's discussion; quarterly exams; and a final examination at the end of the course. Each book covers 10 weeks, but the resources were made to cover twelve weeks of study, with the first and the last as introduction and review respectively. These books were imported from Kenya and therefore very expensive, but it was highly patronised because almost all the churches using it were being sponsored or subsidised.

In sum, the introduction of TEE has been of immense help, especially for the AICs, as they have had to remain in their contexts and yet acquire theological education and serve their churches faithfully. TEE has been called "the Bible School going to the people" and the text as "the book is the teacher", which is more than an adequate description of what it does. It has trained and empowered more people at a given time than the average theological seminary can. It needs to be enhanced, but it has been embraced. OAIC/TEE is now planning to write an HIV&AIDS manual, given the Organization's involvement and work in the filed of HIV&AIDS.

Primary Source: Rosario de Lugo Batlle, Doctoral Thesis: *A Formative Self–Evaluation of the Theological Education by Extension Kenyan Model Project of the Organization of the African Instituted Churches.*

Helena Hooper

helenhoopgh@yahoo.com

QUESTIONS FOR REFLECTION AND DISCUSSION

1. *Why are the African Instituted Churches found primarily among the poor, semi-literates or illiterates, and marginalized on the fringes of society?*

2. *What does this case study mean by "traditional" African ways of worship, reading and hearing the Word of God, ways of dressing, songs and welcoming?*

3. *How has the OAIC initiated its TEE programs throughout Africa?*

4. *What is the role of the text and what is the role of the facilitator in the Dialogical Method, according to this case study?*

5. *What are the objectives of the OAIC/TEE programs?*

The Extension Programme of the Senate of Serampore College

by Roger Gaikwad

How Did the Senate of Serampore College Come into Being?

"Expect great things from God! Attempt great things for God!" This was the mission-stirring slogan articulated by William Carey to the dormant self-complacent church in England on 31st May 1792, based on the text from Isaiah 54:2-3: "Enlarge the place of thy tent, and let them stretch forth the curtains of thine habitations…" Popularly acclaimed as "The Father of the Modern Protestant Missionary Movement", William Carey along with his colleagues, Joshua Marshman and William Ward established their mission base in 1800 in Serampore, which was then a Danish Colony. At a time when the British East India Company did not allow missionary work to be done within their territory, the Danish authorities supported missionary activity. Among the missionary endeavours of the Serampore Trio was the founding of Serampore College in 1818 for "the instruction of Asiatic Christians and other youths in Eastern Literature and Western Science". The aim of the College was to provide instruction in every branch of knowledge to promote the welfare of the people. The College was made accessible to all, declaring that "no caste, colour, country shall bar anybody from admission into the college".

In a period when the Indian subcontinent was under the onslaught of European colonies and their commercial enterprises, being divided into several small kingdoms of Hindu and Muslim rulers, when the caste system, patriarchy and a kind of feudalism dominated society, when religion was characterised by cumbersome rituals and practices, Serampore College was a beacon of light educating people in the humanities, science and theology. It was to play an important role in the renaissance of India during the nineteenth century. In 1827 King Frederick VI of Denmark granted it a Royal Charter empowering it to confer degrees, like the universities of Kiel and Copenhagen. While the Arts and Science departments were subsequently affiliated to Calcutta University, the Theology Department continued with its programme of studies including awarding degrees.

When the British East India Company under pressure from the British Parliament opened its doors to missionary work in 1813, different missionary bodies started working in India. Many of them set up Bible schools to train evangelists, catechists, deacons, elders and pastors. Some of these grew up to become theological colleges and seminaries which sought affiliation to Serampore College. This eventually led to the establishment of new structures within Serampore College called the Senate of Serampore College and the Board of Theological Education through which churches, theological institutions and church related agencies have become partners in theological education ministry. Today the Senate of Serampore College (SSC) has about 50 institutions affiliated to it including 2 in Sri Lanka, 1 in Bangladesh and 1 in Nepal. It has blossomed into an ecumenical university having affiliated institutions from various traditions: Orthodox, Mar Thoma, Church of South India, Church of North India, Presbyterian, Baptist, Brethren, Methodist, Lutheran, Evangelical Church of India and Pentecostal. All of them follow the rules, regulations and curricula of the SSC. These institutions enjoy a semi-autonomous status having the provision to conduct examinations in a certain number of subjects as well as the provision to offer special contextually related papers (whose syllabi, however, have to be approved beforehand by the SSC).

The main objective of the majority of the theological institutions within the Serampore family until the early part of the twentieth century was to train pastors. This was done through residential training programs. In other words, students would have to reside within the campus of a theological institution for a period of time till they finished a particular course. The two main programmes which the SSC introduced were the Diploma or Licentiate in Theology (L.Th.) and the Degree of Bachelor of Divinity (B.D.). Some of the early graduates were also employed by churches or governing boards to teach in their respective theological institutions. In the middle of the twentieth century the Master of Theology (M.Th.) programme was introduced. Thus the foundation was laid to build up a body of Indian theological scholars who would take over the teaching and administration of theological institutions. In the early part of the sixties, two more residential programs, namely Bachelor of Religious Education (B.R.E.) and Master of Religious Studies (M.R.S.), were started.

These programmes created an opening for training candidates who would not necessarily enter ordained ministry, but still serve the church in other ministries. In other words, the SSC was creating an opportunity for training lay persons who could also be engaged in full-time ministry in the churches. By the beginning of the seventies, the L.Th. programme was upgraded to a four-year Bachelor of Theology (B.Th.) Degree Course. This move was an affirmation of the situation that the educational levels of the laity in general (including in rural places) were improving and so they required pastors with a slightly higher level of theological training. In fact the 1970s saw the first scholars earning Doctor of Theology (D. Th.) degrees from the SSC. [Prior to the 1970s most of the academically bright persons and ecclesial leaders were sent to foreign countries for higher theological studies.] The SSC had thus come of age to offer the entire range of residential theological education programmes available in Western universities.

In most cases candidates undergoing education in residential theological institutions were mission or church sponsored candidates. This implied that all the expenses of the candidates were taken care of by the sponsoring agencies. In some cases theological institutions offered scholarships. The SSC also started offering scholarships to some candidates doing theology at the post-graduate and doctoral levels. Candidates from certain states in North East India have been enjoying government scholarships. However, what has been realised over time is that theological education is an expensive training; very few individuals can afford to bear the cost of such education. Many churches which were earlier receiving foreign support now find it difficult to sponsor candidates for residential theological studies. Ever increasing costs of living and the lowering of interest on bank deposits and other effects of globalisation have further made residential theological education an expensive proposition.

And yet the importance of theological education is increasing in the subcontinent. The SSC, which has inherited a system of theological education which is western in structure, perspective and content, has been making endeavors to evolve contextually relevant education. After independence the countries in the sub-continent have been faced with the challenges of nation-building in all spheres—social, economic, political, scientific and technological. Churches have been grappling with the challenges of standing on their own feet, of cultivating Indian identities, and developing relevant forms of ministry. From the 1970s the SSC started giving special attention to issues related to economic poverty, indigenisation of faith and practice, plurality of religions and cultures, and re-definition of mission. Gradually other issues have also been included in the curricula for special consideration: patriarchy, caste system, tribal concerns, urbanisation, ecology, globalisation, and the communication and information technology revolution. Thus the SSC spells out its vision and mission:

We believe that the Triune God has offered the possibility of renewal of life and hope for the entire creation in and through Jesus Christ and that, as an instrument of God, the Church is called to be involved in God's mission of liberation, reconciliation and community building among all peoples through varied forms of ministry.

Set in the midst of people of other faiths and ideologies as well as situations of life-negating forces, we are called upon to equip the whole people of God to respond to the contextual challenges critically and creatively by being faithful to the Gospel of Jesus Christ.

In the light of this faith and self-understanding, we seek to equip ministers, leaders, scholars and the whole people of God to be committed to creative discernment of and active participation in God's liberative mission in the world at large and in South Asia in particular by providing programmes of theological study and ministerial formation at various levels through affiliated colleges and institutions. [Constitution: One National Structure for Theological Education in India (Serampore: Senate of Serampore College, 2005, pp.4-5)]

However the impact of the teaching and practice of the Western missionaries is so deeply rooted, and people's love for traditions is so strong, and the ecclesial structures are so dominating, that the acceptance of what is being attempted through the curricula of the SSC is rather gradual. Furthermore, the attractions of globalisation and prosperity gospel preaching and the phenomenon of charismatic cults are posing a greater challenge to the theological education programmes of the SSC.

WHAT ABOUT THE PROGRAMME OF THEOLOGICAL EDUCATION BY EXTENSION?

Since residential theological education was meant for training full-time church workers, mainly pastors, the concept of external (non-residential) theological education during the first half of the twentieth century generally implied that some theological education needed to be imparted to lay people. Some of the churches and theological institutions made such education available through Bible Correspondence Courses. The implication was that lay persons should be literate enough to do such courses. A second implication of such a programme was that its objective was mainly to provide some Bible knowledge to the lay persons. Such courses were taught in two ways: (1) topic-wise focusing on the understanding of salvation, Christian living, and other important articles of faith and practice; and (2) study of the books of the Bible. Such courses, whether in English or in regional languages, were largely modelled on the programmes conducted in the West. In some cases different levels or grades of Bible Correspondence Courses have also been introduced.

Yet another mode of external theological education is the so-called Mobile Theological School programme conducted by a few theological institutions and churches. The institutions draw up a curriculum for external and largely self-study theological education. A team of teachers visits a particular place where interested candidates from the surrounding region come to attend a series of classes conducted by the teachers for two or three days. Some books or reading materials are sold to the candidates. The candidates are then expected to study the particular subjects on their own, following the syllabi given to them. They may take the help of pastors or other knowledgeable persons in their locality. At the end of the stipulated academic term they are expected to write examinations which are conducted by the theological institutions with the assistance of pastors in those regions. Certificates are awarded to the successful candidates. In such a programme the candidates usually go through courses in Old Testament, New Testament, Theology, History of Christianity, Religions, and Practical Ministry. Usually the courses are taught along traditional Western lines, though attempts are made to relate the courses to the context of the students. A few institutions do teach some courses on social analysis and liberational, ecumenical and ecological concerns.

A reverse format of the Mobile Theological School programme is where students travel to theological institutions on weekends or bi-monthly or whatever the period of frequency is. Here too the candidates are given lectures, buy books and reading materials, even use libraries and resources available on internet (if they have access to it), and finally write examinations. Churches have found such programmes of largely external private study helpful in training their lay leaders, elders, deacons, Sunday School teachers and so on. Some churches are also thinking of making such training mandatory for church members if they are to hold any office in the ministry of the church. Usually the expenses involved in such programmes are not so high; individuals or the churches of which they are members pay the necessary fees and bear the costs.

There are also special institutions which are exclusively providing external theological education. The Association for Theological Education by Extension (TAFTEE) has been involved in offering non-residential theological education since 1971 to those who are not able to spare their time, spend their money and move out of their homes to a campus for formal residential theological education. TAFTEE offers programmes at different levels: Certificate in Biblical Studies (CBS), Bachelor of Theological Studies (BTS), Master of Theology (M.Th.), and M. Phil/Ph. D. at the research level. At the initial two levels the candidates attend periodic classes under the guidance of a supervisor in their own region. The Regional Supervisor even conducts the tests and examinations. At the higher levels the candidates have to attend periodic sessions at the TAFTEE Centre.

Thus, there are different kinds of external programmes of theological education. These are, however, not run by the SSC. Some of the theological institutions and churches have been making suggestions to the SSC to recognise these courses and to grant some sort of a certificate to the successful candidates. The objective of most of these programmes is to inform and train the laity and thereby edify the church. Usually such programmes are not linked with ordination of the candidates as pastors.

WHAT ABOUT THE EXTENSION PROGRAMME OF THE SENATE OF SERAMPORE COLLEGE?

Right until the 1980s the SSC offered External B.Th. and External B.D. programmes. These programmes were in fact a replica of the corresponding residential B.Th. and B.D. programmes as far as the courses and their syllabi were concerned. However the external candidates were not subject to the rigor of periodic academic tests, submission of assignments, practical work requirements and college term examinations. All that they were required to do was to write the university examinations at the end of the academic year. This provision of external studies provided an opportunity for qualified lay persons to go through the same academic learning which candidates in residential institutions underwent. Such a programme had its problems. It facilitated academic education without the personal formation and practical training that was provided in a residential institution. The external candidates did not have to study all the year round. Only a month or so before the examinations they would try to collect notes from some resident theological student, look up university question papers of previous years, make a calculated guess about the possible questions which could be asked in the next examination, study accordingly, and then pass the examinations with good grades! Once they successfully completed the examinations, some of them even staked their claim for being ordained for full-time pastoral ministry! The SSC realized that the external programme was creating an obsession among some of the laity for obtaining a degree, or it was fostering a professional objective without a vocational spirit. Hence there was a need to bring in a change in the external studies programme of the SSC, which happened towards the end of the 1980s.

India was going through a difficult period during the 1980s. The Khalistan Movement in North West India and the Government's army operation against it led to the assassination of Prime Minister Indira Gandhi in 1984. Religious communal tension was being created between Hindus and Muslims in certain regions of the country by political forces. There was also resentment in certain quarters against the operation of the Indian Peace-Keeping Force in Sri Lanka. The country was also passing through an economic crisis. The movements of OBCs (Other Backward Classes) and Dalits (outcastes) and tribals for their rights and special provisions for their development were also becoming strong. There were also scandals of corruption in the Government. The 1990s saw problems escalating further. There was nation-wide uproar on the part of upper caste and upper class citizens against the Mandal Commission Report (which recommended reservations for backward communities), which the then government in power approved; the assassination of Prime Minister Rajiv Gandhi in connection with the Sri Lankan problem; the demolition of the domes of the Muslim Babri Masjid by certain Hindu groups, which once again caused nation-wide unrest; and the opening of India's economy to the forces of globalisation. It was within such a context that the church and theological institutions had to give expression to their faith and mission. Already in the SSC liberation theology and inter-religious dialogue were considered as important constituents of the framework for theological education. The movements and theologies of women, Dalits, and tribals were also being included as special courses in the curriculum. So when the SSC introduced new programmes of external theological education all these factors influenced the objectives of the programme.

The objectives of the Diploma in Christian Studies (Dip.C.S.) programme were stipulated as follows:

1. To provide an opportunity in the Indian context for the study of Christianity, its history, faith and practice;

2. To make (students) aware of the life, teaching and work of Jesus Christ in the Indian context;

3. To interpret the Bible, its formation, and its significance for Christian faith in the Indian context;

4. To provide an opportunity … for the study of the interaction of Christianity with people of other faiths and cultures;

5. To study the interaction of Christianity with the socio-economic and political realities of India/South Asia.

The Objectives of the programme of the Degree of Bachelor of Christian Studies (B.C.S.) would be to:

1. develop "Kingdom of God" values (with special reference to Justice, Peace and Integrity of all Creation);

2. create critical consciousness and openness, to analyse cultural, social, economic, political and ecclesiastical values;

3. provide tools for interpreting the Word of God in different contexts in society;

4. enable persons to become effective witnesses in the context of their varied and diversified vocations;

5. provide theological education as a transforming influence in personal, ecclesial and societal life.

The SSC resolved to keep the Dip.C.S. programme open to all, that is to Christians as well as people of other faiths and ideologies. However the B.C.S. was meant for Christians only. The academic requirements for pursuing the diploma course were kept low: successful completion of higher secondary school. Even those who had completed only high school studies could be eligible to register provided they had done either two years of some other studies or five years of some employment. Subsequently the SSC has resolved that those who have not been able to complete high school can also do the programme provided they pass an entrance examination and are at least 20 years old. The admission requirement for the B.C.S. programme is university graduation. There is a provision for non-graduates to do the programme provided that they are 25 years old or older, and they should successfully write an entrance examination. There is also an opening for persons who have done the residential B.Th. course to register for the BCS programme. Thus, some full-time church workers including pastors are enabled to refresh and upgrade themselves through the B.C.S. programme.

In the Dip.C.S programme candidates have to do ten papers in two years. Six papers are required and four optionals have to be done.

Required Papers

1. Introduction to the Life, Teaching and Work of Jesus

2. Survey of Biblical History

3. The Bible: Its formation, interpretation and significance for Christian faith

4. Christian Faith Affirmations

5. Christian Worship, Traditions, Rites and Rituals

6. Origins and Development of Christianity in India

Optional Papers

7. The Life and Thought of Paul, the Apostle

8. Selected Literary Texts from the Bible

9. Titles and Images of Christ in the Bible

10. Christian Responses to Other Faiths

11. Indian Christian Spirituality

12. Contemporary Challenges and Emerging Theologies

13. Christian Ethics

14. Indian Interpretations of Jesus Christ

15. Introduction to Communication

16. Introduction to Indian Philosophy

17. Introduction to Psychology

18. Introduction to Social Sciences

In the BCS programme candidates have to do 13 required papers and 9 optionals. Instead of 9 optionals, candidates can opt to do 7 optionals and write a thesis (extended essay of around 12,000 words). Candidates who have a B.Th. Second Class (55% to 65% marks) will be required to do only 14 papers or 12 papers and a thesis.

Required Papers

1. Understanding the Old Testament

2. Re-reading Old Testament Texts from Liberation Perspectives

3. Understanding the New Testament

4. Jesus as presented in the Gospels with study of selected texts

5. Understanding Christian Faith

6. Introduction to Christian Ethics

7. History of Christianity in India

8. Selected Events in the History of Christianity with emphasis on Ecumenical Movement

9. Outlines of Major Religious Traditions in India

10. Christian Responses to Multi-Faith Society

11. Introduction to Christian Ministry

12. Introduction to Communication

13. Christological Issues: Classical and Contemporary

Optional Papers

14. Contemporary Missiological Issues (compulsory optional)

15. Re-reading selected Texts from the Book of Psalms

16. Re-reading of Selected Texts from Wisdom Literature

17. Re-reading of the Gospel of John

18. Re-reading of the Letters of St. Paul

19. Contextual Theologies

20. Modern Religious and Secular Movements in India

21. Christian Education and Social Change

22. Introduction to Counseling

23. Communication Ethics

24. Professional Issues in Christian Perspectives: Medical–Healing Ministry

25. Professional Issues in Christian Perspectives: Labor and Industry

26. Professional Issues in Christian Perspectives: Social work

27. Professional Issues in Christian Perspectives: Teaching

28. Professional Issues in Christian Perspectives: Legal

29. Professional Issues in Christian Perspectives: Professional Ethics

30. Christian Perspectives on Contemporary Issues: Ecology

31. Christian Perspectives on Contemporary Issues: Conflict Resolution and Peace Building

32. Christian Perspectives on Contemporary Issues: Human Rights

33. Christian Perspectives on Contemporary Issues: Women in Church and Society

34. Christian Perspectives on Contemporary Issues: Globalization

35. Christian Perspectives on Contemporary Issues: Communalism and Fundamentalism

36. Understanding Social Analysis

In the case of both programmes the academic year begins in February and ends in November. Reading materials are provided to the Dip.C.S. programme candidates. They are expected to study on their own. They could make use of libraries. They could also take the help of pastors or other resourceful persons. BCS candidates are not only provided with study materials but they are also expected to attend a contact seminar every year at which they are given an orientation about the papers they have selected for study. Besides using libraries, the candidates could again take the assistance of qualified resource persons in their study process. In order to strengthen this programme the SSC appointed a Director in 2002 and even set up an extension programme centre in Kolkata called SCEPTRE, at the inauguration of which Dr. Ross Kinsler was specially invited to deliver a public lecture and subsequently to led two consultations, one in North India and the other in South India, on "Diversified Theological Education". Some of the institutions affiliated to the SSC also serve as regional facilitating centres for the Dip. C.S. and B.C.S. programmes. In such situations the institutions are given some degree of autonomy in conducting examinations in certain B.C.S. subjects and in evaluating the answer scripts. As far as examinations (which are conducted in the last two weeks of November) are concerned, candidates may write the same in either English or any regional language approved by the SSC.

The following statistical records indicate the number of registrations for the two programmes over the past 16 years:

Year	B.C.S.	Dip.C.S.	Year	B.C.S.	Dip.C.S.
1990	37	4	2001	213	85
1991	52	14	2002	206	128
1992	50	17	2003	232	96
1993	82	19	2004	211	126
1994	98	5	2005	178	106
1995	99	26			
1996	97	23			
1997	106	19			
1998	110	18			
1999	112	18			
2000	82	9			

Another programme following the external education format, offered by SSC to full-time church workers, is the Doctor of Ministry programme. Started in 1998 this programme is also coordinated from SCEPTRE, Kolkata. The objectives of the D. Min. programme are:

- To analyse the candidate's own behaviour patterns, to deepen personal formation, to engage in critical reflection, and to equip with necessary academic and professional skills needed for the ministry;

- To make the candidate's own ministerial involvement and experience a basis for theological learning and reflection;

- To provide tools to analyse the contemporary socio-political, religio-cultural contexts of the society and interpret their Missiological implications for the Christian faith.

Candidates should have completed at least five years of service after B.D. or B.C.S. in order to be eligible to undertake D. Min. studies. Such persons will have to pass an entrance examination conducted by the SSC before they are registered. The successful candidates first attend an orientation seminar followed by a foundational collegium on two main topics: (1) Church and Ministry, and (2) Re-reading the Bible through Faith and Contextual Perspectives.

The next collegium is on "Issues in Ministry". The candidates have to select any four of the following:

1. Religious Pluralism and Fundamentalism

2. Poverty, Economy and Justice

3. Ecology and Environment

4. Rural Development or Adivasi/Primal/Tribal Culture and Development

5. Ecumenical Relations Today

6. Contemporary Trends in Mission and Evangelism

7. Women in Church and Society

8. Human Rights in the Indian Sub-Continent

9. Changing Family Patterns in India

10. Ethical Issues in Local and Congregational Contexts

The third collegium is on Research Methodologies. During this collegium the candidates are exposed to and trained in different methodologies. So also they are made to write out their initial dissertation-project proposal. Another collegium to follow is the one on the area of specialization which the candidate has selected. This area of specialisation is usually related to the dissertation-project which the candidate intends to undertake. The following are the available areas of specialization:

1. Liturgy and Worship

2. Preaching

3. Pastoral Care and Counselling

4. Christian Education

5. Leadership and Church Administration

6. Ministry of the People of God

7. Communication

8. Women and Children

9. Religion and Culture

10. Mission and Evangelism

After each of the collegiums the candidates are expected to write assignments. Thus they have to write a total of 10 assignments over a span of two years. Following all the collegiums and the satisfactory completion of assignments which are examined by the resource persons who taught in the collegiums, the candidates have to write Comprehensive Examinations on all that they have studied during the course of two years. Only if they pass the Comprehensives will they be allowed to go ahead with their dissertation-project, the proposal of which has to be approved by the D. Min Committee. The dissertation-project must be completed within three years. Since 1998 till 2006 the number of candidates registered for D. Min. is 147.

WHITHER THE EXTENSION PROGRAMME OF THE SSC?

If the extension programme of the SSC has to be strengthened and made more meaningful, then the following concerns need to be addressed:

1. The Extension programme of the SSC is quite rigorous. People engaged in their day-to-day work find it very difficult to give adequate attention to their studies. There is an inherent danger that the candidates may treat their studies as an academic exercise and not relate it to their day-to-day life. Besides, the question papers for their examinations are set, and their answer scripts are examined by theological teachers from residential institutions. Therefore, once again there could be the danger that the question paper tests more of the academic knowledge of the candidates and less of their faith responses and issues of practical discipleship.

   Even the D. Min. programme seems to be quite demanding. So far only four persons have successfully completed the programme. Perhaps the programmes of the first two years need to be stretched to three years so that the candidates could do justice to the collegiums they attend and the assignments they have to write. The dissertation-project could be completed within two years since the work is to be done in the very place where the candidate is doing his/her ministry. Therefore the programme could still be completed in five years.

2. The external programmes still seem to be modelled after the residential B.Th., B.D., and M.Th. programmes of the SSC. Keeping in mind the caption of diversified theological education, the SSC would have to evolve appropriate programmes for the laity and full-time church workers. Moreover, quite often the programmes tend to train and equip "keepers of aquariums" rather than "fishers of humans"; the missional dimension of the life and work of the church would have to be strengthened.

3. Much also needs to be done in terms of providing theological literature in regional languages. This is particularly the problem of people in North India and in certain parts of North East India. While there is plenty of literature available in English and in South Indian languages, the issue is whether the literature facilitates the attainment of the objectives of the programmes or whether they are largely academic writings. Hence in due course of time special literature would have to be prepared for the B.C.S. and D. Min. programmes.

4. Another concern is the encouragement that needs to be given by ecclesial bodies to church leaders, deacons, evangelists, lay leaders, counsellors, Sunday School teachers, local preachers and others to equip themselves better through the extension programmes of the Senate. Theologically educated lay people should not be seen as a threat to ordained ministers; rather a perspective, an atmosphere and an ethos of growing and partnering together in faith and practice should be cultivated. The importance of Theological Education by Extension for the several diverse ministries of the church should be highlighted without the necessity of priestly ordination.

5. A fourth concern is that the present programmes require a certain level of education which makes them beyond the reach of many people, particularly those in rural areas who have not had the opportunity to pursue regular school education. Hence there is an urgent need to introduce a Certificate Course in Christian Studies. A consultation will have to be called to draw up a plan and methodology. Such a course could also be worked out in conjunction with short term laity/ catechist/evangelist training programmes run by some churches and theological institutions in India.

6. A fifth matter is facilitation of issue-based programmes. Churches are interested in short term non-formal programmes on contemporary issues such as HIV/AIDS, Globalisation, Ecology, Human Rights, Dalit and Feminist Concerns, Religious Fundamentalism and Communalism, Missiology, Leadership Training, Ministry to Children, Campus Ministry, etc. SCEPTRE could prove to be instrumental in facilitating such non-formal programmes.

The SSC is presently engaged in a process of curriculum revision. In a couple of years the extension programme of the SSC may have different orientation content and format. It will hopefully affirm much more vigorously and vibrantly that theological education is for all people of God and that theological education should endeavour to be holistic.

Roger Gaikwad

sceptrext@vsnl.net

Questions for Reflection and Discussion

1. *To what extent do the accredited theological education programs of India/ South Asia follow the patterns of Europe and North America? To what extent do they follow indigenous patterns of South Asia?*

2. *What is the mission of the non-residential Diploma in Christian Studies and the Bachelor of Christian Studies underlying the stated objectives of these programs?*

3. *What are the basic components of the Dip.C.S. and B.C.S. educational model? How does this model compare with other TEE programs?*

4. *How does the D.Min. program integrate theory and practice of ministry, reflection and action?*

5. *What recommendations for strengthening these diversified programs does the author offer?*

Chapter 6: Asia and Australia
The Institute for TEE in Nepal

by Peter Bisset

The Institute for Theological Education by Extension in Nepal (ITEEN) was founded in 1995, initially as SEAN Nepal, to help meet the teaching and training needs of the fast growing Nepali church. It set from the beginning a clear target group as follows:

> *The target group is Nepali church leaders and lay people who are unable to go to residential college to study, as they cannot afford it but have to continue in their work to support family and/or have very little formal education.*

ITEEN set out from the beginning a very clear vision that was grounded by clear aims and measurable objectives.

> *To see poor Christians benefiting by being able to take these extension courses and poor churches, which are unable to send their leaders for residential training due to lack of finance, being able to afford these courses to train their own leaders "on the job".*

The tools for the vision were to have available in contextualised Nepali the South American SEAN TEE courses that can even be done by a person who is only just literate. It is planned also to add relevant grass-roots TEE courses from other author bodies and to write some material of their own. The vision was taken forward in the following way.

Stage 1 —Contextualization and Translation of "core curriculum" SEAN student books and tutor manuals—begun 1995

Stage 2—The establishment and running of a TEE programme to serve the Nepalese churches—begun 1999, with this objective:

To equip the lay members and leaders of the church adequately through TEE courses.

- To motivate, equip and train for service the vastly untapped source of leadership and, in so doing, not to by-pass nor disqualify the very type of ordinary folk whom Jesus originally called to be His disciples.

- To encourage thorough discipling and leadership training within individual churches, enabling them to become more mission orientated in the process.

- That, through the programme, from scripture, and under the Holy Spirit's guidance, the tools, material and structure needed are provided to *"train workers and leaders on the job"*. As they mature in their faith and spiritual life, and discover and exercise their particular gifts, they develop an effective ministry and glorify the Lord in their life and work.

Socio-Economic Profile of Nepal

The Kingdom of Nepal is one of the least developed countries in the world with approximately 42% of the population living below the poverty line. Agriculture provides a livelihood for over 80% of the population and accounts for over 40% of its Gross National Product. Over 85% of the total population lives in rural areas of the country. Despite almost 50 years of development efforts, Nepal remains one of the poorest and least developed countries in the world with an estimated population of 27 million in 2005 with 42 per cent of the population living below the national poverty line. The country also faces environmental problems due to increasing population, poverty and dependence on subsistence agriculture. Recent political instability and the deteriorating situation arising from insurgency remain a threat to development efforts. Illiteracy is also problematic, with rates for men at 35 per cent and twice that for women at 70 per cent. The total fertility rate is estimated at 4.2 lifetime births per woman, and maternal mortality ratio is estimated at 740 deaths per 100,000 live births. Women's unequal access to health care and education contribute to the high levels of female mortality and morbidity.

The population is young, with a median age of just 20 years. In the Second Long-Term Health Plan (1997-2017), the government emphasises developing special programmes for population and reproductive health, including adolescent reproductive health. The National Reproductive Health Strategy and the National Adolescent Health and Development Strategy, identify adolescents as a critical component of the reproductive health package, including the distribution of contraceptives to unmarried adolescents. The threat of HIV/AIDS is a major concern in the country. The prevalence of HIV infection among sex workers and injecting drug users has increased. A National HIV/AIDS Strategy has been developed.

Poverty reduction has been and continues to be the major focus of the government's policies and programmes. The government expressed its commitment to implement the reform agenda as envisaged by the Poverty Reduction Strategy Paper (Tenth Five-Year Development Plan 2002-2007), including broad-based growth, social sector development and improved governance. The government has also prepared a Health Sector Reform Strategy, now in the initial stages of implementation. The government is preparing a Population Perspective Plan to integrate population, reproductive health and gender concerns into sectoral development policies and programmes.

Geography and Demographics

The Kingdom is located in South East Asia wedged between China on the edge of the Himalayan mountain range and India on the Indo-Gangetic Plain. Nepal is a country of large geographic diversity. There are three main geographical regions including the Terai region, the Hill region and the Mountain region. Mt. Everest, the tallest mountain in the world, is located in the northern area of the country.

Nepal is a multi-lingual, religious and ethnic society. The National Language Policy Advisory Commission has listed 60 living languages in the Kingdom. According to the 1991 census more than 50 percent of the total population has Nepali as their mother tongue followed by Maithili (12%). Other main languages are Bhojpuri, Tharu, Tamang, Newari, Magar, Rai and Abadhi. The major caste/ethnic groups identified by the 2001 census are Chhetri (15.8%), Brahmin Hill (12.7%), Magar (7.1%), Tharu (6.8%), Tamang (5.6%) Newar (5.5%), Muslim (4.3%) Kami (3.9%), Rai (3.9), Gurung, (2.8%), Damai/Dholi (2.4%).

Nepal is constitutionally a Hindu Kingdom with Hinduism accounting for over 80% of the population with Buddhism practised by approximately 11% and Islam accounting for 4.2% of the population. Nepal was declared a "secular" state in June 2006 by the re-instated House of Representatives. This should have far reaching implications for the Christian Church in Nepal in the future. According to the official census only 0.4% of Nepalis are Christians. However, the estimated number is nearer 3% or 700,000. Also a more accurate figure for Buddhists is nearer 20% when you extrapolate it from the caste figures. However, the Hindu majority has been keen to have the Hindu population statistics as high as possible to continue to justify its insistence on being a "Hindu" kingdom.

The population of Nepal was 22,736,934 as of the 2001 Census as compared to 18,491,097 reported in the 1991 Census, representing a 2.25% growth over the past 10 years. According to the World Bank, the estimated population as of July 2003 was 24.2 million. The mix between males and females is almost equal with males accounted for 49.96% of the total population and females 50.04%. According to the Central Bureau of Statistics in 2002 14.2% of the population lived in urban areas while the remaining 85.8% lived in rural areas.

Over 80% of the population is involved in agriculture with over 90% of women working in the agricultural sector. *Only 1.8% work in the professional and technological sector, 6.2% in services and 4.2% in production.*

Economic Indicators

According to the Asian Development Bank, approximately 42% of the population lives below the national poverty line of NRs 4,400 ($77) per capita per annum, which is based on minimum caloric intake, housing, and other non-food standards. However, this figure varies widely across the country. While only 23% of the urban population does not have sufficient income to meet basic consumption needs, 44% of the rural population falls below the standard. Geographically, the incidence of poverty in the mid-western and far western development regions greatly exceeds the national average, as does the rate in the mountain districts.

According to the Asian Development Bank (ADB), Nepal's economic performance weakened in FY2002, registering negative growth for the first time in the past 20 years. Gross Domestic Product (GDP) contracted by 0.6% after posting a growth of 4.6% in FY2001. This was primarily due to a series of domestic and external shocks, especially escalating after the insurgency and an irregular monsoon season. The agriculture sector decreased, registering a 2.2% growth in 2002 compared to a 5.5% growth in FY2001. Manufacturing production dropped as the industrial sector output fell by 3.3% in FY2002. Tourism arrivals decreased 40% in FY2002, while tourism receipts declined 33%. Inflation increased from 2.4% in FY2001 to 2.9% in FY2002.

Gross Domestic Product grew by 2.3% in 2003 as compared to a negative growth of .6% in 2002. GDP in 2003 was US$5.7 billion. According to the ADB, the budget deficit (after grants) was 3.3% of GDP in FY2002 as compared to a deficit of 4.5% in FY2001. This was primarily due to the sharp decrease in development expenditures. The value of imports decreased by 11.4% in FY2002 due to a weaker demand, particularly due to a decrease in manufacturing and development activities. The value of exports declined by 18% in FY2002 due to a drop in ready-made garments, woolen carpets and pashmina.

Government

The Kingdom of Nepal is a parliamentary democracy and constitutional monarchy. Nepal's parliament was dissolved in May 2002; however, a bicameral parliament consisting of a National Council and a House of Representatives existed prior to it being dissolved. The monarchy is hereditary and with legislative elections the leader of the majority party is usually appointed prime minister by the Monarch. The king dismissed the government in February, 2005 and declared a state of emergency, placing opposition figures under arrest. He assumed direct control of the government as chairman of a new cabinet. By April 2006, when the king offered to restore a democratic government, the situation in the country had become even more troubled, with the pro-democracy demonstrations and the government response to them increasingly confrontational and violent. The reinstatement of parliament in April ushered in a rapid series of governmental changes. The re-instated government responded to the Maoist rebels' three-month cease-fire with an indefinite one. The monarchy was stripped of its powers and privileges, although not abolished, and Nepal was declared a secular nation. The government began talks with the rebels, who in June agreed to join an interim government, although the question of rebel disarmament needed to be resolved.

Education Profile

The schooling system in Nepal has been divided in four levels including a) primary (grade I-V), b) lower secondary (VI-VIII), c) secondary (IX-X) and d) higher education. Education in Nepal and primary education in particular have developed significantly since 1971 when the New Education Plan was introduced. The number of primary schools increased from 10,600 to over 26,000 between 1971 and 2001. Between 1991 and 2001, on an average more than 900 new primary schools were added each year and the number of primary school teachers has reached nearly 100,000 in 2001. The lower secondary level begins at grade 6 and is completed at grade 8. Most of the lower secondary schools are either integrated with the primary schools or with the secondary schools. The number of lower secondary schools increased by nearly three times between 1971 (2,700 schools) and 2001 (7,289 schools). On an average, nearly 400 new lower secondary schools were added each year. The secondary level of education in Nepal comprises grades 9 and 10. Like the expansion of primary and lower secondary level schools there has been a substantial increase at this level as well. For example, between 1971 and 2001, the number of secondary schools increased by more than four fold, from 918 to 4,350. Due to high drop out rates in earlier grades, the current net enrolment rate is approximately 20%. Higher secondary education, which comprises schooling in grades 11 and 12, is relatively new in Nepal's educational history. Approximately 65,000 students were enrolled at more than 500 higher secondary schools in 1999. Tertiary education is being provided through the umbrella of five universities, Tribhuvan University, Mahendra Sanskrit University, Kathmandu University, Pokhara University and Purwanchal University.

According to the Ministry of Education, the enrolment rate at the primary school level has been increasing over the years, however, the completion rate at the primary level is still low and a substantial work needs to be done to improve the graduation rate at the primary level. The net enrolment rate for the primary level of education is 80.4% while the rates for boys and girls were 86.0% and 74.8% respectively in 2002. The over-all dropout rate during 2002, according to the Ministry of Education, in the primary level grade 5 was approximately 17.7% while for the boys and girls separately were 18.4% and 16.9% respectively. The net enrolment rate in the lower secondary level is 33%. Despite a large increase in number of schools, the number of children enrolled in these schools is still low indicating a high dropout and low percent graduating to lower secondary schools.

According to a World Bank Report in 2000 Government expenditures on education as a share of GDP continually increased between 1981 and 1993, from 1.4 to 2.5%, and remained constant at approximately 2.7%. As a share of total government expenditure, the trend in education expenditure is generally similar, having increased from 9.4 to 13.4% between 1981 and 1993 and remained around that level for the following four years before again increasing to 13.9% in 1996/97. For the fiscal year 2002, the government increased its expenditures on education to 15.4% of its overall budget. The 2001 census data indicates that the overall literacy rate was 53.7% of the total population aged 6 years and over. Gender differences in literacy were 65% for males and 42% females. The literacy rate has increased gradually over the last 45 years from a low literacy level of 5.3% in 1954.

Health Profile

According to the World Health Organization (WHO), life expectancy of males and females is 59.5 and 60.2 years old respectively. The child mortality (per 1,000) for males and females is 81 and 87, respectively. AIDS was first identified in Nepal in 1988. Since then, AIDS cases have been steadily increasing. As of October 2001 cumulative HIV/AIDS cases had reached

1,564, based on the number of people who have tested their blood at health centres. Because a very limited number of persons have been tested for HIV/AIDS, it is likely that this figure could be much higher. According to the World Health Organization the estimated HIV prevalence in Nepal in 2000 was over 30,000 or close to 0.3% of the total 15-49 year old population. Based on this estimate, the number of AIDS deaths that could be expected in the year 2000 was close to 3,000 and was expected to double to approximately 6,000 by the year 2005.

Information Communication Technology

According to the Untied States Central Intelligence Agency, the number of telephone lines in use approximated 236,816 in 2000, while the total number of mobile phone users was unknown. As of 2000, there were 6 Internet Service Providers in the country. The number of Internet users was estimated at 60,000 in 2002. The Internet code for the country is np. The number of mobile phones users has grown rapidly during the last 2 years with 2 major providers in the country now.

HISTORY OF CHRISTIANITY IN NEPAL

It is amazing that in just over 50 years three percent of the population have become followers of Christ. Nepal's Christians have seen unprecedented growth in this Hindu kingdom over the last 16 years in particular, since in a limited way freedom of religion came to Nepal after multi-party democracy came to Nepal in 1990.

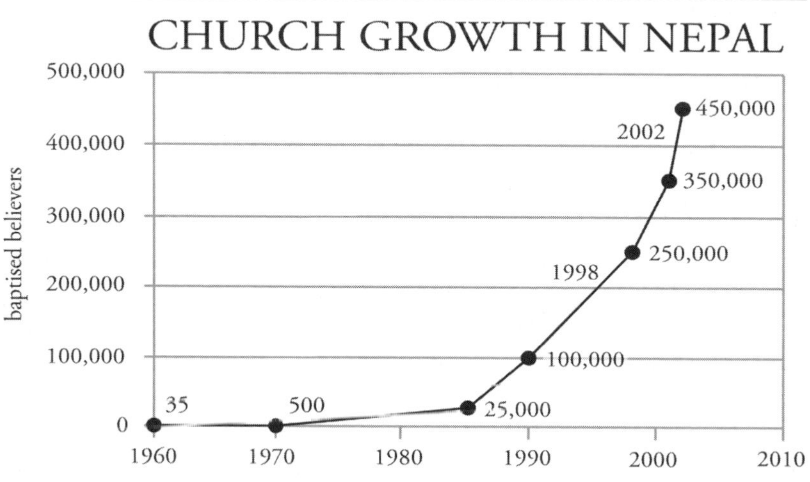

The present estimate (2006) is that there are around 700,000 Christians in Nepal. If there are now around 750,000 Christians in Nepal, it has increased by 450,000 since 1998. This means that nearly two-thirds of the church is from just born to only 8 years old in Christ. This is incredible church growth and a wonderful problem to have! Another amazing thing about the growth of the church in Nepal is that converts have come from every level of society and caste including the high castes. It is the only place in the world where this has happened among Hindus.

The earliest Christian contact with the land of Nepal took place in 1662 A.D., when the Italian Capuchin priests passed through Nepal en route to Tibet. After the return of these visitors to Europe, they encouraged the people to go to India, Nepal, and Tibet to evangelise them. So in 1703 the Capuchin fathers were assigned by the Roman Catholic Church to evangelise in North India, Nepal, and Tibet. They made their base at Patna in India and several came to work in the Kathmandu Valley, the city-states of Newars, from 1707 to 1769. However, when the Gorkha king Prithvinarayan Shah conquered Nepal, he expelled the priests and the group of Newar Christians, accusing them of being agents of European colonial power.

From then until 1951 a firm Nepalese policy excluded all foreigners and Christians. Such policy was made on two main considerations. Independence from foreign power must be maintained, and the Hindu kingdom must be kept undefiled and the Hindu structure of society kept intact. Hence, foreign religions must be excluded. So the nation of Nepal was completely closed for almost two hundred years for any Christian missions. But the missionary work continued among the Nepalese who were living outside of Nepal. For two hundred years many missionary agencies and individuals thus stood praying and knocking at the door of Nepal.

Another important achievement was the translation of the Bible into the Nepali language by the Serampore Trio. The first New Testament was published in 1821 and is the first printed book in Nepali literature. The full Bible in Nepali was published in 1914, and the Revised Bible was published in 1977, and New Revised Version was published in 1998.

Before the door of Nepal was finally opened for foreigners to enter, missionary work started in the Indian borderlands. In Rupaidia, India, mission work started as early as 1921, and the Nepalese going to India and coming back to Nepal were preached to and evangelised right on the border. Nautanwa was another important centre in the border area to evangelise Nepalese people. From this place thousands of Nepalese passed each year between India and Nepal. Through the work of these border-based missionaries, within a short period of time a few people became Christians and dedicated their lives to the Lord. After sixteen years of continuous work on the Nautanwa border, they formed a band that is known as the Nepali Evangelistic Band (later to become the International Nepal Fellowship). At the beginning they concentrated their work among the Nepalese in India.

Though Nepal was not open for the Gospel, much was happening in the border areas. The missionaries and new converts living in the Nautanwa area formed a Gorkha Mission, which undertook to preach and sell scriptural literature at the border points. Some went to Nepal to live and work and witness, but they were immediately expelled from the country. Several attempts were made by several people to enter the country of Nepal and share the Gospel. Many of those people were arrested and finally expelled from the country. This situation continued until 1951.

Though democracy was declared and foreign investments were sought, the new government's attitude towards Christianity was similar to the previous government. The revolution of 1951 opened the door of this nation. Foreign agencies were welcomed to assist in national development. Therefore, in 1951 Christian missions were permitted to enter the land under certain conditions. The conditions were:

- They were to serve the people in such useful ways as should further the cause of nation-building;

- They were to follow the rules of the department to which they were connected; they were to travel, and

- Live only as their visas allowed; but they were not to propagate their religion or convert the people.

Catholic Jesuit missions entered Nepal in 1951 and boarding schools were opened. The International Nepal Fellowship (formerly Nepali Evangelistic Band) entered Nepal in 1952 and opened a hospital in Pokhara, West Nepal. Other mission agencies also started to come to Nepal. The largest mission organization is the United Mission to Nepal (UMN), which was formed in 1954. It is a co-operative effort of many missionary societies, spanning all continents, many denominations and interdenominational mission bodies. The mission has concentrated on various programmes and projects, which contribute to the development of the nation as a whole. The emphasis of UMN has been on health, education, vocational training and agriculture development. There are other mission agencies including Evangelical Alliance Mission, and Seventh Day Adventist Mission that are mainly concentrating on medical services.

Along with this brief history of mission agencies, it is appropriate to discuss the growth of the church itself in Nepal. After 1951 small congregations were established in various parts of Nepal. Some of the earliest congregations were established in Pokhara, Nepalganj, and Kathmandu. In the fifties and sixties only a handful of Christians were found in Nepal. During the seventies the churches started to grow in various parts of Nepal. Christians were not allowed to preach, and conversion to Christianity was prohibited. The Nepalese law stated that conversion to Christianity meant one-year imprisonment for the convert, three-year imprisonment for the preacher, and six-year imprisonment for the one who baptises. After the 1960s until the 1990s such laws were in effect and many Christians were imprisoned because of their faith. The church experienced severe persecution during the 1980s.

In 1990, there was an agitation against the existing rule, wherein the king was absolute monarch. Then the king declared democracy, and the multiparty system was restored. The king was willing to remain a constitutional monarch. The church experienced some freedom after 1990, but the attitude of the government toward Christians remains the same. In some places there are still arrests. Christians have been imprisoned. The government does not acknowledge a Christian presence, and does not register Christian churches and organizations.

In spite of all these pressures, the church in Nepal is growing. There are small and large congregations all over the country. The church faces a great challenge to witness to the people and also to disciple its converts and develop quality leadership. Developing ministerial courtesy among the new churches and denominations is another challenge the Nepali church faces. There is a genuine concern among some of the leadership that in order to establish God's kingdom in Nepal we need to work together. Our united effort will convey a better message than our single effort. This does not mean we need to be uniform in everything we do. We need to have the unity of the Spirit. Our main motive should be to establish the kingdom of God.

Evaluation Report of ITEEN 5th–26th March 2003

For too long Theological Education by Extension has been frustrated and handicapped by a number of factors:

- The educational technology and methodology of classical TEE, including its disciplines and administration, has been too often misunderstood, ignored or been inadequately taught in Bible colleges and missionary training establishments.

- There remains confusion still among many donor agencies and accreditation organizations as to what actually is TEE and what it is not.

- Enthusiasts have rushed into TEE without adequate preparation, realistic funding or proper administration.

- Programmers have failed to build up from grass-root levels.

The ITEEN programme in Nepal is a refreshing and encouraging example of what can be achieved through a very carefully planned and realistically funded TEE programme—a programme that is nationally owned and exceptionally well managed. After three very full weeks of travelling and interviewing church personnel across Nepal, the Evaluation Team is certain that this low-cost "grass-roots" ITEEN programme is absolutely relevant to the discipleship and leadership training needs of the majority of the economically poor but fast growing churches of Nepal.

The Team is convinced that ITEEN has demonstrated responsible and accountable stewardship at an exceptionally high level. The staff have been careful and thorough in all aspects of their work. They deserve further support at a time of rapid growth in their ministry. The Team would strongly recommend that other organisations involved in modern mission and church growth strategy be encouraged to study the valuable lessons that ITEEN provide.

The Evaluation Team

M.S. Rana, Former Director of the Nepal Gospel Outreach Centre, Deacon of Gyaneshwor Church, Kathmandu.

Sam G. John, B.Th., B.D., M.Th., Former lecturer, Kerala Bible School, India. Missionary in Nepal 4 years and Pastor of the Brethren Assembly, Dharan.

Michael Huggins, NDA., CDFM, Field Director, Oxen Ministries. (Chairman)

The team were helped immensely by the total co-operation and assistance of all the members of the ITEEN Staff:

Peter Bisset, NDA, CDFM, CBS, Director

Tanka Subedi, Dip.Th., National Coordinator

Mrs. Rita Subedi, Dip.Th, Translator/Programme Co-ordinator (part-time)

Miss Yasodha Devi Malla, Secretary

Miss Shivu Nepali, Computer Operator

Sarju Sar T.R., Field Worker

Kamal Gharti, Office Assistant

The evaluation was undertaken during the period between the 6th and 25th March, 2003. Members of the team reviewed available documents:

1. Proposed foundation aims and objectives

2. ITEEN Project Proposal & Details

3. Minutes of Meetings

4. Annual Planning Objectives

5. Annual Budget details and summaries from 1999 to 2003

6. Six month trial balances comparing to budget

7. Annual Income and Expenditure accounts comparing budget to actual

8. ITEEN Monthly reports including both enrolment and completion summaries

9. ITEEN Forum

10. In-service training reports

11. Tutor training assessments

12. ITEEN programme forms

Members of the team held interviews and discussions with each member of ITEEN HQ Staff, some members of ITEEN Board, including past and present Chairpersons, 72 course tutors, 140 course students, 20 church leaders.

Members of the team travelled to some 10 districts and held interviews and discussions with pastors, tutors and students from the following areas: *Banepa, Bhaktapur, Bhimad, Chitwan, Dharan, Dhulikhel, Dulegauda, Ghorahi, Gobardiha, Hetauda, Jajarkot, Janakpur, Kathmandu, Kohalpur, Lamahi, Lamjung, Ovari, Pokhara, Sindhupalchouk, Surkhet, Tulsipur.*

During each interview, the Evaluation Team sought to obtain the following background information from the person involved: name and age, ethnic grouping, from which area and church, whether an ITEEN tutor or student or both, how many years a Christian, previous religious background, level of education, which ITEEN courses completed or now doing, favourite lesson and why, main blessing through doing the ITEEN courses, any other comments or testimonies.

Of the people interviewed:

- 119 were male and 109 were female.

- 70% were converts from a Hindu-related background—the remaining 30% were from Buddhist or Christian backgrounds.

- The average age was 26.

Members of the team sat in on a three-day tutor training Seminar from 11th to 13th March 2003 at Nayagaun, Pokhara, run by the ITEEN staff Members of the team had the opportunity to examine all ITEEN courses.

ITEEN Staff and the Fulfillment and Monitoring of Achievement of Goals

The Evaluation Team found it an immense pleasure to meet, work along side and interview all the ITEEN staff. Each member of staff proved to be motivated, hard-working and capable of remarkable initiative. All were mutually supportive. The team were impressed by the quality of attention and courtesy the ITEEN staff showed to all callers at the office, however humble.

Since the beginning of its ministry, ITEEN has maintained its goals by setting forth clear annual achievement targets and supporting budgets. It has been obvious from interviews that these goals are clearly understood, shared and owned by all the ITEEN staff.

The Evaluation Team was also impressed by the careful choice of in-service training provided to the members of the staff. ITEEN has a policy of regular staff meetings and assessment in all aspects of its work.

ITEEN recognises the fundamental need for good group leaders—good tutors—for the success of a TEE programme. In order to meet this they have established a policy of holding monthly three day tutor-training seminars for ten months of the year. ITEEN plans to extend this to twice-monthly seminars to meet the fast growing demand for such.

Financial Policies

The ITEEN budgets are both realistic and thorough, yet clear and easy to follow. Based on the proposed targets for each year, they cover all aspects of income and expenditure in detail. *Income* is generated through the programme, from donations from within Nepal and grants from outside Nepal. *Expenditure* covers, firstly, a careful assessment of capital expenditure, and, secondly, the recurring expenditure linked to staff (both direct and indirect), office, repairs and maintenance, training, transport, public relations and specific costs relating to the ITEEN project. A double entry system of accounting is used.

ITEEN has maintained a flow of reporting that is consistent and easy to understand. A careful control is kept on the budget. Actual expenditure is carefully monitored during the year through quarterly, and now monthly, trial balances. This is an outstanding discipline within the organization of ITEEN, expressed through both internal reporting between staff and external reporting which has a refreshing transparency.

ITEEN has an independent audit which is undertaken before the close of the first quarter of the following financial year. The audit is carefully studied and appropriate action is taken to recommendations within the audit. ITEEN tutors and church leaders are becoming aware of the need to work together towards a policy of sustainability and are facing up to the challenge of this valuable work becoming sustainable within the Nepalese church economy.

ITEEN has made it very clear to all pastors and tutors that foreign aid has to be perceived as short-term pump-priming and that somehow the programme has to become sustainable through disciplined yet voluntary support within Nepal itself.

ITEEN has calculated that at this stage in its development, to train a student through ITEEN for 12 months costs 1000R (£10). Based on the completion of a maximum of three courses in a 12-month period, the most ITEEN can expect to receive from each student would be around 110R (£1.20) from the sale of the course books (e.g. *Abundant Life* @ 30R, *Abundant Light* @ 30R and *Life of Christ Book 1* @ 50R).

ITEEN is challenging each tutor-training group, however economically poor, to help meet the shortfall in running costs by making some sort of contribution as a demonstration of their commitment to the work of ITEEN and is asking:

1. How can ITEEN raise funds in Nepal?

2. How can individual ITEEN groups help also?

ITEEN has calculated that after 2-3 years costs will fall from 1000R per student per year down to 600R (= 50R a month).

The Extent that ITEEN Contributes to Social and Spiritual Change among the Poor and other Disadvantaged Groups

The Evaluation Team were able to interview a random selection of over 200 people studying and tutoring within the ITEEN programme, and from that collected detailed testimonies that clearly demonstrate the effect of this TEE material on the breaking down of tribal, caste and gender barriers within both its administration and in the groups; the training, motivation and equipping of even the low caste and semi-literates for remarkably effective and much needed service in the church and wider community.

> *I was illiterate. I bought a Bible and God helped me to learn. My son wrote my (dictated) answers to the ITEEN course. I was unable to memorise the stages in the life of Christ, but God gave me a vision and taught me. I still remember all the stages in the Life of Christ. I never went to any literacy class; I learned to read and write by the ITEEN courses. I was first in the group with the highest mark.* —Mrs Maya Gautam, pastor's wife, aged 43, 11 years a believer

I am from a Hindu background. At 26–27 I read literature about Christ and found what I was seeking—Jesus came not for the righteous but for sinners— it really spoke to me as I am a low caste person. So I looked for a church. Result: A dysfunctional family came to the Lord and have become a good Christian family—now consistent father and mother have a good relationship, father has left his bad behaviour. All the family believes now—we have 3 daughters and a son. My favourite lessons are from Abundant Life—*"How to overcome the World and Satan" (9 & 11). I have also completed LOC 1-3 and am now starting* Abundant Light. —Indra Bahadur Nepali, aged 36, tutor and student, 8 years a Christian*

During the interviews the Evaluation Team listened to many other such testimonies as to how the teaching of the ITEEN courses motivated the students. One pastor's wife, for example, herself only just literate, started a ministry of teaching illiterates to read. Other students have testified how they learned to read and study through ITEEN.

A number of "Help" ministries have started to develop. The following is an interesting testimony regarding self-help through the honouring of God's word:

*Most new believers are poor. When we give the "Abundant Life" course to them we can see changes in their lifestyle. They stop drinking. They become clean—slowly they become better off financially. Take for example my own family; they were very poor. The family were drinking and smoking a lot. They were dirty and unhealthy. When they did "Abundant Life" they stopped drinking and gradually everything began to change. Now they have enough for food, clothes and shelter and are no longer poor—yet they haven't received any financial support from outside. Cleanliness helps them not to get sick, and they save the money they would have spent on medicine. In their studies of the Bible 1 Corinthians 3:16 is the main verse which affected them. —*Pastor Tiara Chaudhari, new believer, but after doing *Abundant Life* he became a leader of a small church and is now a tutor

Tanka Subedi, the National Co-ordinator of ITEEN, is himself one of the members of Pokhara Christian Community, which has initiated "Asal Chhimekee Nepal" (Good Neighbours Nepal), of which Tanka is secretary. Its aims and objectives are:

Health: To provide Health Care Assistance to the poor and the communities of the remote areas in Nepal.

Education: To support schools located in the remote areas of Nepal by providing assistance for teaching and physical development to improve the quality of education. To encourage girls into education up to higher level and in the future to establish a model education centre.

Rehabilitation: To rehabilitate victims of political conflicts, addictions, prostitution and minister to the needs of street children.

Agriculture: To seek improvement in traditional agriculture to increase the income of farmers.

Environment: To raise awareness of environmental safety issues by using various methods, i.e., organizing activities, distributing booklets, etc.

Income Generation: To provide training in skills required to run small businesses, based on the requirements of the market. (Micro Business Enterprises—granting loans of up to $2000 to start businesses. Funding helped through Jhodas Int. USA)

Helping Government: To feed back valuable information acquired through the work of the organization that would help Government policy.

Emergency relief work: including victims of landslides. (On average some 50 people die each year through landslides)

ITEEN has also set aside a fund out of which money is occasionally given to churches to help victims of internal disasters.

The Extent to Which ITEEN Meets the Needs of the Local Church

Relevance of Courses to the Local Church and Culture

As the team interviewed more and more pastors, students and tutors, it became very clear that this ITEEN programme is extremely relevant to the needs of the churches. Believers, even the semi-literate, are being thoroughly grounded in the faith. This grounding is tested both through the tough TEE tests they have to pass and is also tested within their daily struggles and temptations and honed within their growing church responsibilities. The culture is multi-tribal, of Hindu background and very poor—yet churches are growing through the thorough training, motivating and equipping of humble men and women for service, people who would most likely be disqualified for such in the West through its antiquated theological caste system!

I have done 5 months of pastoral training and many other trainings, but I have found ITEEN courses more effective and practical. I desire that every Christian may do ITEEN courses.

Most churches have no Bible Study groups. ITEEN has given them the opportunity to incorporate Bible Study groups as a normal and essential part of church life. My longing is that ITEEN will be able to expand more, for all churches here in Nepal need to avail themselves of their training ministry. When my children grow up I would very much prefer them to study through ITEEN than go away to Bible College. I have noticed that students returning to the churches from Bible College are not very interested in others going. I don't know why. This generation of Christians is very poor. They cannot attend Bible College by themselves—they have to obtain some sort of scholarship, which is not easy. Where the Bible college trains one person, ITEEN trains a group—and for less money. Before I heard of

ITEEN I was given the opportunity to go to Bible College, but I remembered my important family responsibilities at home and declined to accept. This is a situation repeated often across Nepal. In our church we have three Bible College graduates, but only one is a full-time church worker, the others have town jobs, however there are many ITEEN students working for the church.

It is my opinion also that, in terms of producing actual church workers, the training of ITEEN is much more relevant to the needs of the church than the training in a distant Bible College. —Ram Prasad Sharma, leader and church planter

ITEEN plans to add two more courses to its programme in order to bring in further relevant teaching:

- The translation and transculturalisation of the course "Family Life" by the Christian Leaders' Training College of Papua New Guinea. CLTC produces parallel and complimentary TEE material to SEAN.

- ITEEN is seriously considering the possibility of writing its own special TEE course to meet teenage needs—covering areas including personality development, relationships, peer pressures, time management and the media.

Meeting Semi-literate and Illiterate Needs

At 45%, literacy is still a problem in the villages and the more isolated but well populated hill regions of Nepal. ITEEN has already approached Focus Radio for permission to convert their radio adaptations of SEAN's "Abundant Life" and "Abundant Light" into Nepali. At no cost to ITEEN, Loknath Manaen, former Chairman of the Nepali Bible Society has acquired available broadcasting time for such material from the Moscow Radio Station. There may also be radio stations in India that would be interested. There is great interest in the possibilities this "Radio Arm" could present. The technique of linking this radio (and even cassette) ministry with the main ITEEN programme could be introduced as a feature of future tutor-training to help the illiterates and semi-literates.

Relationships with Church Leaders

The ministry of ITEEN is to serve the churches of all denominations, in strengthening and equipping the membership, however humble, into service and ministry.

The Evaluation Team observed how well ITEEN seeks to work through church leaders. No student can register to do an ITEEN course without the written permission of his or her church leader.

Acceptance and Use of ITEEN Training within Churches

We were able to interview church leaders from the National Churches Fellowship of Nepal, Brethren, Baptist, Assemblies of God, Friendship Church,

Believers' Church, Agape and independent groups who enthusiastically paid tribute to the ministry of ITEEN.

Nepal has many very isolated areas; many are several days' walk from the nearest road and bus pick-up point. Not all the churches yet know about ITEEN. It is still very early days.

However, there are some church leaders who do not want to relate to ITEEN.

- A few have their own programme and don't feel a need to involve ITEEN.

- Some want total leadership control in all things and see any "parachurch" help as a threat to their own position and power.

The Extent to which ITEEN Enables Students to:

• positively understand the main teaching of the Bible

The people interviewed showed a remarkable understanding of the structure and teaching of the Bible. Even students just part way through the basic foundational course were able to explain their faith clearly, and many were already using their knowledge of the Bible to witness to their families and friends.

ITEEN has introduced special examinations for both the foundational courses—*Abundant Life* and *Abundant Light*.

At one church the Evaluation Team met a group who were just completing Book 6 of *The Life of Christ* and would be applying for the SEAN Extension College Basic Diploma in Pastoral Theology. They were all now enthusiastic church workers. Questioned as to their educational background, one left school when he was 10, one was studying at undergraduate level, and the remainder left school between the ages of 12 and 15. To have reached this Diploma, each would have had to have completed 190 lessons, attended 98 group meetings and undertaken over 100 written tests and exams—some 600 study hours.

> *My mother couldn't read but has learned to read through doing the* Abundant Life *course. One lady was shown a vision how to read, for she couldn't read and was very upset, so she prayed to God. In a vision or dream she saw the Nepali script and understood it. She then sat up and then awake read the whole of the lesson. She has been able to read since. Regarding the ITEEN Tutor training, this helped me very much and gave me considerable encouragement. I learned how to run the course, be an effective group leader—I am most excited by the training by being able to teach others also. My favourite lessons are: "How to pray" and "How to study the Bible" (Abundant Life 7&8). These have very much helped the group in prayer. —Mrs. Kailas Lama, aged 32, tutor for mothers' group and a teenage and student group*

I have learned more in one year through ITEEN courses than in the previous 13 years. The materials have helped equip me to be a leader. —Min Thapa, aged 32, youth leader, Deacon and responsible for church music

Just as Nepal has basic needs of roads and water for survival and economic growth, so the churches have basic needs for Abundant Life *and* Abundant Light. —Nepalese Church Pastor

- **grow in Christian character**

The Evaluation Team witnessed exciting evidence of this in probably every student and tutor interviewed. They positively radiated Christ. Many gave testimonies as to how various lessons had resulted in radical changes in both attitudes and behaviour.

For example, Mrs. Laxmi Adhikari, aged 28, 6 years a believer, told the team that she has received so very many blessings through ITEEN courses. She found that she could now explain her faith much more clearly. She saw her most challenging lesson to be forgiving others—to build the habit of learning to forgive others. The Evaluation Team were very impressed as to how very clearly students could articulate their faith and testimonies.

Another example is Mr. Dil Kumar Subba—he is a labourer on building sites. He has had very little education or opportunity to study. He had been a Christian for a number of years, but did not know how to pray. He enrolled with ITEEN and is currently up to LOC Book 3. He is now very bold and can lead house Bible Study groups, pray and teach the Word.

- **develop and use Christian ministry/service skills**

The Evaluation Team interviewed a number of pastors—some themselves studying or tutoring through ITEEN, a few with Bible College diplomas or university degrees. All witnessed the profound effect that the ITEEN programme was having on the life of the church. The various giftings of the students become apparent as they progress through the courses, and therefore the churches are able to grow their own workers. Evangelists (friendship and lifestyle evangelism is a hallmark of nearly all their believers), youth workers, helpers, administrators, Sunday School teachers, teachers, people with pastoral hearts, and future leaders are being trained and proven within their churches and communities through the ITEEN programme. Teenagers/youths take literacy classes. Youths sometimes lead the service and take cell groups in their villages.

I have studied so far up to Life of Christ *Book 3. My favourite LOC lesson is "Proofs of the Bible". I found Tutor training quite different from other training— like being in a family. So I was not frightened. Everybody was happy. We learned a lot of things.* —Miss Usher Guam, aged 22, ITEEN Tutor and Student

Equipping the Believer for Suffering and Persecution

Linked to the growth of the ministry of ITEEN is the constant threat of persecution. The Constitution of Nepal is confusing over the matter of religious freedom. Its opening statements include subscribing to the United Nations Convention on Human Rights, which includes freedom of conscience and religion. However, it has also incorporated into the constitution old laws relating to a person changing his/her religion (one year prison sentence) and that of causing another to change religion (up to 6 years in prison).

The World Hindu Federation is putting pressure on the Nepali Government to suppress this Christian growth. It is suspected that Chief District Officers from the Home Ministry have been instructed to enforce the laws relating to change of religion and proselytising, which has already led to arrests. Believers face serious problems, ranging from cultural expectations to open persecution.

In Dharan the Evaluation Team interviewed a brother and two sisters (18 and 20) who are ITEEN students and believers but have parents who are still Hindu. All three bubbled over with their love for Jesus and their appreciation of their ITEEN training. The Team learned later that the girls are regularly beaten by their father because of their Christian faith. There is a serious problem also facing the brother who wants nonetheless to honour his father. When his father dies he is expected by his family and community to publicly undertake the Hindu funeral rites expected of a son to get his father through to heaven.

The Evaluation Team also interviewed a young church worker in Dharan who had been thrown out of his home by the rest of his family for becoming a Christian.

The ITEEN training seeks to equip all believers to understand and face suffering and persecution. For example, in the home study of lesson 11, frame 10 of "Abundant Life", the student learns:

> *Persecution takes many forms. Sometimes it is just unkind words or teasing. At other times it may be in the form of threats or physical harm, and in some places it has meant imprisonment and even death…*

Later on in the lesson, following a scriptural meditation on Jesus, the student is asked which of the following thoughts can give you strength when the people of this world ill-treat you:

> *My relatives should not treat me like this.*
> *Jesus also suffered persecution and hatred.*
> *If things go on like this, I shall give up following Christ.*

Then in the group meeting there is opportunity for members of the group to share, discuss and pray over such situations that affect them personally, their church or their country.

The Evaluation Team interviewed a man whom they knew had been imprisoned for becoming a Christian. When the matter of his imprisonment was raised, he lightly dismissed it with the words "It was only for a year."

Growth of the Ministry of ITEEN

The growth of the ministry of ITEEN has been truly remarkable. The number of registered students was 250 in 1999, 450 in 2000, 1049 in 2001, and 1750 in 2002. The difficult and exacting translation programme has rapidly progressed so that now ITEEN has material on hand to take students up to the level of SEAN Extension College Intermediate Diploma of Pastoral Theology. Within a year or more, material for SEAN Extension College Advanced Diploma in Pastoral Theology will become available in Nepalese.

It is clearly evident that this growth is nowhere near its peak. The evidence is that many more Christians are willing to do the ITEEN courses if approached, but ITEEN is concerned that if the work grows too fast its existing resources and personnel would become severely over-stretched and standards would suffer. Already everybody in ITEEN is working very hard, usually six days a week plus overtime, and it is obvious that more staff and larger facilities are already needed. Rita Subedi, for example, has to cut down time on translation because of increased tutor training needs. These the Evaluation Team will quantify in their recommendations.

Some Reasons for ITEEN's Effective Ministry

- The firm foundation of prayer and work of Christian witness in Nepal, especially these last 50 years

- ITEEN networks with other Christian organizations working in Nepal

- ITEEN has clear objectives and practical and obtainable goals and has not been distracted by accreditation issues.

- The Director and the National Coordinator of ITEEN are very competent men of vision

- Members of ITEEN's staff are very motivated and work within a genuine Christian family atmosphere

- Grant money has enabled ITEEN to establish a very effective and well disciplined administrative structure with solid financial policies.

- ITEEN maintains careful financial management, transparent accountability and good stewardship

- ITEEN has organised a plan of studies recognised and accepted by the churches

- ITEEN has firm enrolment requirements for all its students

- ITEEN has kept a strong emphasis on regular and thorough training to establish a growing pool of effective tutors within the churches

- Discipline and high standards are built into all aspects of ITEEN's work, both of which are carefully maintained

- The ITEEN programme meets the needs of the national churches at "the coal face"

- ITEEN's Education policy starts effectively at the "grass-roots" level of need in the emerging churches and then builds upwards on a firm foundation. Traditional Western Theological Education has been likened to a fireman's ladder with the first 20 rungs missing—ITEEN has sought to provide those missing rungs to serve the churches so that people of little education, yet willing workers for Jesus, have been able to "train on the job" and serve their churches effectively. In the process, they can obtain the SEAN Extension College Certificates and Diplomas that carry the prestigious names of Dr. John Stott, Dr. Michael Green and Rev. Steve Chalk as Patrons and which are signed by Martin Goldsmith as Dean of Studies.

EVALUATION TEAM'S RECOMMENDATIONS
New Staff Appointments

The Team is concerned that the National Co-ordinator carries a very heavy work-load at a time of rapid expansion. It is convinced that he urgently needs an Assistant who can also support the Programme Coordinator and Administrative Assistant. The Team believes it is vital that immense care be taken in this choice and that both the Director and National Coordinator be permitted to have the final say of the choice.

The Team also recognised the dedication, initiative and courage of Sarju Sar, the ITEEN Field Worker. He regularly makes long and difficult journeys. As the ministry of ITEEN grows, this may mean Sarju having to travel more often into the less accessible regions that do not possess proper roads. Furthermore, in this work Sarju faces the risk of hostility and imprisonment. The Team would recommend that a second Field Worker be appointed.

Tutor-Training Needs

At present ITEEN undertakes 10 tutor-training seminars a year. The demand for such training far outstrips the supply. ITEEN recognises that the effectiveness of the tutor-training seminars would be reduced if the number of participants per session were increased above 15, so they would strongly prefer to hold a further 10 sessions a year (two a month during the training periods).

The Team considers that the current space available at ITEEN would be insufficient to serve the administrative and Tutor-training of ITEEN to meet the current growth. The current 1,700 registered students could double within 18 months to around 3,500.

The Evaluation Team recommends that a new combined administrative and tutor-training centre be sought or built within the next two years: ITEEN would like to be able to move their office from Pokhara to Kathmandu; the existing ITEEN staff is happy to move to Kathmandu; ITEEN believes that they would be more able to recruit the additional staff they are seeking from that area.

The Evaluation Team would also recommend that financial help be given to ITEEN to update their office equipment. The existing equipment consists of 3 computers—all quite old and running on Windows 95. One of the three is not working properly. It was purchased 5-6 years ago. The other two will soon be too old for typing. ITEEN also has three printers, two of which are good, but the other no longer economic to use.

The Team recommends the purchase of:

- Two good computers—one for the Computer Operator and one for the National Co-ordinator.

- A colour printer which would be used especially for tutor training.

Purchase of the following equipment would greatly help ITEEN's ministry:

- Binding equipment

- A Power Generator (for office and training)

- A Multimedia Projector (for the training)

- A TV and VCR (for the training)

- Musical instruments (for the training)

ITEEN Transport

The Evaluation Team is concerned that ITEEN does not have a passenger and material carrying vehicle of their own. ITEEN staff often have to undertake much travel. At present this is carried out using buses, hired cars and the staff's motorcycles (even on journeys of over 150 kilometres). The Team was able to inspect the Indian-made Mahindra diesel "Voyager" at a trade fair in Pokhara. This is a robust vehicle that can seat up to 8-9 people and is marketed at almost half the cost of its competitors. It currently costs in total R1,500,000 =£12,500 (Ref. Appendix 18). The purchase of this vehicle would greatly facilitate the growing work of ITEEN. Also, the National Coordinator's motorcycle is now very elderly and unreliable and needs replacing. Additionally, the Field Worker needs a motorcycle.

Tutor-Training Video

The Evaluation Team was very impressed indeed by the content and effectiveness of the ITEEN Tutor-Training Seminars. The Team recommends that ITEEN be funded to produce a video of their Tutor-training seminars that developing TEE programmes in other countries could use. The Team suggests that initially there be English explanation summaries over-voiced at each stage of the video, which could be transferred to other languages.

Accreditation

The Evaluation Team accepts that accreditation by Asia Theological Association could be helpful, especially if ATA then follows the example of some leading South and North American Bible colleges who grant generous academic credits to students who enter college with SEAN diplomas.

The Evaluation Team is nonetheless concerned that an "academic caste system" is not forced on these emerging Nepalese churches, and takes note of the analysis of A. J. Barratt in "Issues facing Latin America":

> *Traditionally the churches in the more advanced Western countries have followed the principle of the colleges fixing the parameter of Theological Education according to traditional recognised curriculum and then allow this to shape the destiny of the church. In the West this has resulted in a universal highly middle class, highly academically trained ministry—de-churching the masses and disqualifying for ministry the very class of people Jesus chose as His disciples.*

The Team believes that the Western Church could in turn learn much from this ITEEN experience, even to the extent of a radical re-thinking of the traditional approach to accreditation, especially the classification of what is and what is not "Higher Theological Education". The Team would argue that:

- It acknowledges the need for evangelical scholarship, but questions, in the light of the continued church decline in the West, that evangelical scholarship should automatically be the recognised accredited training route for church leadership and be repeated in the emerging countries as such.

- ITEEN has repeated the original South American experiment, which proved that it is possible to train effective leadership "at the coal face" through a disciplined TEE programme. The Evaluation Team would pose the question as to whether, if TEE was replaced by a more traditionally recognised training system, that system would have been able to produce the same or better results, let alone have expected those it had trained to return to their rural origins.

Classical TEE with its home studies, group dynamics and associated ministry assignments is able to change people in the three key areas of "Knowing", "Being" and "Doing". It can be a tough and difficult system, but it does produce remarkable results in all three aspects.

Churches are declining in the West. Unlike the churches in poorer and humbler countries, Western Churches have still not learned how to seriously envision, train, equip and mobilise their people, the ordinary people of God, into tough, costly and effective service that takes territory from Satan. From this Nepalese experience the Evaluation Team would advocate a re-thinking of the classification of all aspects of Christian training in the West, especially where such training is to be exported elsewhere. Perhaps the time has come for Christian service education to be disassociated from the secular/Greek pattern where "increased knowledge" is elevated as "higher". One tends to focus on an elitist system that leap-frogs the need for disciplined training at "grass-roots" level. Is western theological training handcuffed to a now out-dated accreditation system? A few years ago Milton Barker, of the Evangelical Foreign Missions Association, wrote the following:

> *We are not training the right people.*
> *We are not training the right leaders.*
> *We are training them in irrelevant concepts.*
> *We are segregating our trainees as professionals.*
> *We spend too much money doing it.*

Traditionally one would classify the SEAN Extension College Intermediate Diploma as "diploma level", though not officially accredited. The Evaluation Team believes more emphasis should be placed on the word "appropriate" and that the word "higher" no longer be used when discussing aspects of

Christian service education. The accreditation that the Evaluation Team recommends as being of prime importance is the value that these growing Nepalese churches place on their members discipled and trained into various ministries through the ITEEN programme.

Peter Bisset

bisset@gmail.com

QUESTIONS FOR REFLECTION AND DISCUSSION

1. *What is your general impression of the relevance of ITEEN to the socio-economic and spiritual needs of the people of Nepal? How does your own theological education program relate to the basic socio-economic and spiritual needs of your people?*

2. *How is the rapid growth of ITEEN related to the rapid growth of the churches in Nepal? What do the testimonies in this case study indicate in this regard?*

3. *What aspects of ITEEN were examined by the 2003 evaluation team? Has your own theological education program undergone similar evaluations? If not, why not? If so, what did they find?*

4. *What are some of the reasons for ITEEN's effective ministry, according to the evaluation team? Do these reasons apply to your own program?*

5. *How does the case study deal with "accreditation" and "higher levels" of theological education? How does your own program deal with these matters?*

St. Mark's National Theological Centre, Australia

by Stephen Pickard

THEOLOGICAL EDUCATION IN AUSTRALIA: THE CONTEXT

The paper is in four sections. First, it briefly outlines the context for theological education in Australia and identifies some of the questions that arise for theology. Second, it traces the recent development of TEE in Australia. Third and more fully, it considers a case study on TEE with reference to a theological institution of the Anglican Church of Australia. Finally, it offers reflections, assessments and proposals regarding "E" world education within the context of the future church.

Australia is the largest island continent on earth. It is also the driest with over 70% desert or uninhabitable land. Australia covers seven and a half million square kilometres of earth. The population of 20,000,000 hugs the narrow coastal strip of the continent, and over 80% of the people live in the major urban concentrations of the six state capitals on the coast. Our cities face outwards towards the Pacific, Atlantic and Indian Oceans. The rural population is sparsely distributed. The first Europeans to settle in the country were convicts and military in 1788. Convict transportation continued until the 1840s. A convict settlement is a far cry from the quest for religious freedom of the first "Pilgrim Fathers" to the United States. The harshness of the continent and the intense isolation engendered by a six-month sea voyage to the other side of the world had a profound influence on the pattern of settlement and the Australian psyche. It meant that settlement was concentrated in a limited number of seaports separated by vast distances, even by modern standards.

This has meant that regionalism has dominated Australian life socially, economically, politically and religiously. Consequently there are often intense rivalries between states and capital cities and a corresponding parochialism in most things including religion. This is a consequence of what has been aptly termed "the tyranny of distance".

Religious rivalries reflect those imported from the mother country. For example, many Irish Catholics were transported to Sydney and eventually clashed with the dominant Church of England. Today the Catholic and Anglican churches of Sydney are powerful, conservative and intolerant. To a large extent our religious tensions are the result of imported religious species struggling to assert their identity in a foreign colonial setting. Denominational rivalry and jealousy from the UK has taken root in Australia. This has made ecumenism difficult and frustrating.

Theological seminaries for most denominations were established in the capital cities in the nineteenth century and provided the main source of training for clergy for the churches. Within each denomination each state tended to have its own clergy training institution or two if, as with the Anglicans, there was pressure to serve different constituencies, e.g., high church and low church varieties. The brand of theology was derivative and reflected the concerns and prejudices of the home church.

Since the Second World War Australia has had successive waves of immigration from Europe and Asia and the Middle East. This has increased the Roman Catholic proportion of Christians and has also meant that Australia has become one of, if not the most multicultural and religiously diverse countries on the globe. How this mix will develop in the twenty-first century remains to be seen.

The above is the larger context for theological education in Australia. Religious patterns followed regional settlement along a coastal strip with vast distances between main centres. Independent seminary theological education for clergy of different denominations has been the result. This has stretched resources. As the influence and public voice of the churches has weakened in a highly secularised country, the strain has begun to tell. Seminaries have closed, others have shrunk; and those that have survived have usually done so because they have entered into new partnerships. Partnerships are essentially a recent development and are either in new theological consortia (but still retaining their own identity and financial independence) or with universities. The universities are state secular institutions which from the beginning were unsympathetic to the establishment of departments of divinity. The churches were so strongly confessional and internally divided that they were not able to muster any significant response to the university prejudice against religion.

This has ensured that theology has struggled to be anything more than a service activity of the churches for the purpose of providing clergy.

The isolated and harsh realities of Australian life have bred a pragmatism and resourcefulness as well as an impatience with anything intellectual. Australians will hold state funerals for tough sportsmen and women but hardly celebrate writers, thinkers and crafters of new ways. These attitudes are also reflected in the churches which are similarly impatient with theology and keen on producing disciples who get things done without too much fuss or reflection on what or why.

The above context indicates that a major continuing challenge for the Church concerns its ability to creatively adapt in a new environment. Inculturation of the Gospel has been a challenge. For economic, social and psychological reasons Australians have tended to remain in adolescence under the wing of the mother country, often rebellious if in the end compliant. The maturation of a people takes a long time, and European presence in Australia is a relatively recent phenomenon compared with the ancient peoples of Australia. But in a highly multicultural society and with the emergence of religious pluralism the churches of twenty-first century Australia creative adaptation to the local environment is critical.

One consequence of this is that mission in the Australian setting requires an incarnational model of being church. This has to be reflected in worship, theology and discipleship. An incarnational model will have to be one that embeds the faith at the local level, that takes seriously the cultural and social realities of the place, and that struggles to find a truly indigenous voice. This is a particular challenge in a country where distance between cities and towns and a highly dispersed rural population make good quality communications absolutely critical. The rural people can easily feel disenfranchised in Australia.

Seminary theology has been orientated to immediate practical ministry needs. But theology too will have to find its own authentic Australian voice if it is to contribute to the needed transformation of the churches and bear witness to the coming kingdom of God. How then will theology play its part in the equipping of the people of God for a new kind of engagement in Australia? What structures will best serve the future church? In a resource-depleted church what new possibilities are there for theological education that is truly for all the people rather than restricted to the clergy? These are some of the questions arising out of the Australian context. Today there is much talk about a mission-shaped church and an emerging church. A mission-shaped theological education is a natural corollary of this. The next section offers a brief introduction to the way theology has begun to move beyond the seminary and into the wider church and society and respond to the problem of "the tyranny of distance". It is at best a brief sketch.

EXTENDING THEOLOGICAL EDUCATION: INITIAL DEVELOPMENTS

For many years in Australia the General Board of Religious Education was a leader in the development and furtherance of theological education. GBRE had its origins in a decision of the National Anglican Church in the 1940s to develop resources to allow clergy who lived at some distance from the main theological colleges to complete their basic theology qualification (i.e., Th.L.; Licentiate in Theology). Later, when the Australian College of Theology began its Diploma of Ministry and opened this to lay people, GBRE developed correspondence-type courses to serve this constituency. This signalled a move of theological education beyond the walls of traditional seminary education in the Anglican Church of Australia. GBRE developed shorter and longer courses to help people of the churches explore their faith in the context of lay ministry and vocation in the world. This involved the distribution of notes and booklets to people spread throughout Australia. The nature of the material was such that it was user-friendly for denominations other than Anglicanism.

In the early phase of TEE resources were, by today's standards, quite basic, even primitive. "Correspondence Course" was the basic nomenclature. It would have been regarded as something of an upgrade when tapes accompanied notes sent out to students. Assignments were duly sent in, marked and returned, and it was at least theoretically conceivable that students could phone their tutor for conversation. In the 1990s the correspondence courses were supplemented by residential workshops. These were held in Melbourne and other places where clusters of students gathered for two or three days for theological reflection and encouragement.

During the mid-1980s Australian Universities began to move into the computer desktop world. Some universities with a focus on the rural and country sector—in contrast to the universities of the metropolitan centres— saw the importance and advantages of a more intentional online approach to delivery of higher education. To this extent they were following trends in the public and commercial sector. The University of New England was an early pioneer in this. This University combined its distance education stream with a commitment to residential workshops. In this they were followed by Charles Sturt University, which later became the birthplace of the School of Theology through St. Mark's National Theological Centre.

Australia has always been quick to employ the latest technologies, and the education sector has been part of this. To the extent that some theological institutions had associations with local universities, they too began to harness such technology. However, there was always going to be a lag in the take-up of such technology because of resource problems and the seminary context for theological education. This latter feature meant that churches still prized residential training over more dispersed models. To this extent Theological Education by Extension belonged to a lay model of theological education. Trinity Theological School is an example of an institution that has managed to retain its emphasis on residential life and adopt part of its programme to online education. In 2000 it introduced online delivery for its Diploma of Ministry and Graduate Diploma of Theology.

Two factors have emerged in Australia in recent years to change the traditional approach to seminary education. First, the churches have increasingly struggled to resource their education and formation programmes for ordinands. Second, the ministry of the whole people of God has undergone a remarkable explosion over the last fifty years. Both factors have conspired to push theological education in new directions. In respect to the former issue dioceses have begun to trim their education budgets and explore ways of formation and education for ministry that do not cost as much and do not require the dislocation of ordinands and their families. This has meant that distance education programmes in theology combined with local formation programmes have taken root. With regard to the latter issue, the emergence of lay ministry has meant that theological education is now seen as a task for the whole people of God and can no longer be confined to or be defined by the seminary/residential context. This raises the very practical issue of how the baptised will be resourced to become disciples in a brave new world, which is mobile, fast-changing and increasingly uncertain. In such a world technology exercises remarkable power for good and ill. Increasingly the "E" world is a feature of the cultural landscape. It offers a companion technology to the emerging understanding of ministry, vocation and Christian education. Exactly what kind of companion is the matter to be discussed in what follows.

The above developments provide some markers for the new environment for theological education. These developments relate to our understanding of the church and its theology of Christian formation. The recent history in this respect has been both exciting and at times full of tension. There remain a number of unresolved tensions to do with preparation of candidates for ordination and the common ministries of the church. And the issue of residential life in an intentional religious community has not disappeared but rather begun to resurface in new and quite exciting ways. For example, in my own context a number of student houses have been established in local parishes. Students sign up to a religious covenant and participate in the daily life of prayer in the church. Some students are ordinands, and others pursue other vocations. It isn't seminary, but it is residential and religious and linked to theological education.

There is no doubt that the theological scene has radically changed from thirty years ago, and there is no turning back. Flexi-mode theological education is part of this. But how? The following is a case study of one institution's attempt to reinvent itself within the new context of the "E" world and theological education.

A New Experiment in Theological Education: The "E" World and St. Mark's National Theological Centre

In 1995 St. Mark's National Theological Centre entered into an agreement with Charles Sturt University to become the founding institution of the School of Theology in the Faculty of Arts in the largest rural-based university in Australia. CSU has over 40,000 students throughout Australia and internationally. The agreement enabled a small theological institution to locate its educational work within a sophisticated and resource-rich infrastructure. The revolution that this link created is still in process a decade on. In 2007 St. Mark's will celebrate its fiftieth anniversary. The brain-child of Bishop Ernest Burgmann in the 1950's, St. Mark's was established not as a seminary, but a place to foster engagement between theology, the church, academy and society. It had from its beginning a brief to be a place for what has now become know as "public theology". St. Mark's was "public" before the name was invented for theology. Until the mid-nineteen nineties St. Mark's had principally served the churches of the Canberra region and had a reasonably good track record of engaging with issues of church and society in the national capital of Canberra. Burgmann had initiated the dialogue with the political and social world of the fledgling national capital and had seen St. Mark's as "the church's window on the world".

Burgmann had harboured a vision for the institution to play an active and prophetic role for the nation. Students studied at St. Mark's whilst living within the Canberra community. It was not a residential institution. It drew people into its orbit from all denominations and none, lay and ordained, men and women. Its excellent library and intimate chapel provided the ideal resources. However, it struggled for adequate resources from a local diocese which was essentially rural and cash-strapped. The issue of resourcing bit hard in the early nineteen nineties, and it became the catalyst for an innovative partnership with a multi-campus flexi-mode learning university. Because it was a newer university serving the vocational and professional needs of rural NSW and beyond, the prospect of adding theology for ministry to its offerings seemed unproblematic. It is one of the blessings of so-called post-modernism. The ground of tradition has been disturbed, and even for secular institutions older ideologies are more difficult to sustain. Witness the stark contrast of the attitude of Charles Sturt University to a university like the Canberra Australian National University (ANU), which was powerful, resource-rich and ideologically unsympathetic to the teaching of theology. This latter institution was not keen to partner a relatively weak theological institution like St. Mark's—at least not ten years ago!

So out of a search for a partner in higher education to "hitch its wagon to" there emerged a remarkable association. There was a surprising and, on reflection, quite natural reciprocity between the aims of St. Mark's and CSU. The fit was very good. From the universities' point of view theology could fit within a vocational and professional university environment. Furthermore, to have a good quality site (St. Mark's is on prime real estate in the parliamentary triangle) in the nation's capital, offering a new niche area for its expansion was extremely attractive. At the heart of the agreement was the intention that St. Mark's would develop a truly national theological programme through the university distance education focus. Without this it is hard to imagine the partnership would have been either desirable and/or practical. The other ingredient was the passion and commitment from the University and St. Mark's through its then Director, Jeff Driver (now Archbishop of Adelaide) and the Bishop of the Diocese of Canberra and Goulburn, George Browning.

In 2005 the School of Theology celebrated a decade of operation. Over that period there has been a remarkable growth in student numbers from 90 involved in largely undergraduate programmes to 400-plus enrolled in the full range of courses from undergraduate certificate to research doctorates. The partnership is such that student enrolments are fully funded through the Commonwealth Government Higher Education allocations made to all universities. Faculty remain contracted to St. Mark's, but are accredited as Academic Associates in the University. The School has taken on board new partners from other denominations and has agreements through the University to provide theological programmes with overseas institutions (Hannam University in South Korea and Pacific Theological College in Fiji). These days it is a powerful ecumenical institution offering a critical and vibrant theological resource for the nation. This has been a boon for those living in rural Australia and for busy people often isolated in the large cities.

In the basic undergraduate Bachelor of Theology students enrol from across the nation but principally from the country rural sector. The Distance Education mode makes the programmes available to people who would not normally have such access. The key here is the development of learning materials—not teaching materials—for the online environment. This includes: *Subject Outline* (introduction to the subject, syllabus, resources available, university protocols, assignments, reading lists); *Study Guide* (13 week programme designed to lead students into the particular field of study offering guidance, commentary, questions and tasks that include web based materials); *Reading Bricks* (key readings referred to in the study guide). The package is sent to students in hard copy form though the material is also available to students online through the university web-based system.

In the early start-up phase in the mid-nineteen nineties the development of learning materials had to adjust to the online environment, and this took time and energy. The transfer of lecture notes into a learning package was neither that simple nor that effective. A more interactive package was required and the adjustment to a new kind of pedagogy required the assistance of a university skilled in this delivery. Correspondence had to give way to new learning modes in an emerging "E" world.

Interaction between lecturer and students takes place through e-mail, telephone, "subject forums" and "chat rooms", and residential schools. The Forums are the key to good quality interactive learning. Students "post" to the forum their reactions to materials and topics and respond to each other and the lecturer. Another element in the programme is the judicious use of residential periods where students travel to the home base of the subject (Canberra campus) for 2, 3, 4 or 5 days of face-to-face learning with the lecturer. Not all subjects have a residential built in; some residentials are optional and a limited number are compulsory. It is almost possible to undertake the entire degree via DE, however, our experience over ten years has been that students find the balance between online, hard copy material and residential face-to-face an optimal way in which to undertake their study. Residential periods are known well in advance, and it is rare that students are unable to attend for work-related reasons. Moreover, our experience has been that through residentials students who don't know each other but live close to each other actually connect and maintain contact through and beyond their studies. Here the online community meets face to face, new networks are established, and this in turn draws others into the learning process. The online mode of theology draws students together not simply online but face-to-face.

The above programme is most appropriately termed "flexi-mode learning". It is ideal for busy people who need the freedom to structure their learning in a way that fits their work and family and pocket. The online environment presumes access to the net and this has become a standard requirement for most universities. The quality of the Internet connection in some remote areas can cause difficulties from time to time, though in this situation the hard copy material is available. The programme requires commitment from lecturers (learning facilitators) and willingness to explore new ways to develop material for the online learner. University resources and expertise have been a critical element in the development of enhanced pedagogy for theological teachers.

Because St. Mark's was established as a broad-based ecumenical institution for lay and ordained alike, the growth of TEE through the university partnership has meant that theology is essentially a lay enterprise. Second, it has opened up this work to women as well as men. For the first nine years of the School women constituted about 60% of the enrolments in theology and most of these in distance mode. This change in the demographics of the theological student is critical. The first five doctorates awarded in theology through the School have been women—mostly lay. Furthermore, well over 50% of students come from non-metropolitan Australia. Today the School has 20 Ph.D. students and an equal number of students enrolled in the professional doctorate programme (Doctor of Ministry). Most students are dispersed throughout Australia.

When an institution moves into flexi-mode delivery it makes it possible to draw upon the expertise of lecturers/teachers who also live at a distance from the main institution. Teachers too can be drawn from a variety of places, be linked up with the School at St. Mark's, come to residentials and meet their students, and become part of the teaching community. It enhances their own pastoral and professional life, for it offers them fresh ways in which to express their gifts. Not only does TEE in our experience generate new networks of students across many boundaries of denomination, gender, geography, culture and profession, it also generates a community of teachers committed to the learning task. This has been our experience. However this also has its challenges. Good communication is probably the key as well as careful assessment as to who might operate best in a flexi-mode learning environment. Older teachers seem to find it harder than younger ones and hence they require more careful attention.

The impact on ordination training in the Anglican church has also been significant. With poorer dioceses unable to afford to send students to a residential seminary, they have had to develop alternative means of preparation. In a number of dioceses candidates enrol in the Distance Education programme of the School through St. Mark's. They will attend the required residentials. The local diocese has then begun a cooperative arrangement with St. Mark's for the ordination training programme. Local supervisors and mentors have primary responsibility for a candidate's progress, and faculty from St. Mark's hold a number of residential intensive weekends each year in the local diocese. One effect of this development has been that the local diocese takes far greater responsibility for its own candidates. It is an interesting experiment that continues to attract other dioceses along the eastern seaboard of Australia. One unexpected result of this arrangement is that local dioceses are choosing to send some students to St. Mark's as full-time students/candidates on campus. New confidence has been instilled in an institution that is seen to be creatively responding to the needs of the church. The flexi-mode operation is central to this turn around in attitude. Of course, it is only as good as the people involved. Flexi-mode theology needs flexi-mode spiritual guides and teachers. This cannot be stressed enough. They need to be properly inducted into the resources available and pedagogy of online education. They need to share the vision for a theological community that requires new skills and values the riches of the past.

Preliminary Stock-Take: Flexi-mode Delivery and Christian Formation

It is probably too early to offer definite assessments but the following points seem important:

1. Marketing 'E"-theology is big business

There is no doubt that online delivery has become the buzz-word in theological education in the twenty-first century. This is evident across the denominations from traditional seminaries to newer Pentecostal institutions. The latter are into upmarket packaging of theology, and the former are desperately trying to repackage their programmes to win the hearts and minds of potential students. The advertisements for theological institutions tell the story of the rise of the "E" world culture. The dangers of grandiose claims are all too apparent. The shopfront often has a sign implying remarkable gifts awaiting the buyer of this or that theological product. However, in the "E" world resourcing and delivery are everything. Most institutions fail to understand the difference between marketing and delivery. St. Mark's has invested hundreds of thousands of dollars and an equal number of hours to developing the product. It has been weaker on telling its online story, but after ten years the fruits of the labour are beginning to bring rewards. We have discovered that there are no cheap options in online education. It doesn't save money. It represents a major investment of resources, time and energy.

2. Online belongs to a balanced theological portfolio

St. Mark's has struggled to find the balance that builds online learning into a larger and richer account of how students learn and what the optimal conditions are to enable this. Online has not replaced face-to-face learning, but what it has done is begin to break down distances between people who wish to study theology and deepen faith. This is why the older phrase "DE" (Distance Education) is positively unhelpful and tells the wrong story. Online and E-learning does not generate distance between people. Rather, it enables distance to be overcome. In doing this it opens up new possibilities for people and reconnects them. Online is more often the means by which face-to-face engagement occurs. The St. Mark's approach has been to weave together the new with the old. There are tensions, and the art of compromise is highly prized in our faculty. We have only recently begun to loosen our grip on compulsory residentials. Having established a reputation over ten years for good quality theological resourcing and having striven to maintain a balanced policy between compulsory and optional residentials, we now leave students more choice in the knowledge that the word is out that residentials at St. Mark's offer high value. We have instituted a billeting system for students to reduce costs. It is working well. Students learn that online is entirely compatible with face-to-face. Getting the balance is the key.

3. The online classroom is different

One of the real challenges in online theology is to develop resources appropriate for online learning. St. Mark's has benefited greatly from the wisdom and expertise of the University staff in this area. The idea that you simply transfer lecture notes into web-based learning is a misnomer to say the least. The possibilities for web-based learning are immense. Even after ten years we recognise we have a long way to go. The main issues here are imagination, time to develop resources and expert advice. In our context the time factor is the greatest challenge. St. Mark's, like most theological institutions in Australia, operates on a shoestring budget with very good people working extremely hard to offer quality learning environments. The online classroom is different, and it needs extensive commitment of time and resources to realise its potential. This also goes for students, for they too need to be prepared to invest their time and commitment into the learning process in order to maximise its benefits. The classroom is part of a larger "E" world which also includes a good quality web site that is easy to access and journey in. It makes the seeker more sympathetic, the prospective student more keen to pursue the trail, and the enrolled student happy within the environment.

4. "E"-learning can enhance Christian formation

The experience of St. Mark's over the last ten years is an example of a renewal in theological education. This has occurred in the context of the assimilation of its programmes into the infrastructure of a modern secular online university. Theological education is not co-terminus with Christian formation, though I hope it has many points of overlap. The formed Christian life is a work of a lifetime, and to the extent that St. Anselm's "faith seeking understanding" belongs to that maturation of the ecclesial self then theological education has a significant part to play. How significant? For some it has been a negative thing and has left students with an acute sense of the dislocation of their theological learning from their lived experience. This has led to the entirely false supposition that Christian formation does not take the mind seriously and the understanding is enhanced beyond theological study as such. Theology is marginalised, and the church loses its capacity for critical reflection upon practise.

Our experience at St. Mark's has proved far more positive. In our context theological education has been a gathering exercise. Through the online world students have been drawn together, have discovered new possibilities for interaction, and have been drawn more deeply into the life of faith seeking understanding. Very few of those who begin study ever stop. The educative process bites deeply; a pedagogy has emerged that weaves the online into other modes of learning. This overflows into the local church, which can also grow through a more educated laity and leaders. The growth in the sense of the self as an ecclesial self (and all that this entails) is what Christian formation is about. We have found that our venture into the "E" world has enhanced rather than diminished that ecclesial formation. Of course, we have a long way to go, but the key is getting the right recipe for the ongoing nurture of Christian discipleship in the world.

Conclusion: "E"-Learning in a Decomposing Church

The larger scene for the church—of the West at least—is one marked by a profound and unfinished decomposition. The reasons are many and complex, and this is not the place to even attempt to rehearse them. What we are acutely aware of is the breakdown of community life as it has been known through the traditional institutional structures of our social life. Australians participate in these wider developments. Our society is increasingly fragmented; community is an elusive thing. The individual is unconnected. This suits a market economy which prizes outputs and cannot honour the value of human life.

We live in increasingly fluid and uncertain times. What we shall become is unclear to us. There is also a sense that new possibilities are emerging within the ruins of the old; new networks of people linked across boundaries of space, culture and religion are not unfamiliar to us. The possibility of new religious communities where Christian discipleship is nurtured and empowered for mission is not a fanciful dream but a reality for increasing numbers of the young. New monasticism is a worldwide movement with a great deal of internal variety but sharing passion for God and authentic life.

In such a context good news will be that news that reconnects people and builds new community. In this context good news will point to the fundamental connectivity between people, God and the environment. Joining people back together again is a work of the Spirit of God. But this re-creative community spirit operates through the life of those communities dedicated to such a mission. The church in Australia has such a mandate, and it is a major challenge. To be in God's mission in our place is to be involved in the overcoming of distance between peoples. This 'distance' exits socially, economically, geographically and religiously. Theology has a part to play in this reconnecting activity of the Spirit. And in a small but not insignificant way TEE contributes to the mission. The case study bears witness to the way in which online learning in the right kind of environment can begin to break down distance, begin to form new networks of friendship and learning and remind the people of God who they are.

The "E" world of theological education can be a companion technology to the above developments. It can also be a problem. Our experience at St. Mark's gives us cause for hope that the wisdom of the online community of faith and seekers alike can contribute to the revitalising of the church as a learning community which can creatively respond to a mobile and rapidly changing culture and can do this in ways which draw people together rather than further fragment them. The spirit of the "E" world is essentially a community forming spirit, and when this arises out of the ashes of the old, then the people of God will know that even technology can play its part in the purposes of God for a new faithful sociality to welcome the coming kingdom.

Stephen Pickard

SPickard@csu.edu.au

St Mark's National Theological Centre, Canberra

QUESTIONS FOR REFLECTION AND DISCUSSION

1. *What were the limitations of traditional residential seminary education for the Australian context? What new possibilities have emerged through St. Mark's alternative approach?*

2. *What is now the stated or implied mission of St. Mark's National Theological Centre? Why is St. Mark's now tied to Charles Sturt University?*

3. *What are the main components of the new educational model at St. Mark's? Which of these components are available in your context?*

4. *How does St. Mark's respond to the multiple needs of the Australian churches: training and formation of ordinands, equipping the whole people of God, advanced theological research, and in-service training of pastors?*

5. *What preliminary evaluations of the new "online" model of theological education—after ten years—does this case study offer? What are the prospects for this model of theological education for Australia's "decomposing church" and "secularized society"?*

Chapter 8: Latin America

Latin American Biblical University

by José Duque

It is with real pleasure that we present this summary of the educational model of the Universidad Bíblica Latinoamericana (UBL) and explain how and why we developed it. UBL's educational project is being carried out not only in San José, Costa Rica, but in numerous churches, Bible institutes and theological education institutions in many countries of the continent. It includes two major programs. One is a university academic program, which combines residential and extension components. The other is a more diverse and dispersed program through the Pastoral Bible Institute (IBP), open to churches and institutions and movements throughout the region with minimal academic prerequisites.

This case study begins with a summary of our vision for theological education today in Latin America. Then follows an in-depth analysis of the social-cultural context with a critique of the dominant pedagogy and our option for change. The third section explains the basic components of the educational model of the Latin American Biblical University, and the fourth section focuses on our Pastoral Bible Institute.

Summary

Following military repression and political corruption in the 1970s and 1980s, the leaders of Latin America discovered that the return to political democracy was not only possible but advantageous for the dominant national and international economic powers, because "free market" ideology and mechanisms enabled them to continue and intensify their concentration of wealth without the embarrassment of former human rights scandals. Today economic inequalities, tied to long-standing cultural and racial discrimination, are reaching unprecedented levels. Exploitation by global financial and corporate forces has now advanced to the point of economic devastation, i.e., massive poverty and ecological destruction throughout the region. This causes unconscionable levels of malnutrition, disease, unemployment, street children, prostitution, hopelessness, and violence of all kinds.

Educational and religious institutions tend to reinforce these developments as they appeal to both rich and poor with offers of personal advancement in this life or the next. Protestantism continues to gain followers among the nominal Catholic population, and it is said that 80% of the Protestants are Pentecostal, with limited theological capacity or inclination to meet the social challenges of our time. Local preachers and international evangelists appeal to the majority poor and elite rich with their apocalyptic rhetoric, "spiritual warfare", and prosperity theology. Liberation theology made powerful inroads among important sectors of Catholicism and Protestantism in the 80s and 90s, but it was repressed by political and religious authorities, and generally today Christian education in the churches and theological education of all kinds and at all levels do not offer effective Latin American theologies for liberation from this economic, cultural, and spiritual malaise.

A New Model

The UBL, founded as a Bible school in 1923, later known as the Latin American Biblical Seminary, and recognized as a university in 1997, has developed an evolving, diversified model of theological education that tries to incorporate the advantages and limit the disadvantages of both residential and extension approaches. It currently enrolls over 2000 students throughout Latin America at the B.Th., L.Th., and M.Th. levels. These students participate in two-month intensive courses at the Costa Rica campus, relate to a network of centers in their own countries, participate where possible in local extension groups for weekly seminars and occasional intensive courses led by traveling UBL professors and/or adjunct faculty, and use a growing body of study modules and alternative learning modes prepared and supervised by the central faculty. The UBL also serves a much wider constituency through intermediate-level study materials (Pastoral Bible Institute) and other services utilized by various autonomous institutions and churches in the region.

The UBL has played an important role in the development of a regional association of theological institutions and its accreditation system. When recognition of theology by Costa Rica's Ministry of Education became possible at university levels, the UBL went through a lengthy accreditation process, which now gives our students access to new educational and professional possibilities. But the faculty has had ambivalent feelings about the whole matter of accreditation, because these standards are not capable of evaluating—and may in fact undermine—critical elements of our mission. Following is a brief summary of these critical elements, which do not correspond to the usual criteria for accreditation—such as academic level, class hours and number of courses, faculty degrees and publications, library size and reading requirements, physical plan and budget—which are usually considered to be essential for higher theological education. In fact, in some Latin American contexts the whole institutional apparatus may be useless, unattainable, or detrimental for the essential mission of theological education, which we understand to be a movement as well as an institution.

A Theoretical Framework for Theological Education
"Seek First God's Reign and God's Justice." Matthew 6:33

Theological education has developed primarily as a vehicle for the training and formation of servant leaders (lay and ordained, some paid and most voluntary) to lead the churches in their multiple ministries. Before considering the content and methodology of our programs of theological education, it is very important to set them within a theoretical framework that includes and explains the concentric relationships between these servant leaders, their faith communities, the peoples of Latin America, and God's Reign.

We have chosen as our motto Jesus' words in Matthew 6:33: "Seek first God's Reign and God's Justice." The general goal can be expressed as follows: To form servant leaders who will be able and committed to accompany, build up, and guide their faith communities and agencies toward holistic witness and service among their people in faithfulness to God's Reign and God's Justice. The following diagram sets forth these relationships for discussion, planning, and evaluation.

GOD'S REIGN AND GOD'S JUSTICE
THE LATIN AMERICAN PEOPLES
OUR FAITH COMMUNITIES
SERVANT LEADERS
THEOLOGICAL
EDUCATION
SERVANT LEADERS
OUR FAITH COMMUNITIES
THE LATIN AMERICAN PEOPLES
GOD'S REIGN AND GOD'S JUSTICE

We continue to plan and evaluate our educational model in terms of these dynamic relationships, recognizing that servant leaders are not created by any theological institution but rather emerge out of the life of faith communities engaged in the struggles of their peoples. We live in a complex world; our churches and organizations are imperfect and fragile; we are all clay instruments in the Potter's hands. Theological education is simply one element in the midst of God's work for human transformation.

Theological Education and Human Transformation
"Behold, I make all things new." Revelation 21:5

Education can be defined as a process of change. Theological education is a process of personal, ecclesial, and social change in terms of God's Reign and God's Justice. It is important to consider how our programs prepare our students to be agents of personal, ecclesial, and social transformation. The students come from throughout the churches, among all social sectors (gender, age, ethnicity, race, economic condition, geographic location, etc.) with special concern for the marginalized, so that we may all work together to bring about the changes that God wills for God's people and for all creation.

We know very well that human beings do not change easily, whether personally, in the churches, or in society. On the other hand, we know that God is Sovereign over our lives and over all of life. God can bring about change in persons, in the churches, and in the social order. Throughout the Old and New Testaments God struggles to free humankind from sin in order to live in fullness and dignity. Biblical-theological-ministerial formation is deeply concerned with this divine mandate.

ECCLESIAL TRANSFORMATION

PERSONAL TRANSFORMATION   SOCIAL TRANSFORMATION

As students, faculty, and administrators we all carry the responsibility to plan and evaluate all our programs in terms of these three dimensions of our mission and of the dynamic relation between them.

The Hermeneutical Circle
"Have this mind, which you have in Christ Jesus." Philippians 2:5

In the past theological education emphasized academic or intellectual formation, centered on the biblical-theological content of the faith, later added the practical application of the faith in ministry, but dealt with the social, cultural, and historical context in a very secondary way. We have come to see that these three basic ingredients should be present throughout the entire formation process, that the interrelation or tension among the three is what gives them meaning, and that the constant circulation between them can be the dynamo that drives the curriculum as well as present and future ministry.

As church leaders, teachers and students, we tend to see our context, faith, and practice of ministry from a privileged perspective. So it is important to analyze our local and global context from the perspective of the poor and marginalized, to re-read the Bible from that perspective, and to develop pastoral models from that same perspective. Jesus did this, becoming a human being and taking the form of a servant, humbling himself even to death on a cross. Others have done likewise throughout history, and today many are experiencing a similar change in their Christian vocation.

RE-READING THE BIBLE

ANALYSIS OF REALITY   PASTORAL PRACTICE

All three elements of the hermeneutical/pedagogical/spiritual circle must be contextualized, locally and globally, which is facilitated through the decentralized and centralized dimensions of our model.

Three Fundamental Dimensions of Learning
"Speaking the truth in love, grow up in Christ." Ephesians 4:15

Educators have long emphasized that learning is not just the accumulation of information/concepts/knowledge. Of equal or greater importance are skills, on the one hand, and attitudes, values, and commitments, on the other. This is so, above all in theological education which is ministerial formation. Intellectual development must be accompanied by complex and diverse abilities and by attitudes/sensibilities/commitments oriented to God's Reign and God's Justice. It is evident that these three dimensions are not nurtured primarily in the classroom. They must be identified and proven and refined in daily life and in the practice of ministry under appropriate conditions and guidance.

Reflection on these three fundamental dimensions of learning might begin with the truth and the love that we are to pursue in Christ and in building up the body of Christ. We need to ask ourselves how we are developing and integrating all three dimensions in all our courses and throughout our programs.

ABILITIES

KNOWLEDGE   ATTITUDES

Here again we affirm the importance of combining the local, decentralized component and the residential, centralized component in our educational model.

Theological Education as Self-Development in Community
"All are members, though many, of the one body." 1 Corinthians 12:12

Recent experiments in decentralized theological education have affirmed that true learning is a process of self-development with appropriate resources and with effective accompaniment. Our students are generally mature leaders of churches and local communities. They bring to theological education a wealth of experiences, concerns, questions, and goals. Our programs build on those previous experiences, respond to their present realities, and help them to advance toward future ministries in church and society. The students are the subjects of the process; they should play a central role in the design and execution of the program. Our role is to accompany them in an affirmative, creative, and critical manner and also to ensure their access to essential resources for their growth.

RESOURCES

SELF-DEVELOPMENT   ACCOMPANIMENT

This and all the previous perspectives on the enterprise of theological education do not easily fit the categories of accreditation and standards. Our concern is not so much for each individual in isolation but in relation to a faith community in service and witness to the wider local and global community in pursuit of God's Justice. The barefoot farmer, the household grandmother, the professional pastor and lay leader, the theological scholar, the community organizer and social activist all equally are called and need to be equipped within their very diverse, complementary ministries. If grades, diplomas, accreditation, and standards place some over others, perhaps far above others, we must question their value, and we may have to look elsewhere for the values of God's Reign. The UBL may some day conclude that its mission is best served through its non-accredited Pastoral Bible Institute (IBP), which is open to all in their struggles for life, liberation, and justice.

CONTRADICTIONS AND POSSIBILITIES
OF THE HISTORICAL CONTEXT

Every socio-historical context has two aspects that alternative forms of theological education cannot ignore: on the one hand, the contradictions and ambiguities that are produced in various social relations, and, on the other hand, the aspirations, dreams and vindication of the struggles and theoretical contributions that bring about transformation. Following are some of these aspects of the contextual reality that have influenced the development of the UBL educational model.

Ambiguities and Contradictions

In Latin America and the Caribbean the hermeneutical circle has become the ideal tool for the contextual reading of the Bible; it was found to be very valuable not only for the ministry of the Word, but for all other ministries. This tool provided a valuable instrument for the church, as the people of God, to carry out its mission and to respond in a responsible manner to the challenges, needs and aspirations that appear throughout the stages of history.

The hermeneutical circle has been an essential tool for the required reading of the context. Thus, we learn to read, from a historical reality, discourses, actions and many hidden intentions in the subjunctive. This has led us to discover much that was hidden, for example, the official educational discourses that today are linked to neoliberalism and globalization. Contextualized education has had to confront the ambiguities of education influenced by the interests of neoliberal globalization, which more or less follows these ambiguous and contradictory tendencies:

1. Lecture-based education, protected in the educational system. The professor has the knowledge and the students are the object of this knowledge. The students receive the pronouncements of the professor.

2. A competitive education and, therefore, exclusive to some degree. Rote memory is the primary learning method utilized: all education takes place in the classroom and neither the abilities nor the skills of the student body are taken into consideration. Information technology (computers) is now competing with this type of classroom learning, but that technology is accessible only for those with adequate financial resources.

3. An a-critical education based on functional instruction. It is dogmatic and pre-established. There is no development of critical thinking or reflection, because its principal method is empirical. The students memorize long-established pragmatic formulas or rules. The didactical methodology is its favorite tool, because it is functional. This begins to cultivate a fear of independent thinking in the students because the teacher imposes his or her way of thinking, the only one permitted, and that criterion is not open to question.

4. Fundamentalist and doctrinal. Theological education suffers from being subjugated to fundamentalism. This occurs when this spiritual movement opposes all rational and contextual theological study, taking out of context Paul's words: "… the letter kills, but the Spirit gives life" (II Corinthians 3:6). This method demonizes theological reflection and systematic studies, eliminates pedagogies and disparages hermeneutical methods. In addition, it forever silences the gifts of science and knowledge stressed by the Apostle Paul (1 Corinthians 13). This irrational dogma excludes diversified methods because it limits the biblical text to just one literal meaning.

5. Mono-intelligent. Its method utilizes only mathematical logic, a literal logic, and no other understanding. This is knowledge without wisdom, because it is mechanical education.

6. Education to make money. Neoliberal education is based on an ambitious calculation to make money. You study to become rich, to gain prestige, to take advantage of others, to make a profit.

7. Fragmented education. It is monolithic education that isolates diverse types of knowledge and learning. In some universities general studies have been eliminated because time is "lost" for concentrating on one specific specialty. And, with that, diversified and interdisciplinary education disappears.

8. Education as a profession. This education has the objective of earning degrees. It is a meritocratic education, motivated by benefit calculations. More than anything, it is bureaucratic and cultivates competition. Professionals accumulate degrees to move up the ladder; it is education that promotes getting to the top.

9. Automated education. In the education market there are offers on the Internet that focus on degrees and not on formation. They offer both undergraduate and postgraduate degrees in the style of fast-food restaurants. Professional and even theological degrees are offered without classroom instruction, without reading books, without professors, without exams and in the least time possible. The only requirement that is not negotiable is paying the respective fees. The degrees, of course, are written in English.

10. However, by far the worst scenario found in education is the use of spirituality, of religion and of theology for ideological and materialistic purposes. Religion is one of the fields used to legitimize war, material prosperity and the media fascination for making money (*Da Vinci Code*).

11. Critical education is risky. Many prophets who are educators and/or students have died in Latin America because of their patriotism or because of their choice to work for change. This was why a group of Jesuit professors was murdered in El Salvador in 1989. They were killed because of their critical thinking, because of their prophetic denunciations. Thousands of others were assassinated or disappeared during the Cold War era in Brazil, Argentina, Chile, Bolivia, Uruguay, Peru, Ecuador and Central America. Even today in Colombia professors and students who resist the unipolar structure are assassinated, disappeared or exiled. In the current global village, under the direction of a superpower, critical education is a motive for death. This week, the news of the selective killing of university professors in Iraq made us shudder in horror. To date 250 professors have been assassinated, and there are an unknown number of disappeared in that country. According to UN reports, 84% of the educational institutions in Iraq have already been burned or bombed (www.nodo50.org.irak).

Conditions and Sources of Inspiration for Change

Following are some of the considerations and sources that have contributed to the development of the educational model of the UBL. The idea for creating this educational model did not fall down from the sky, but came out of the context where this school is located.

1. *The crisis.* One of the factors that made us consider and organize a new educational model was the crisis that the institution was experiencing. This dealt with a crisis in the traditional residential model, which had been influenced by the ambiguities and contradictions previously mentioned. The discourse had developed in accordance with the changing context, but the subjects of education (students) were not adequately defined. We said that we served the churches, but we did not define exactly who in the churches or to which church we were referring.

2. *Changes in the context.* Without a doubt change in the socio-political and economic context, which had developed in the region during the "Cold War" (1950-1990), was a contributing factor. Social and political movements were in constant turmoil. There was a revolutionary environment that had an impact on religious activity. The revolutionary and changing atmosphere brought about a cruel and dehumanizing response from the principal capitalist structure. The U.S. used its National Security Doctrine to inspire military regimes throughout the continent which violated the human rights of the civilian population through torture, exile and repression. Nearly

half a million people were assassinated and disappeared during that period. Pain and death are still the sad inheritance of that era.

3. *The Latin-Americanization of Human Sciences.* In this context of change, the educational sciences contributed to the search for alternative didactic and pedagogical methods: the pedagogy of the oppressed (Paulo Freire). Also, a Latin American Philosophy emerged that incorporated the identity of the Indigenous and Afro-American peoples. Likewise, the economy, with the theory of underdevelopment and dependence, demonstrated by scientific criteria the causes of misery. A critical sociology distanced itself from functionalist sociology and identified with the social subjects (agents); from this new social space it contributed to the interpretation of grass-roots social movements. More recently, the natural sciences have contributed to discovering the risks to and the importance of the environment.

   Finally, the sciences and interdisciplinary processing contributed enormously to uncovering the reality, to unmasking the numerous ambiguities and contradictions that the interested powers use to conceal the truth in order to make money, dominate and exclude.

4. *Latin American Liberation Theology.* Without a doubt, this is another factor that contributed enormously to the formation of the educational model of the UBL. Its contribution came, basically, from the methodology of this theology: it recommends starting from the historical reality and transcending the dualism of spiritual experience. Also important was the methodology of the circular hermeneutic that makes it possible to read the scriptures in their pre-text, text and context. This theology shook the foundations of vertical ecclesiology and established the foundation for an ecclesiology based on the model of a shared table, the communion table, a table for equals. That is when women, the Indigenous and Afro-Latin American peoples and other people who are discriminated against because of the color of their skin, migrants, handicapped people, sick people and all those whom Jesus recognized as "little ones" began to claim their rights.

5. *The Ecumenical Movement.* The ecumenical movement in Latin America and the Caribbean has led people out of the four walls of the churches and inserted them in other social arenas. It has brought to the fore issues that are vital to the life and mission of the church and theology—issues like human rights and social and economic development. Migration and the recent emergence from violence, the

integrity of creation, HIV/AIDS, and other current priorities have had an effect on the UBL curriculum. We must not forget to mention the importance that the ecumenical movement, particularly the WCC, has given to education. Beginning in the 1960s the first Theological Education by Extension (TEE) consultations began to be held, and since then we have strengthened this emphasis. Subsequently, the fund for ecumenical theological education institutions was created, which has now been inherited by the Latin American Community of Ecumenical Theological Education (CETELA).

We could continue to discuss other factors that have contributed to the development of the educational model, but because of space limitations, I will mention only a few more: the ethical, political, pastoral and evangelical orthopraxis option.

The Option to Change Theological Education

What we have then is a general context that demands that we redefine theological education. "Do not pour new wine into old wineskins…" (Matthew 9:17). Today, the cry of many social movements that have gathered at the World Social Forum (WSF) is that "Another world is possible." Yes, another world is possible, and another kind of theological education is also needed because another church, as the people of God, will need to transform its ministries.

With the challenge that another education is possible, which we assumed with all our strength, the next step was to make a transcendental decision: to opt for change. But this option required at least three more basic ingredients: a theoretical framework, a commitment to unity, and a coherent spirituality.

Preparation of a theoretical framework

This was a very difficult task that required a great deal of consultation with Latin American theology, pedagogy and many sister institutions and relevant documents. This task is ongoing and remains open.

A commitment to unity

This kind of work must be done by a team or it won't get done. In our case, we had an internal "community" that was accustomed to the residential model, and because of that we needed to work for several months to come to the needed consensus. It was not total, but it was sufficient. This internal community was composed of administrators, students and professors. It had, and it has, the characteristic of representing a majority of the nationalities and denominations in the region, men and women, and diverse theological orientations. However, this internal body was not sufficient for building a diversified model. We needed help from sister institutions that were already working with different educational models. After long consultations, what we now know as a "Brotherhood/Sisterhood" of theological institutions was organized. In the beginning 16 institutions participated—from Mexico, Guatemala, Honduras, El Salvador, Costa Rica, Cuba, Colombia, Venezuela, Ecuador, Peru and Bolivia. This unity among many diverse institutions constituted the resources and visions that contributed to the creation of the diversified model that the UBL is now developing. The initial objective was to create a theological school with an evangelical, ecumenical, Latin American and Caribbean perspective to share faculty, library, pedagogical and economical resources.

A coherent spirituality

We wanted to use our formation, vocation, different charisms, commitments and option for the "little ones" in service of others. To serve the church as the people of God we focused on what we called "ecclesial movements," which meant something more than ecclesiastical institutions, more than orthodoxy, and more than education itself: it dealt with a lifestyle, an ethic, a vision, and transforming commitment, whose horizon seeks to faithfully follow Jesus: the kingdom of God and God's justice, which includes the integrity of creation.

Education for the whole church and for all of society

This has been another factor in our theoretical framework that I would like to underline, because we have written little about this, but it has oriented our diversified model. If we say that our education is not exclusive, the correlation is that it is an inclusive education. This means that it is for everyone who is a part of the church and belongs to the people of God. This principle from ancient Israel transformed the 16th century Reformation into the "universal priesthood of all believers." The charisms and ministries are for all believers.

This principle is not a part of the life and mission of many churches, because the "ordained" ministry excludes a large majority of the faithful. This kind of exclusion was passed on to the universities, and since that time formal theological education has excluded those who are not seeking an ordained ecclesiastical ministry. This formal education often excludes not only laymen but also women, because of their gender.

To overcome this contradiction, the UBL not only affirms the universal priesthood in its curriculum, but makes the formation of all God's people accessible. It also concludes that formal education and non-formal education can achieve the same formation objectives. This will be possible if we want it to be.

In order to fulfill this objective to serve in the formation of the entire church, the UBL created a parallel institution, the Pastoral Biblical Institute

(IBP), with an open, informal, diversified, integral, decentralized and contextual methodology. In Latin America access to education is very limited, but today, the PBI serves in nearly every country in the region.

We conclude this section by mentioning some of the components of the UBL's diversified model, as proposed for education by extension: pedagogical diversification, hermeneutical diversification, diversified methods and curriculum, methodological and cultural diversification. It is an open curriculum.

PRIORITIES AND COMPONENTS OF OUR DIVERSIFIED MODEL (UBL)

A Network of Centers and Institutional Partners

Students and churches and partner institutions have responded to the need for accompaniment by developing national and regional centers that organize and facilitate academic processes, intensive courses with UBL professors and/or local adjunct professors, bibliographical and curricular materials, and special theological events in their respective countries. Centers/partners are located throughout Latin America and the Caribbean:

Central American Evangelical Center for Pastoral Studies, Guatemala

Reformed Theological Community, Honduras

Caribbean Theological Center, Costa Rica

José Chuquín Center, Colombia

Ministerial Program of Open Theological Studies, Colombia

Mennonite Seminary, Colombia

Open Program for Theological Training, Venezuela

Indigenous Theological Study Center, Ecuador

Latin American University Center, Peru

Pilgrim Seminary, Peru

St. Paul Seminary, Peru

Andean Ecumenical Institute of Theology, Bolivia

Martin Luther King, Jr. Center, Cuba

Center for Pentecostal Studies, Chile

Old Testament Professor José Enrique Ramírez describes a recent experience:

> *In December of last year I was invited to give a course in Biblical Studies in Santo Domingo (Dominican Republic), held on the campus of a Pentecostal seminary. The participants were both Catholic and Protestant theological students. On the first day I looked out at a class of about fifty students varying*

in age, religious background, and academic training and realized that I was facing a group with extraordinary pastoral experience.

Preferential Option for Women, the Indigenous, Afro-Latin Americans, and the Poor

Based on Galatians 3:28, virtually all the work of the UBL contains a commitment to gender, racial, and economic justice. One course required of all students deals with gender as a fundamental axis of spiritual-theological-social concern, and this dimension appears in all courses and research projects. A special process has incorporated Indigenous students and faculty in the analysis of historical and cultural and spiritual distinctives of diverse Indigenous peoples of Latin America. Among the theses of 2004 graduates are these themes:

- A woman from Peru: "Toward a Pastoral Ministry with Women in Rural Peru, from a Gender Perspective"

- A woman from Venezuela: "The God of Abundance"

- A woman from the US: "Women as Foreigners in Israel: Exegetical Study of Ezra 9 and 10"

- A woman from Colombia: "When Bodies Speak: A Reading of Luke 13:10-17"

The Integrative Seminar

One of the requirements for all degree students is attendance on campus for the two-month intensive Integrative Seminar, equivalent to two courses, which focuses on a critical current issue of mission in today's world. Three professors, representing Bible and Theology and Pastoral Studies, and often invited specialists guide the students in plenary sessions and in group work according to their academic field. In 2006 the issue was "Water as Gift and Right for Life." The Dean explains the relevance and urgency of this issue:

Water is essential for God's purpose to make life sustainable, and it is a necessity for human dignity. Our ministry emerges when we appropriate this creative action by God and make it part of our culture to preserve it and not damage it, ensuring life for future generations.

Curriculum

Students choose to take the Bachelor's Degree in Bible or in Theology and Ministry, which requires 122 credits. They may then proceed to the Licenciate or, with faculty approval, the Master's in either field with 11 additional units and a thesis and additional practical assignments. Students may require scholarship aid in order to return to campus for an extended period (up to one year) for research and the writing and defense of a thesis.

Three Phase Courses

Intensive courses at the various centers and partner institutions throughout the region often have three phases. The first phase, which may take one or two months, is organized locally by announcing the subject, distributing the syllabus, making reading and other assignments, and holding one or more meetings with students who enroll. Later the UBL professor or another invited professor comes for one to two weeks of intensive work that will build on the preparations of the first phase. Following that intensive period, students will carry out final readings, reports and other assignments to complete the course with the guidance of a local coordinator or adjunct professor.

PASTORAL BIBLE INSTITUTE (IBP)

We understand our educational philosophy to be that thought developed and socialized among those of us who are part of the UBL, by which we intend to guide and shape the formative practice of our educational model through the Pastoral Bible Institute. Our methods are contextual, dialogical, liberating, biblical, and creative. Our objectives are:

> *To equip the participants to understand and confront the great spiritual, economic, and social challenges of our communities and peoples in the twenty-first century.*

> *To discover in the Bible the will of God for personal, ecclesial, and social transformation here in Latin America.*

> *To develop practical and pastoral abilities of leaders in the context of their families, churches, and communities.*

The Pastoral Education Course (CEPA)

The IBP has prepared study materials for 30 courses organized in 6 areas: The Ministry of Administration, the Ministry of Education, the Ministry of the Word, Spiritual Ministry, the Ministry of Evangelism, and Specific Accompaniment Ministries. Additional materials are being prepared. All of these materials make use of the Hermeneutical Circle. Our intention is to promote a permanent process of analysis of biblical-theological foundations and ecclesial practices in terms of the Latin American and Caribbean reality.

Each institution or church making use of these materials may sign an agreement with the IBP and elaborate its own curriculum in keeping with its necessities and challenges.

- The IBP does not matriculate students directly.

- The IBP offers orientation and accompaniment to other institutions, centers and churches through agreements or letters of intention.

- The IBP can provide orientation regarding the application of study methods.

- The IBP can provide guidance regarding academic administration.

- The IBP provides study materials for students and manuals for facilitators.

- The IBP offers training for facilitators.

- The IBP accompanies sister institutions in their education programs.

A Systemic Model

A system is a group of dynamically structured elements whose totality generates certain properties. These properties are, in part, independent, but at the same time they influence each other. Consequently, to understand the behavior of a system you must take into consideration not only its elements and properties, but also the interactions between those elements and properties and the products that result from the totality of the interactions. In the General Theory of Systems it is common to distinguish the *suprasystem,* which refers to the medium in which the system develops, and the *subsystems* that are components of the system. According to Katz and Kahn all systems are open because the elements that compose them exchange information, material and energy with the outside environment and demonstrate the capacity to adapt to the environment.

This theory is applicable in all sciences. In the case of social sciences, mainly in psychology, sociology and theology, a member of a system that manifests problems, for example, within a family, is not seen as sick, but as the expression of a dysfunctional system. Therefore, the search for a solution to the problem is not only in a change that the person can make but in a change of the structural system of the family itself.

If we review socio-historical reality from a systemic perspective, we realize that it is organized by innumerable structured systems in which life is produced and reproduced. Thus, all human relations present in the production and reproduction of life participate in a complex variety of well-structured systems.

However, within this multiplicity of systems there are a large number that choose to oppress, marginalize, exclude and alienate a large part of their members. These may be social, religious, economic, political, pedagogical or any other kind of cultural systems; they possess a venom that is threatening to life itself. They can be macro-structural systems (*suprasystems*) or the micro-systems of daily life (*subsystems*). In other words, these are systems that are found in numerous areas of vital human relations, which, whether intentionally or not, are dehumanizing.

Nowadays, many of these systems are not only recognized as inhuman but have been correctly identified as evil, and it has been possible to denounce them. However, they still operate and impose their unscrupulous irrationality in the name of order, authority and other values, while they hide the pain and human misery they produce.

You can observe this reality in a patriarchal system, for example. Although there are tender demonstrations of love in the warmth of the daily home life, unequal and unjust relationships are maintained in the family. The same can be said of certain religious systems that were constructed in a specific time and context to respond to the needs of the community of faith at that time and that have been perpetuated as absolute systems with practices today that can be clearly seen as flagrantly exclusive and that marginalize broad sectors of the people of God.

This tells us, then, that systems like the two we just discussed, can simultaneously include truly humanizing practices as well as the opposite, dehumanizing practices. Therefore, a *machista* father can demonstrate tender, fatherly relations with a loved one and simultaneously appeal to the cruelest types of authoritarianism in his relationships with other people. So then, there is no doubt that in the dualistic behavior of this father, which is peculiar to a patriarchal system, the cruel authoritarianism dominates by far the tender feelings. Because of this, the systemic model is not limited to accompanying a person (in this case, the one who suffers the consequences of an authoritarian father) but to all of the members of the family system because one or the other of them is product and member of a system that generates those kinds of interactions. The system needs to be restructured to avoid these interactions.

From a theological point of view, the boundaries of life are found in changing personal and social structures in order to make the Kingdom of God and God's Justice possible, and because we are all sinners we all need to be transformed.

Theory of Gender

There is a difference between sex and gender. When we speak of sex we refer to the biological difference that exists between a man and a woman. We are different. Our genitals are different; our bodies are different. There is a visible difference that is easy to determine. We are sexual beings, we have a defined sex: we are women or we are men. We are born with this difference; it is a natural characteristic. Our sexual body constitutes our most perfect manner of relating with other human beings. Our body is a wonderful gift; it makes it possible for us to be humans, able to reason, love and be loved.

Gender, as a concept, has existed for many years. However, in the 1970s it began to be used in the social sciences with a new meaning. It is this meaning that we will consider now.

We are born as male or female, but little by little we become "men" and "women." This may seem strange, but it is so. From the time we are born we are conditioned according to what society has determined corresponds to our gender. If we are little girls, the attitudes and skills "of girls" are instilled in us and the same is done with little boys. They are given the training that will guarantee that they grow up to be "men."

This means that a given society has established what is proper for women and what is proper for men. It has established its own "models" of femininity and of masculinity and requires everyone to adjust to these patterns. That is why we say that we are molded to become more and more like this model, which is invented by each society according to its interests and needs. Therefore it is said that gender is a symbolic construction that contains a group of attributes that are assigned to people based on their gender. These attributes are biological, physical, economic, social, psychological, erotic, legal, political and cultural characteristics.

How is the model imposed? This task begins in the family, continues in formal education, is justified in churches through religious standards, and is constantly accentuated in the mass media: radio, television, newspapers, etc. An entire group of supposedly "formative" situations manage to convince us that to be happy we must adapt to a determined way of being. For example, we are taught that women are born to "give ourselves," to continually give ourselves for the good of men, who become our owners. We frequently hear advice like this:

> *A little girl should be sweet.*
> *Sit down properly and don't go out alone.*
> *You should be a homemaker, industrious, quiet and smiling.*
> *A little boy should be strong.*

He should not show fear or weakness (don't cry).
Learn to walk alone and, above all, don't give in.

All human beings, regardless of their sex, can develop different kinds of values, and can and should aspire to develop according to their personality or to their desires and aspirations. However, the "social models" that are imposed on us intend to assign a masculine personality to the values that represent dynamism, courage, rational thought, and finally, the capacity for full achievement in a successful future.

Women are urged to be passive, submissive and to conform. We are made to believe that they are naturally sweet, patient, sentimental, incapable of correct thinking or of making important contributions to humanity.

However, we know that this is not the reality. For thousands of years women have actively contributed to the cultural progress of our towns and cities. They are great creators of culture. Because of what they do, the quality of life in our communities has improved, and there has been progress in the relations between towns.

However, intelligent relations between women and other people and with nature are manipulated when they are made invisible in historical accounts. This is done to avoid contradicting the schemes that have been proposed for femininity and masculinity. There has been an attempt to maintain, at all cost, the image of passive women and dynamic men.

While it is true that the difference between males and females is obvious, giving "negative" values to women is a cultural fact, in other words, it was created by society. As a consequence, any woman who leaves what is considered to be her "natural sphere" (if she decides not to have children or not to dedicate herself to homemaking) is pointed out with contempt. On the other hand, what is "proper for men," whether it is to fly through the sky, dive into the oceans, discover new worlds, or carry out anything that is beyond the immediate, what is near, what is "natural" is seen to be fine. So, men are allowed to plan their future. Women, however, must submit to a plan designed by others.

Assigning what is "feminine" or "masculine" is a social interpretation of our biological condition. It is not something that we are born with. For example, we think that a woman is feminine if she is flirtatious, if she shows weakness before men and asks for help. On the contrary, a man is "very masculine" if he is dominant, authoritative, etc. We think like this because we have been taught or indoctrinated to believe this.

To pigeonhole all women in "feminine" activities and all men in so-called "masculine" activities, in addition to denying the individual preferences of each person, establishes a gender hierarchy. This leads to domination-submission relationships between the masculine and feminine genders.

Understanding the concept of gender allows us to incorporate a new way to analyze situations that we have lived in for a long time in our lives and work. We are able to consider taking into account that men and women are treated distinctly by society and that men are the most privileged. Biology does not determine our gender identity and behavior; rather it is the fact of having lived the experiences, rituals and habits attributed to a certain gender since birth.

The category of gender lets us see the world clearly, and we see that it is divided into two parts, like a large pie: one part is called masculine and the other feminine; it was determined that men would be responsible for the part called masculinity. Women are in charge of the second part, and it was called femininity. Such a division responds to the interests of the economic, political and ideological order, which has emerged from patriarchy, which wants to exercise control over the lives of people. It is an arbitrary and rigid division.

Pedagogical Option

The process of pastoral counseling and accompaniment is a process of mutual service: yes, to serve in the church and in society. There must be symmetrical relationships when training pastoral agents and accompanying people in a structure of service. There must be a relationship of equals in regard to gender, race, ethnic group, confession, nationality and academic level. Systems are needed that provide for equal relationships that are in solidarity. Also, a preferential option for "the little ones", those left out, is needed.

The teaching/learning process includes all the dimensions of life in society. It has to do with all human relations as well as with nature. It is a continuous process in all micro-social spaces (personal, family, local) as well as in macro-social spaces (school, work places, neighborhood, society). It is a process—transforming church, social, family and personal commitment—that tests the development of capabilities, knowledge and attitudes. All of life is a process of healing, accompaniment and pastoral counseling. This process produces a knowledge of reality in order to escape manipulation, whether it be religious, political, pedagogical or cultural. It illuminates reality.

This deals, then, with creating together a pedagogical, semantic and epistemological place—a place to process and share information, a place for training, for carrying out the transformation. It is, therefore, a liberating place—a freeing place, pulled along by the dreams of church and society where everyone has a place with dignity and justice. It is theologically carried by the images of the Kingdom of God and God's Justice, which Christians have dreamed about for so long.

Incarnate and Contextualized Pastoral Ministry

The incarnation of God into our human condition, into our history, and into our reality has marked the path of our faith. From there comes the urgent need to contextualize the church, theology and pastoral work. Pastoral ministry embodies the Gospel in specific situations, with its own needs and answers to a historical moment, a *kairos* moment, reading the signs of the times. This means not only knowing the concrete and harsh information about reality, but trying to explain all that remains hidden and produces pain, precariousness and human injustice. For that we turn to the social sciences to help us understand the causes, structures, ideologies and strategies of systems that marginalize, oppress, exclude, destroy and bring death. We seek to understand reality in order to become incarnate in that reality and try to follow the messianic model of Jesus Christ. It is impossible to propose a universal and unique pastoral ministry, because the proposals are constantly being evaluated, revised and renewed, because it is a personified pastoral ministry.

Integral Pastoral Ministry

Integral pastoral ministry rejects dualism between the spiritual and secular kingdoms. The unity of those two kingdoms is a Biblical principle that agrees with the eco-systematic perspective that insists that all systems are interrelated and should be taken into consideration when analyzing a problem. Therefore, there is only one history in which the secular and spiritual world mutually effect each other and are equally important. We reject those spiritualized pastoral practices that intend to protect the "saints and chosen ones from the temptations of the flesh."

Hopeful Pastoral Ministry

The work proposal is for a pastoral ministry committed to people who suffer; those who hope against all hope (Romans 4:18). Without abandoning a share of the utopia that characterizes the Good News, pastoral projects must be rooted in realistic hope. This stance goes against the pastoral attitude that promotes passive expectations and proposes magical and exaggerated solutions that, if not fulfilled, it is because "faith is very weak."

Participative Pastoral Ministry

It is important to rescue the inclusive participation of all the ministries and gifts that God gives to those God chooses. Pastoral ministry is nourished by the flow of ideas and proposals for change that come from the critical reflection of the person cared for and of the members of the system to be structured. Projects that someone wants to impose from "above" or from "the outside" are often rejected and destined to failure. We are against the practices of "specialists" who have a messianic complex and believe that they are the repositories of truth, and who develop a managerial type of pastoral ministry that does not provide an opportunity for empowering individuals or the group. We do not accept the pastoral practice as an opportunity for exercising personal power that can result in the domination and exploitation of others, because it makes it difficult to respect the rights and development of autonomy.

Considers People to be Subjects

The objective of pastoral ministry is that the people fulfill the role of active agents and change their own situation of injustice. Pastoral service encourages people and collaborates with them in the process of "becoming aware" of their situation and of getting ready to struggle against it. The people are not considered to be invalids, incapable, ignorant or helpless. A good pastoral approach encourages, empowers, promotes freedom of choice and facilitates personal and collective growth. Thus, pastoral service must believe that people are important to God, to the church and to society, and it does not take away their place as agents of change of history, believing that suffering is not a private but a collective matter. Pastoral service must develop by caring for both dimensions: the personal and the collective.

Taking into Consideration the Complete Society

People are part of a society that has mutually dependent systems (school, church, work place, neighborhood, socio-economic and political situation, etc.). Therefore, pastoral practice must have a structural and integral vision. Much of pastoral work erroneously tends to be carried out within the four walls of the churches in expectation that the people "who need God" will come there to look for consolation. The teaching/learning process should be made available for all the members of the society and not only for a particular faith community.

Its Horizon is the Kingdom of God and God's Justice

We are not tossed about by every wind of doctrine. Our horizon is focused upon the Kingdom of God and God's Justice. Biblical theology emphasizes that the center of Jesus' preaching was the message of the Kingdom of God (Mark 1:14-15). Jesus himself announces it, makes it present and projects it into the perspective of fullness of life. This means that the ministry of Jesus was a historical manifestation of the first fruits and a foretaste of the Good News of the Kingdom.

The Kingdom of God is the central theological idea in Latin American theological reflection and pastoral ministry. We have sufficient biblical-exegetical basis to know that the church is not the Kingdom of God, as had been boldly announced in other times. The church does have a commission to announce the Kingdom and to demonstrate concrete first fruits and foretaste in the relationships within the community.

Human history can condense first fruits and foretaste of the Kingdom of God. We can say that a social justice project that is inclusive and symmetrical for everyone is in the perspective of the Kingdom of God. But, although redemption includes all of creation, no socio-political project should be confused, in any way, with the Kingdom of God. The social commitment to construct societies with just systems here and now is part of following Jesus, although the fullness of definitive life will only be possible when the Kingdom is fully here!

Motivates Full Growth

Leaders in faith communities must seek to be qualified and know how to encourage spiritual growth. The key to human fulfillment is to have an open, nourishing and joyful relationship with the spirit of love, source of all life, health and growth. The objectives of the methods for spiritual health and growth are to emphasize the values that guide faith in transcendental moments of life.

An Ecumenical and Interdisciplinary Pastoral Ministry

Pastoral service extends to all people, men and women from all confessions and denominations—Christian and non-Christian—and from contexts of Indigenous and African roots where ancient and mestizo religions survive. Among this diversity are conservatives, liberals, radicals and fundamentalists. This description is, then, multi-religious, multi-ethnic, multi-theological and multi-racial. However, despite this rich, exceptional plurality, transforming ecumenical relations are not necessarily established automatically.

Today, the barriers of separation, exclusion and oppression that exist and function in social systems are hidden because of the fallacy of globalization and the free market, which is presented as the way to freedom. This fallacy constitutes the greatest challenge to ecumenism today in our pastoral service. Ecumenical unity is the road to reconciliation of humanity in justice and peace. But the light of wisdom must be ignited to overcome the darkness of this fallacy. Therefore, ecumenical relations are an alternative, a cultivated need and an organized resolution.

Now that the pastoral service we propose tries to have an integral perspective, it has to work with other disciplines, such as, for example, economics, health, sociology, anthropology and other related disciplines. To work as a multi-disciplinary pastoral team is ideal, but we recognize that it is not always possible to do so because of the high cost. The only way to do this is by means of volunteer work by professionals. When it is difficult or impossible to organize a team, the process of pastoral accompaniment should not be detained. Without pretending to be a "know-it-all," it is urgent that pastoral agents learn about various matters in order to carry out the accompaniment, by making the necessary adaptations to create alternative forms of service.

Conclusion

Among those who have taken at least 50% of the Pastoral Bible Institute program, there are many people, facilitators and students, who affirm that they have completed the objectives of the program; in particular they have experienced what we call an "epistemological breakthrough." In other words, they have experienced a transformation in the way they see the Gospel, the church and the world. There has been a qualitative leap in their worldview. We could say that, theologically, a conversion in their worldview of faith has taken place, which has changed the way they live the Gospel. This change affects the way they think, biblically and theologically. But, also, it changes their personal, daily and community lifestyle. Those testimonies have touched us greatly, and at the same time they challenge us to move forward and to improve our work.

However, we also have heard some testimonies that show a kind of frustration because they cannot achieve concrete changes, because their ecclesiastical structures do not permit it. It is as though the formation was for someone else, but not for themselves. For example, in some churches there is no opportunity for women's ministries.

While it is the church leaders who have encouraged the IBP program, they don't find enough tools in the program to restructure the structures, to implement new ministries and to leave the four walls of the church to serve in the "city," that is, in society. This shows that the program, from the point of view of worldview, is well received, but we still lack tools to help transform structures and ministries.

Warning: Despite our interest and desire for articulation between theory and action (praxis) of this educational proposal, we are still very far from optimal in this regard. As in all human projects, we live with ambiguities and contradictions inside our institution. We are still seduced by our rationalizations, by our academic careers, by holding on to power, and we continually flirt with legality in detriment of service. That is to say, we are not yet presenting an ideal performance of our objectives, but it continues to be a learning process that must mature among all those involved in this academic proposal. Despite our ambiguities and contradictions, the impact is sufficiently recognized, that is, within our modest capabilities. However, we are always willing to listen with attention and sensitivity to the criticisms, because the more serious these are, the more they will teach us. We believe that self-praise makes us arrogant, while outside evaluation builds us up.

There has been continuous growth since we began this program. Recently we were invited to work with the pastoral team of the Church of God in Lima, Peru. This is one of the largest Pentecostal churches in that country with approximately 160 local communities that are generally very poor. They asked the UBL, with some insistence, that we help them begin an IBP program.

We were also invited to participate in a meeting of the National Education Commission of the Methodist Church of Peru. As a result they have asked me to advise this commission and to help implement the IBP program in the entire national church, as a consultant.

"The harvest is plentiful but the workers are few" (Mt. 9:35). Currently there are about 1,500 students in this program among institutions that have a direct agreement with the UBL. There is a similar number of institutes and churches that have not wanted to make an agreement with the UBL but that are freely using our materials without such an agreement. This also makes us extremely happy.

This has been the collective work of Nidia Fonseca, Sara Baltodano, Ross Kinsler and José Duque. However, this was discussed among the entire teaching staff and with those in charge of the program in the different countries.

José Duque

eteduque@gmail.com

Questions for Reflection and Discussion

1. *What is your evaluation of the educational contradictions and ambiguities enumerated in this case study? Are these contradictions and ambiguities present in your context? If so, how does your approach to theological education deal with them?*

2. *What conditions and sources of inspiration for change are mentioned in this case study? What are the basic ingredients of this institution's option*

for change? Are these conditions, sources, and ingredients relevant for your own institution or program of theological education?

3. *What are the priorities and components of this educational model? Are these priorities and components relevant for your model of theological education?*

4. *Summarize the theory of gender set forth in this case study. What theory of gender is articulated and practiced in your program of theological education?*

5. *What are the distinctive components of the Pastoral Bible Institute of the UBL?*

International Faculty of Theological Education, Argentina

by Norberto Saracco

THE SUCCESS OF A FAILURE

Twenty-nine years have elapsed since the failure that changed our destiny. On May 3rd 1977, the inaugural class of the Centro de Preparación de Líderes Cristianos (Christian Leaders Preparation Center—CPLC) "Emmanuel" took place. More than a starting point, it was a point of arrival. My church, Asociación la Iglesia de Dios (The Church of God Association), ALIDD, had asked me that during my last year of studies at the Seminario Bíblico Latinoamericano (Latin American Biblical Seminary), SBL (San José, Costa Rica), to prepare a project of theological education for the training of church leaders. In fact, several years earlier the church had started the Instituto Bíblico Emmanuel (Emmanuel Biblical Institute), but now I was being asked to do something more complete and organized. For various months I worked on the elaboration of the bases for a traditional program of four years of study with all the subjects usually used in seminaries, including Greek and Hebrew. The CPLC project was an important step forward for the Argentine Pentecostal Church. We had managed to hire several teachers (Pentecostal and non-Pentecostal), who with a good disposition were ready to help us in the adventure. The first registration was of eighteen students, who took classes from Monday through Friday, four hours a day. Before the end of the first quarter, only six were left. Each of the ones who had dropped out had personal reasons to do it. But the truth is that we no longer doubted the great dream was facing failure. We had not succeeded in reaching the church leadership with what we offered. The project was very good from an academic and theological perspective. But evidently it did not respond to the church leadership's needs.

July of the same year arrived and, taking advantage of the Independence Day holiday, a group of churches organized a youth conference. It was in the city of Resistencia, about 600 miles from Buenos Aires. Those were very difficult days for Argentina. A year before, a military coup had taken power. Everything was fear, repression and death. Maybe to take advantage of this small oasis in the desert, more than 1,500 young people attended the conference. During one of the services of that conference, one of the pastors approached me and told me: "Look at the number of young people who want to serve the Lord. Couldn't you do something to help them? Would you be ready to teach them?" This Macedonian call pierced my heart like a dart.

Back in Buenos Aires, I made two decisions: to close the program I had started two months before and accept the challenge from the churches in the city of Resistencia. Thinking of a non-traditional, non-centralized program to respond to the needs of the churches was something new for me. A few years before, being a student in SBL, I had had the privilege of being chosen by Rubén Lores to work with him and with a very reduced number of teachers in designing PRODIADIS (Programa Diversificado a Distancia [Distance Diversified Program]). That foundational experience marked me. Rubén Lores had returned form his study furlough with the "crazy" idea that one day in the near future there would be more than 5,000 pastors in Latin America. If this happened, Rubén said, no seminary could prepare so many pastors, and it could not be done using traditional methodologies. It was true, because what he was stating had also been seen by others since the 1960s, according to the experiences of the open universities in Madrid and London and to the movement of Theological Education by Extension based in Guatemala.

The first step was to offer a program of ministerial formation for the pastors of Resistencia and its surrounding area. The idea was to test the pastors' level of commitment with theological education and at the same time to develop stable relationships of mutual trust, which could give a solid base for a more ambitious program. Twenty-two pastors registered. The number was very important since only three of the pastors in the city did not participate. We could say that it turned out to be a project of the church in that city. Every other week, I traveled nineteen hours by bus to Resistencia and as many hours back, in order to lecture through the weekend. Between classes, students worked with the course on the Gospel of Mark. This was one of the programmed texts used in Guatemala by the founders of the "Theological Education by Extension" movement. The result was amazing. None of the students dropped the class, in spite of their busy pastoral schedules and their numerous ministerial pressures. Though they were pastors, for all of them this was their first theological education experience. They saw they could almost immediately apply in ministry what they were learning. At the same time their preaching and teaching was enriched. In December, at the end of the academic year, in spite of having completed only one programmed course, one with required attendance (every fortnight), the unanimous decision of the pastors was to open the courses to the whole church.

In March 1978 seventy-six students began their studies. We did not have much to offer, though they did not know it. We continued with the system of having weekend classes every other week and using some study guides. All we had were some spare materials which did not provide a coherent and systematized plan of studies. In order to put this in context, we must remember that by then, so-called Theological Education by Extension was in full growth. This favored the fact of being able to think in a non-traditional way of teaching theology. However, there were several problems. Trying to follow the fashion, traditional seminaries opened their extension programs, most of them without understanding the radical change this brought about in the philosophy of education. They mistakenly intended to "extend" the seminary. That is to say, the theological institution remained at the center when, in fact, the proposal was that the church and the student, their interests and possibilities, were to be the axis of the teaching program. On the other hand, a good amount of the materials produced did not comply with the necessary methodological requirements in order to be adequately used. In general, also mistakenly, it was thought that it was a matter of issuing a text with questions for the student to answer. Nobody considered that that text, both in content and in methodology, had to comply with certain programming criteria, which made it pedagogically suitable. In spite of our limited resources, our students remained faithful and enthusiastic, because they valued the opportunity of being able to study in their own context of life and ministry. They looked at theological education as something possible and accessible for all, and not as something reserved to a certain privileged class, of those who had resources and time for it.

FROM DREAM TO REALITY

By the middle of 1978, a few months after having started with the classes, the Comisión de Educación por Extensión (Commission of Education by Extension) of ASIT, the Asociación de Seminarios e Instituciones Teológicas (Association of Seminaries and Theological Institutions), held a consultation on theological education by extension with the purpose of sharing experiences and materials among the theological institutions of the Southern Cone of Latin America. It was on that occasion that we first came in contact with the Compendios de Teología Pastoral (Handbooks on Pastoral Theology). These were six books written by Anthony Barratt and published by SEAN, Evangelical Seminary for All Nations or Anglican Extension Seminary for All Nations. Based on the Gospel of Matthew and following Jesus' chronology, these programmed texts approached basic theology and Christian ministry subjects in an integral way. To us they seemed to be the most coherent and best elaborated of all the ones presented. They also allowed us to count on a two-years program, and they adapted to the methodology we were implementing. We studied the material superficially, and we saw that the content did not raise conflicting doctrinal issues and that its methodology could very well be adapted to what we were developing. The launching of this program, which we called "Certificado en Teología" (Certificate in Theology), produced a true revolution. Students multiplied by hundreds, forcing us to adapt our administrative structure. Up to then, I had carried out the educational project personally with the help of a secretary. In order to respond to the new challenges we organized ourselves in regions, and we put "regional coordinators" at the head of each. The function of these coordinators was to promote the courses in their areas, assisting students, implementing the program and giving exams. With this minimal structure, a central office and regional coordinators, the seminary was established in city after city.

Though the initial growth was explosive, nevertheless the steps we took responded to a vision of the church, of the ministry of theological formation, and of the relationship between both. First, we believe that the local church occupies a central place in the educational process. The church must feel fully involved. In our case, before beginning with the programs of study, we worked with church pastors and leaders, looking for a way in which what we had to offer could serve the ends of the church itself and what they expected from the students. Pastors were so much involved that they knew what was being taught and created spaces for the students' ministries. On the students' side, they had the obligation of applying each week, in practice, something of what they had learned. The result was that the seminary mutually affected both the life of the church and that of the students. Thus, theological formation is not an end in itself but responds to the needs of the church and the mission it carries out.

Second, we saw that theological education could be an instrument for the unity of the church. At the end of the 1970s we were living, as a country, in one of the most difficult situations of our history. Since 1976, a military regime was in power, which attempted to justify its existence on the basis of the deep crisis the last democratic government had undergone. Society was divided and, therefore, so was the church. Taking this reality into account, from the seminary we decided to work in a city only if more than one church invited us and if, at the same time, they were ready to participate together in this ministry. We did very practical things in order to "force" the churches to walk this way. Even if we considered with each of them how they could take the maximum advantage of the programs we offered, at the same time we had meetings with the pastors of the city in order to discuss together a global strategy. Programs were individually applied, but decisions were taken in a collective way. Study groups gathered in each church, but for the exams whole day events were organized, in which the students of the various churches gathered in one place. At first the number of students was so large that we had to use nearby public school buildings for these activities. As a result of this, in many cities pastoral councils were formed, which continue working together till this day as an expression of the unity of the church.

The Power of a Strategic Alliance

Up to that moment (1978-1980), all we had to offer was the "Compendio de teología pastoral," six books comprising two years of study, which we offered as a "Certificado en Teología" (Certificate in Theology) and some other programmed texts (Gospel of Mark, Romans or Jeremiah). As we worked with these materials, we perfected the strategy for their use (later we will explain in detail), so that the program consolidated seriously. Thanks to this the relationship with SEAN (the Anglican group that published the materials) deepened. They saw that our situation was different from what happened with others who attempted to use the same materials. Maybe they followed the "fashion" of theological education by extension but did not fully understand its philosophy and challenges. In our case study groups remained and advanced, and an increasing number of churches embraced the program. At the same time, from the Centro Emmanuel (Emmanuel Center), we had an enormous debt of gratitude towards SEAN, since they had placed in our hands a key tool in order to make our vision come true. In spite of the successes we achieved, or better said, due to them, we were approaching a crisis. The problem was what to do with the 1,500 students who were about to graduate with the Certificado en Teología (Certificate in Theology). They and their churches were asking lots of questions. How will the program continue? What additional study levels can you offer us? How can we complete a true educational program for the church? We did not have a clear answer. We knew we had to do something, and that whatever we did had to respond to the same educational philosophy. But we had nothing concrete to offer.

Logoi, the publishing house located in Miami and dedicated to Christian literature in Spanish, had seen the great need Latin America had for theological formation that would serve pastors already in ministry. From the 1960s on the Latin American Evangelical church had began to grow significantly. The appearance of Latin American evangelists, the development of Pentecostal churches among the masses in great cities, the popularity of ministries dedicated to evangelization, such as "Evangelismo a fondo (Evangelism in Depth)" and "SEPAL," and the birth of the charismatic movement contributed one way or other so that the church in Latin America could begin a period of growth and multiplication. One of the direct consequences of this phenomenon was that people who had not had a formal preparation entered the ministry. Like now, the "spiritual experience" of the candidate for ministry was privileged over and above his or her ministerial formation. Facing this reality, Logoi publishing house launched a project which was called "Seminarios pastorales Logoi" (Logoi Pastoral Seminars). These seminars started in the South of Chile and consisted of three gatherings, one per year, each a week long. The event was especially addressed to pastors. Well-known professors were invited, and the publishing house gave each participant in each seminar a group of books with the purpose that at the end of the program they could count on a pastoral library. The idea was that in returning the next year the pastors would have read the books they had received the year before. Regretfully, the pastors did not fulfill this job. For people not used to studying, the mere fact of having a book in their hands was not sufficient motivation for them to read it. In view of this reality, and knowing of the capacity the SEAN people had for programming texts, Logoi asked them to elaborate some guides to be handed out together with the books in the pastoral seminars. As part of the agreement, Logoi gave SEAN some equipment as resources (typewriters, computers, etc.) and the cost of personnel. But SEAN already had the experience that, in a non-traditional program of open education, materials were important but not enough. By then, there was an exaggerated emphasis on the importance of programmed materials, as if by themselves, almost magically, they could achieve the objectives. The theological institutions, which tried to implement what were called "extension programs," dedicated all their financial and human resources to the production of materials, without paying attention to factors as important or even more important, like implementation and methodology. The consequence was that of those hundreds of programs (more than 400 just in Central America), few survived. Taking this into account, SEAN and Logoi asked Centro Emmanuel (Emmanuel Center) for advice and assistance to carry out the program of pastoral seminars, incorporating new materials and methodology.

The relationship between the three institutions grew, and we realized that each one had its strengths and weaknesses. But if we were capable of working together, each other's strengths could make up for each other's weaknesses. SEAN knew how to program materials, but they had neither the resources to prepare them nor the capacity to implement them. Logoi had resources and a lot of materials, but they did not know how to program them, nor did they know how to use them effectively. In Centro Emmanuel (Emmanuel Center), we had found a way to develop a program with academic criteria and acceptance by the churches. But we now faced a lack of materials to continue and of resources in order to expand. We accepted these realities and decided to carry out a common project of ministerial formation, in which each institution would provide its best. In July 1981, in the city of Salta in the Northwest of Argentina, we signed an agreement of mutual cooperation, and we decided to work together under the name of FLET (Facultad Latinoamericana de Estudios Teológicos [Latin American Faculty of Theological Studies]). The power of this strategic alliance was reflected in the amount and quality of the materials produced and in the growth of the program. In a short time, we had extended the program to twenty-three countries, most of them in Latin America and the Caribbean, but we also reached the USA, Canada, Australia, Japan and Spain.

Here it is important to note, because it has to do with our ministry and mission philosophy, that FLET was never thought of as a multinational corporation of theological education. In most of the countries, national offices were established, always with national personnel and with a great contribution of national resources. The idea was to share a vision for ministerial formation and support those who accepted the challenge with our experience and materials.

The amount of students surpassed 20,000 per year, and for the academic management of the whole project it was necessary to appoint three deans who coordinated the elaboration of new courses (writing, programming, test groups, academic level, etc.). Regretably, this alliance only lasted up to 1994. Personal and institutional conflicts aborted the project, which has undoubtedly been the most ambitious one Latin American theological education has ever had.

The Vision Continues

In a time of crisis in Israel God spoke through the prophet Habakkuk and said, "Write the vision; . . . For still the vision awaits its time; it hastens to the end" (Habakkuk 2:2-3). With these words, God made clear that beyond adverse circumstances the initial vision continued forward. That has been our experience. The crisis of the alliance served to prove the value of what we had built. In almost all of the countries, programs have continued, have adapted to the new reality and have grown in their contextualization. In our case, since 1994 we adopted the name of FIET (Facultad Internacional de Educación Teológica [International Faculty of Theological Education]). We have an average registration of 1,800 students, in levels going from the Certificado en Teología (Certificate in Theology) or Estudios Pastorales (Pastoral Studies) to a Master's degree with official recognition at university level, specializing in mission and ministry. Our vision and mission have not changed since we started the project in 1977. But we continue to incorporate new programs and cancel others, always in search of ways to be sensitive to the situation of the church in its context.

Our Mission

The mission of FIET is to glorify the name of God (Father, Son and Holy Spirit), providing the people of God with biblical-theological education and with tools for an effective ministry.

Our Commitment

1. To serve fully, depending on God, with integrity and holiness.

2. To minister, open to the Spirit, with excellence and quality.

3. To offer pedagogical resources which integrate, in a balanced way, biblical-theological content, ministerial practice and a commitment to the mission.

4. To honor ministries, to respect each congregation's own characteristics and to foster the unity of the church on the basis of a biblically founded faith.

   We do not conceive of theological education as a rigid model to which the church must adapt, but as something dynamic at the service of the church and the mission. This demands a high readiness for change and an open mind to understand new realities from each of the persons involved. As an example, we will consider three of the programs implemented in the last five years.

DIPLOMA EN PASTORAL Y ESPIRITUALIDAD
(DIPLOMA IN PASTORAL CARE AND SPIRITUALITY)
Context Creating the Need

At FIET we made a survey in the city of Buenos Aires in order to know the state of the theological formation of pastors. The result was that, out of the 310 Evangelical churches in the above-mentioned city, 40% of their pastors had no theological preparation whatsoever. Another 40% had taken some kind of course on Bible and Theology, and only 20% had graduated from a seminary. This data confirmed our hypothesis that those who are in pastoral work function without having had any previous formation; they also do not make any attempt to study once they are in the ministry. We know many cases of churches, with which we have agreements to help them in their ministerial formation. Their pastors fully support the project; they send their leaders to the seminary, but they do not study.

A second step in our investigation consisted in knowing the reasons for this phenomenon. We discovered that the pastors who were not studying, but wanted to do so, faced three obstacles. (a) Their complicated and unpredictable pastoral agendas did not allow them to make permanent commitments, certain days, at certain times. Pastors cannot program when church members will get sick, or when they will die, or when a family crisis will break out, neither can they anticipate a problem with church ministries. To the unpredictability aspect, in our context we had to add the fact that pastors make a living by means of a secular job or profession. Only 20% receive a salary or some kind of economic help from the church. The consequence of this situation is that many times pastors enroll in seminaries, but as the academic year goes by and problems arise (they cannot attend classes because of the reasons we have just explained), they end up dropping out. (b) The other obstacle is that those who are in pastoral ministry do not feel comfortable in a class where they receive instruction together with other church leaders, on similar terms. (c) The third obstacle is that, in theological formation, pastors look for immediate answers to their ministerial needs. A program not providing instruments for their immediate ministry does not challenge them.

FIET's Answer to the Need

Taking into account the results of the investigation, we decided to work on a project that might help to solve these obstacles. We had several meetings with pastors in different cities, searching for the characteristics of a program they could attend and which responded to their needs. Thus the "Diploma en pastoral y espiritualidad" (Diploma in Pastoral Care and Spirituality) emerged.

It is a two-year program, and no previous studies are required in order to enter. Classes are held in intensive events, on Saturdays once a month. Between classes, students receive programmed materials, study guides and books with assigned tasks. Only pastors and pastoral leaders attend these classes. The curriculum was elaborated in agreement with pastors, aiming at covering their ministerial needs. The subjects integrating the program are:

1. **Corrientes de espiritualidad (Spirituality Currents).** A historical and thematic panorama of diverse schools in the field of spirituality.

2. **Espiritualidad y lectura de la Biblia (Spirituality and Bible Reading).** Specifics on the devotional reading of Scripture. Differentiation of other reading methods. Exercises, historical examples.

3. **Teología de la espiritualidad (Theology of Spirituality).** Theological foundations of Christian spirituality. Similarities and differences with the spirituality of other religions. Reflection on spiritual experience.

4. **Espiritualidad y señorío de Jesucristo (Spirituality and the Lordship of Jesus Christ).** Importance of the Lordship of Jesus Christ in all areas of Christian life, as an expression of spirituality: church, work, marriage, social life.

5. **Espiritualidad de la oración (Prayer Spirituality).** Reflection on the importance of prayer in spiritual life. Analysis of historical examples of Christian piety. Prayer models, exercises.

6. **Espiritualidad en la evangelización (Evangelization Spirituality).** Evangelistic implications of spirituality. Historical models, methods and programs.

7. **Teología pastoral (Pastoral Theology).** An introduction to pastoral care in a broad sense, as task and ministry of the church. Theological reflection on pastoral care of the great human dimensions.

8. **Culto cristiano (Christian Worship).** Historical review of Christian worship. Elements and symbols of the worship service. Contemporary liturgical models. Contents and dimensions of liturgy.

9. **Resolución de conflictos (Conflict Resolution).** A survey of the different possibilities in mediation. Strategies, methods, exercises.

10. **Ética cristiana (Christian Ethics).** Ethical principles of the Old and New Testaments. Ethics and theology. Bioethics. Euthanasia. Manipulations. Abortion. Capital punishment. Unemployment. Poverty and wealth.

11. **Modelos de iglesia cellular (Cell-Church Models)**. Analysis of the advantages and disadvantages of cell work. Distinction between "church with cells" and "cell-church." Study and application of the diverse models.

12. **Historia de los avivamientos (History of Revivals)**. Survey of diverse revivals in the Christian church. Classification of common and different elements. Possible conditions.

13. **Iglesia con propósito (Purpose-Driven Church)**. Ecclesiological reflection based on a practical analysis of local church life around its purpose. Methods to keep all areas in constant renovation and evaluation.

14. **Aspectos legales de la iglesia (Legal aspects of the church)**. A study about the legal implications of religions in Argentina. Opening of temples, hiring of paid ministers, etc.

15. **Liderazgo (Leadership)**. Biblical and theological bases of Christian leadership. Contemporary models and strategies for coordinating task groups.

16. **Misión integral (Holistic Mission)**. Foundations of missiology, goals, outreach and methods.

Over three years of having this program, 230 pastors and 300 pastoral leaders have studied. One hundred twenty pastors and 250 pastoral leaders have graduated. Another direct result of this project is that ten churches have decided to establish permanent programs of theological education for their members and leadership.

CAPELLANES CARCELARIOS (PRISON CHAPLAINS)

Context Creating the Need

One of the most outstanding present phenomena about the impact of the Gospel on society is what is happening in jails. In recent years, due to the economic and social crisis that Argentina has undergone, violence and crime rates have increased. The prison system has collapsed. Prisons have more than double the population they can properly house. A corruption circle has been formed among the authorities of the penitentiary system and between them and the prisoners. Today jails are true delinquency schools, and most of the ones who are set free commit crimes again. Amidst this situation, the power of the Gospel has begun to impact lives of prisoners and to affect the penitentiary system. It is a relatively new phenomenon (about six years old) but of great significance. Nowadays, in some jails more than 80% of the prisoners have accepted Jesus Christ as their Savior and Lord. The environment within those institutions has changed, and corruption has diminished. According to official information from the government, 60% of those who are released commit crimes again. In the case of the so-called "Evangelical prisons," only 5% do so. Spiritual work in prisons is not carried out by chaplains. Brothers and sisters in the faith voluntarily develop this ministry. According to the laws of our country, only the Roman Catholic Church has recognized chaplains paid by the government. But in spite of not having legislation allowing spiritual work in prisons by Evangelicals and due to the fact that we have had to suffer prohibitions and obstacles to carry out this ministry, results are so many and so visible that the authorities are now considering a way of changing this situation.

FIET's Answer to the Need

Some of the leaders of this prison movement approached FIET to see if we could help them in preparing prison chaplains. None of the ones who are working in this ministry has ever received any formation. There is no seminary offering courses in this area. Evidently, they did not need any preparation to do what they are doing and achieve the success they have achieved. But, at the same time, they are aware that as they advance in their ministry, they have to face more complex problems, which demand another kind of answers. Also, it is well known that, if the authorities decide to recognize a space for this ministry, they are going to demand certain conditions, which will include an appropriate formation.

FIET accepted the challenge and three years ago we started a program of "Capellanía con orientación carcelaria" (Prison-Oriented Chaplaincy). It is a two-year program. With the purpose of creating trust towards the program on the part of students and in order to show that they were respected in their experience and context, during the first two years classes were held within one of the prisons. Students attend classes once a month during four hours. Between classes, they study with programmed materials. In the classes they attend, practical ministry issues are approached from the "professional" perspective of the teacher and from the students' practical experience. In the first group, 125 students registered and 98 graduated. Now, we have two groups, one in Buenos Aires and another in an inland city, with a total of 110 students. We have requests to start this program in several other cities. Also, a provincial government is using our program materials for the formation of penitentiary personnel. The government of the province of Buenos Aires has invited FIET to be part of a Consejo

Asesor en Capellanías (Chaplaincy Advisory Council). The success of this program has been such that we have more applications than we can accept. We have also been asked to start something similar in the field of hospital chaplaincy, which we will do next year.

LÍDERES PASTORALS CARCELARIOS (PRISON PASTORAL LEADERS)

Context Creating the Need

As we have seen in the previous example, preaching the Gospel in Argentine prisons is attaining achievements never seen before in our country. In some of the jails the interns have three worship services a day; they fast once a week; and they tithe from what they receive from their relatives and friends. With these resources, they help families in need outside the prison. This is a very great spiritual movement which continues growing. In these circumstances, the pastoral work of external chaplains is insufficient in order to meet the spiritual demands of hundreds of prisoners.

FIET's Answer to the Need

Taking into account this reality, in FIET we have prepared a program called "Líderes pastorales carcelarios (Prison Pastoral Leaders)." It is an intensive program of biblical and ministerial formation, addressed to the prisoners who have a greater commitment to the Lord and who are in a situation of helping others. This program, which usually lasts three years, in prisons will be completed in one year, due to the evident time prisoners have. We are starting the project with 500 interns in different prisons in the country. They will study with our programmed courses. These brothers and sisters we are preparing in their "Chaplaincy" course will be future tutors and the ones who will implement the project. Various elements come together here, which respond to our vision in FIET. On the one hand, we prepare chaplains according to their needs and context. Second, we place in their hands a ministerial tool (our courses), so that they can multiply their ministerial influence. Third, we integrate the educational process to the mission of the church. In order to pass the course of "Líderes pastorals carcelarios" (Prison Pastoral Leaders), there are two requirements. One of them is academic and has to do with passing the final exams for every subject. The other is ministerial. Each student will have to start a basic discipleship course (eighteen lessons about faith in Jesus Christ and what following Him means) with ten other interns. This means that in fifteen months we will have prepared 500 prisoners to serve as prison pastoral leaders, and 5,000 other interns will have received an initial discipleship course. Thus, we will have affected more than 10% of the prison population of Argentina.

LESSONS WE HAVE LEARNED

In 2007, thirty years will have elapsed since we started this ministry. Many of the things we did were successful, and others ended up in failure. From both we have learned something, and today they are part of our rich inheritance.

1. Every program of ministerial formation must begin in the heart of the church and must remain faithful to it. Theological education is far too important to be left only in the hands of theologians. In Latin America the traditional models of theological education have been imported, and therefore they respond to a different reality. The pastor-theologian model is the one that presupposes that every theology student must in the end become a professional theologian. In practice, this shows some kind of depreciation for the pastoral ministry in itself. The student preparing for ministry who does not end up being a theologian will have "failed." Some institutions try to hide this "failure," granting ministerial degrees as consolation prizes. When the theological institution takes the church seriously, the latter takes the theological institution seriously.

2. In a methodology of non-formal, non-traditional education, firm demands must be established as regards fulfilling times and tasks. The permanent absence of a professor must be replaced with a rigid procedure. This does not mean that the seminary sets the rules without paying attention to particular situations. On the contrary, the standards for work must be set in common agreement, taking into account the characteristics of the context (days to gather, place for the events, schedules, etc.). But once these have been set, they must be respected without exception. If not, the process becomes unmanageable, and students lose interest. At the beginning we had several discussions with the SEAN team around this issue. In their vision they want to make the materials they produce available, without any handicap. Speaking of a minimum managing structure implies personnel and additional costs, that the student must pay. For a time, there was a discussion between a position of free and non-restricted access to the materials and one demanding controlled access implying a cost but assuring quality. At the end SEAN also accepted this possibility when they verified that on one side there were students who advanced and on the other there were students

who had obtained the books but did not achieve anything, and they even ended up with misconceptions.

3. Every educational program must try to be financed in its functioning with what students pay. This is more possible in programs of open education, since they count on a significant number of students, which lowers the cost per student. Nevertheless, here is where the greatest obstacles are found in order to apply this basic principle of administration. Like with other ministries which were born economically dependent, modifying this reality is very difficult. In the case of open education the problem seems to be greater since the argument is: "If we want education to reach the whole church, we must do it with a very inexpensive cost or even free." This is a mistake because it perpetuates paternalism and dependency. It deprives study of its worth (that which does not cost anything is not worth anything); it creates limitations, and teaching is offered using a wrong example. In the case of FIET, we have demonstrated the contrary.

    a. During the thirty years of its existence, the program has been 100% self-financed, including all personnel salaries (there are no hidden missionary salaries).

    b. The student is dignified when he or she pays, making an effort. Several years ago there was a flood in the Northwest of Argentina. Many people lost their houses, and for various months they could not return to their place of origin. At that time, we had almost 100 students who had suffered from the flood and lived in train cars. The study groups were not suspended, because they decided to study in the train cars. Neither did they stop paying. Each morning they sold pastries among their neighbors, who were equally poor, in order to collect the money to pay for their studies. With this attitude and dignity, they overcame the pain of having lost everything.

    c. This way of administering resources makes us all more careful, because every cent has a special value. We have learned to thank God for each cent we get and for each course that is sold. Also, our lifestyles are kept close to those of the students, because we do not handle great fortunes, but what is necessary to live and carry out our ministry. Except for the administrative personnel (secretaries), the rest of the people (coordinators, teachers, assistants, etc.) receive their salaries according to the number of students they have. The idea here is not rejecting or trying not to get external help. But whatever help we get should be used for special projects in order to advance in certain areas, which would otherwise be impossible. Sometimes it is necessary to count on greater facilities, or to buy a certain amount of books for the library, or to invest in the preparation of some personnel member, or to support a project initially. All this is good and necessary, provided it neither affects nor interferes with the normal development of the program. We ourselves have received help to buy Bibles for the prison project, or to pay for the teachers' expenses during the first year of the pastoral centers. This was added to what we were already doing. But if those funds had not come, the projects would have been carried out all the same, only with limitations.

Conclusion

FIET will be thirty years of age, and we are offering a Bachillerato Superior en Teología (BA in Theology) and a Master en Ciencias de la Religión (MA in Sciences of Religion), both degrees with official university recognition. The objective is to take these programs to every corner of the country. We know there are thousands of Christian professionals who are developing a bi-vocational ministry and who have not had the opportunity of getting a theological education. They are now our mission field. We desire to have a subject on "theology of the future," that is to say, to be able to do theology today about facts of tomorrow. This is not futurology, but it is asking science and technology in what direction we are going and thinking theologically about the future. Of course, we continue being committed to the church and to God's mission, at all levels. We understand that as instruments in the hands of God, we must remain open to the Spirit, in order to *discern the times and be useful to God's cause.*

Norberto Saracco

fiet@sion.com

QUESTIONS FOR REFLECTION AND DISCUSSION

1. *What has been the fundamental need of the churches of Argentina that has called for a new approach to theological education? Why has this new approach insisted on the churches' ownership of theological education?*

2. *Why was the traditional approach to formal theological education unable to meet the needs of the pastors? Are these same factors present in your context?*

3. *What are the essential components of this model of theological education? Does your own model of theological education include these essential components?*

4. *According to this case study, why must theological education be self-supporting? According to this model of theological education, how can theological education be self-supporting?*

5. *What surprises you about FIET's Diploma in Pastoral Care and Spirituality? What impresses you about FIET's program for Prison-Oriented Chaplains?*

Chapter 10: Latin America

Central American Center for Pastoral Studies, Guatemala

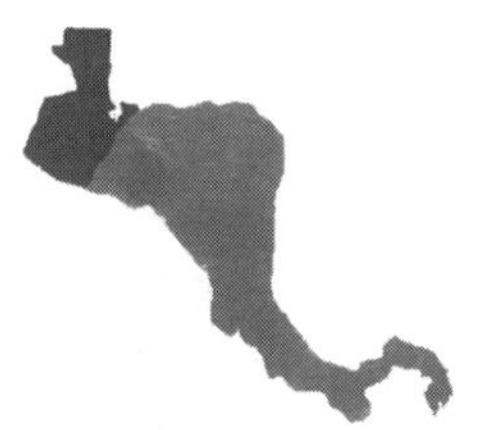

by Judith Castañeda, Elizabeth Carrera Paz,
Rafael Escobar, Dennis Smith

This case study is based entirely on CEDEPCA's Annual Report for 2005. CEDEPCA stands for Centro Evangélico de Estudios Pastorales en Centroamérica. Here "Evangélico" means "Protestant" or "Ecumenical" and includes "Evangelical." The following report begins with an open letter from Judith Castañeda, the General Coordinator of CEDEPCA. Following this letter are statements about CEDEPCA's Roots and Mission and reflections on the Central American context, ending with a typology of the churches of Central America, with which CEDEPCA attempts to work. The second half of the report, as organized in this case study, describes CEDEPCA's diverse programs of theological education: The Women's Pastoral Program; Biblical, Theological and Pastoral Training; Intercultural Encounters; and Publications and Communication Training. The interaction among these diverse programs gives new meaning to the concept of Diversified Theological Education.

Once again in 2005 natural disaster struck Central America, this time in the guise of Hurricane Stan. As always, the people most affected were those living in precarious circumstances: rural indigenous communities and those living on the periphery of major cities. CEDEPCA was able to offer spiritual and emotional accompaniment to victims of this tragedy and deliver food, water and clothing to affected communities.

We also continue to suffer the consequences of a man-made disaster: the ongoing violence that plagues Central America. In Guatemala alone, 565 women were assassinated in 2005. Through all our programs, CEDEPCA continues to work for a life that is just and free of violence.

How easy to feel helpless in such circumstances! In difficult times such as these we must ask ourselves: Upon what resources can we draw when we seek to do good? The first words of John's Gospel affirm: "The Word was made flesh and dwelt among us. . ." As people committed to doing good, we are deeply encouraged by the news that God, in the person of Jesus, is in our midst; God accompanies us in human history.

CEDEPCA is an ecumenical service institution, working in a Central American context marked by exclusion, discrimination and racism. Our ministry offers a word of hope, a space for communion, the living out of solidarity and sorority, and the possibility to share tasks and dreams that will lead us to a full and just life, a life filled with dignity and joy.

We give thanks to God for another year of service to the community. Our thanks, too, to you who live the liberating Gospel message and who, by giving of your time, your resources, your ideas and your labor, have made possible the results reported here.

May the Grace and Peace of our Lord Jesus Christ be with each of you.

Marta Judith Castaneda
General Coordinator

CEDEPCA's Roots

In the seventies a group of evangelical seminary students and professors in Costa Rica joined together to rethink their theology and pastoral practice in light of their particular place and time. They tackled the tough question of what it means to be faithful to Jesus Christ in Latin America today. They were especially influenced by the far-reaching pastoral, theological and liturgical reforms that were sweeping through Latin America's churches. Under the leadership of Dr. Orlando Costas, these pioneers created CELEP, the Latin American Evangelical Center for Pastoral Studies.

For more than two decades of pioneering work, CELEP designed and implemented flexible research and training programs especially designed to respond to the needs of church leaders, women and men, who were serving their communities by doing pastoral work but who had little access to continued theological, pastoral and technical training.

By September, 1985 the Central Americans who participated in this initiative had set up a semi-autonomous regional office named CEDEPCA, the Evangelical Center for Pastoral Studies in Central America. Similar regional initiatives had been set up in Mexico, Brazil and Peru. By 1998, CELEP, the umbrella organization, had devolved into its regional offices.

CEDEPCA's Mission

1. Facilitate theological reflection and pastoral practice that is rooted in our context, liberating and inter-confessional.

2. Accompany and serve those sectors of our churches that are anxious to engage in theological reflection and pastoral practice that is rooted in their own experience.

3. Promote the dignity and self-esteem of women; work to eliminate violence against women; transform and consolidate women's leadership in the church and community.

4. Offer opportunities for reflection and encounter to people from different cultures and with different personal stories so that each participant might understand his or her personal reality in terms of other realities, thus helping to build a more tolerant, just and equitable world.

5. Study the role played by religion and spirituality in the socio-political, economic and cultural life of Latin America. Offer churches elements of social and religious analysis that help them to discern their pastoral task.

6. Support service ministries; offer solidarity and consolation in times of crisis.

From Modernity to Fundamentalism

(The following paragraphs were taken from an article by CEDEPCA staff member, Dennis Smith, and included in CEDEPCA's Annual Report 2005 as part of the Publications and Communication Training department's analysis of the Latin American context.)

This is not what we were promised. The Modern Age, we were told, would bring us all the benefits of reasoned human enterprise: science and technology would grant us control over our environment and freedom from want; mindless passion would yield to understanding; even our inner demons would yield to the bounty of progress. When Brazil embarked on the modern adventure in the 19th century, they chose as their slogan "Order and Progress." That sums it up nicely.

Religion, too, would toe modernity's line. Liberal dictators from Mexico to Guatemala and Brazil saw in the Protestant missionary enterprise a key ideological ally in their battle with 19th-century Latin America's most powerful and richest institution: the Roman Catholic Church. The schools and hospitals built by the Protestant missionaries, together with their entrepreneurial spirit, would bring local culture into line with emerging European and US thought. In addition, the text-based liturgy and rational theological discourse of the Protestants would challenge Catholicism's medieval obscurantism.

Something went wrong on the way to the Enlightenment. Almost two centuries of modernity have taken us through endless political and economic unrest only to leave us where we began: as a source of cheap labor and natural resources for the industrialized North. Some have reaped the material benefits of progress, but today in Latin America the gap between rich and poor, men and women, urban and rural, landed and landless is as wide as any place on the planet.

The system that promised reasoned well-being has brought us exclusion, alienation and exhaustion. Security, the rule of law, social tolerance and broad-based economic development have yet to flourish in Latin America. Not surprising, our commitment to democracy is only skin deep. According to a recent survey sponsored by the United Nations Development Program, 55% of Latin Americans would be willing to accept a non-democratic government if it proved capable of generating widespread economic development. (Latinobarometro: 2004).

The 20th century was to be the Secular Century. Indeed, many religious institutions in Latin America, both Catholic and Protestant, limped into the 21st century in a state of profound crisis. But popular religiosity is a very different story. A new generation of religious entrepreneurs has understood how to accede to the collective spiritual resources of the region, package them in drama and present them to the public with authority and mystery. Such religious spectacles are offered to a population struggling to survive, mired in crisis, anxious to acquire hope, seeking meaning and access to transcendence.

"I Found My Voice"

(Rafael Escobar, the Coordinator of CEDEPCA's program of Biblical, Theological and Pastoral Training, offers the following paragraphs to describe the context and mission of that program.)

In October 2005, Hurricane Stan demonstrated our vulnerability as human beings. Many families experienced suffering, pain and death; the level of destruction was terrible. During this crisis, the population served by CEDEPCA experienced moments of deep solidarity and tenderness. Local churches in the affected communities played an historic role offering emergency housing and food to the population. But these same churches do not have the resources or training to respond to the challenge of reconstruction.

This is our context: on the one hand, we are a people immersed in the consumer society—hypermarkets, cell phones, fast food; on the other, we are a people strangled by insecurity and anxiety. Stan evidenced the great gap between the privileged minority, those who enjoy the blessings of the market economy, and the excluded majority. Today these communities, still isolated due to washed-out roads and bridges, confront the crude reality of hungry children, damaged houses, and lost income. These communities are still haunted by the specters that have always preyed on humankind: famine, exposure to the elements, unemployment, lack of access to education and health care, physical isolation.

We live between fear and hope—the perfect scenario for doing theology, for discerning God's presence in our lives. How does God participate in our daily struggles? How do we nourish the life-giving mystery of God's presence in the midst of hopelessness? How do we discern "tenderness" as a theological category where God's face is revealed?

The truth is that many churches in Central America responded to the disaster by proclaiming that our suffering was punishment from God; such "pastors" are religious terrorists who offer spiritual spectacles, promising relief to anguished souls in exchange for cold, hard cash. At CEDEPCA we insist that this is not relief, nor is it theology. We believe that the moment demands theological reflection and pastoral practice that empower the faith community. It is in local churches that people act out their faith, empowered by the Spirit of Life. As Marcos David Chonay, a Methodist student from Lemoa, Quiche, said: "When I began these studies, I didn't say a word. Now, I have found my voice."

Walking in Sorority

(Betty Carrera, who directs the Women's Pastoral Program at CEDEPCA, offers these reflections on their context and mission.)

2005 was a year marked by pain, suffering and sadness for many women in Central America, especially due to the impact of natural disasters like Hurricane Stan. In Guatemala, for example, the storm affected 14 of the 22 departments that make up the national territory.

We responded to the disaster by accompanying the victims. We were able to share an embrace in solidarity, consolation, a word of encouragement; we planted hope in the midst of hopelessness. Once again God's Spirit reminded us that, in moments of great difficulty, we can pick up the pieces together and rebuild our lives.

I saw how women held themselves as they arrived at the Holistic Health workshop we held at a Presbyterian church in San Antonio Suchitepéquez, Guatemala; their faces were marked with grief; they were dusty, worn, on the verge of giving up. I saw how they sat on the benches, the pain etched into their faces; these women had witnessed the devastating force of water as it inundated their communities. Barely a month had passed since the disaster. I prayed: "Lord, may this workshop renew these women. May they return to their homes equipped with simple exercises that will help them manage the stress produced by this disaster, tools that allow them to care for themselves and celebrate their own worth as human beings. May they share these simple tools with their friends and families."

I thank God that, as the workshop proceeded, those hunched shoulders and tight gestures began visibly to relax. Worn faces began to show rest and relief. There were moments of catharsis and release, tears and laughter. What a joy to see those transformed faces!

In their evaluation of the workshop, participants stated: "Today I took time to breathe, to do relaxation exercises, to meditate. We need to practice these exercises every day! I'll share them with others."

I also observed as our new team of Holistic Health facilitators received their training: they described how the training helped them grow in their personal lives and how thankful they were for this new space in which they could serve. How encouraged we are when we find a purpose in life and feel useful!

This is one of the objectives of the Women's Pastoral Program: to train women to build a concrete connection between their faith and society. To live out the Good News of Jesus is our primordial task: to promote the life and dignity of the dispossessed, the marginalized, those made invisible. Jesus' encounter with the crippled woman in Luke 13 reminds us that we, too, can stand tall with dignity. We can engage life with security and celebrate the value God grants each person.

In all the events we held in 2005 we could again savor the deep grace that comes from working ecumenically. Sister relationships arose naturally: new friendships, new spaces for communion and growth. These are spaces where, as women, we can speak clearly, explore the Bible together, clarify our doubts about our bodies and our sexuality, and question so many things we've been told about the role of women in the church and society.

In 2005 we confirmed once again the capacity of women to rise above adversity with resilience. We confront violence daily, but we train ourselves, in this Decade to Overcome Violence, so that our homes, our workplaces, and our churches become true sanctuaries of peace and so we can live alternatives to the violence we experience every day.

THE MANY FACES OF THE CHRISTIAN CHURCH IN CENTRAL AMERICA: A TYPOLOGY

(As a further orientation to CEDEPCA's context and mission, Rafael Escobar and Dennis Smith have included in the Annual Report for 2005 the following summary of churches of Central America, among whom they carry out their mission.)

Central America is a deeply and vibrantly religious region. In CEDEPCA we are privileged to work with the many expressions of the Christian faith in Central America. Here is a brief typology to help you map the terrain.

1. **The Roman Catholic Church** arrived in Guatemala in 1524 and is the oldest expression of the Christian faith in Central America. Despite adversity, in recent decades the Catholic Church has managed to preserve its institutional integrity while at the same time demonstrating great internal diversity, ranging from the Charismatic Renewal movement to Base Ecclesial Communities, from Jesuit educational institutions to Opus Dei.

2. **Immigrant Churches.** Many ethnic groups, when they emigrate, take their religious traditions with them. In the case of Central America, European immigrants introduced various Christian traditions to the region: the English merchants (including Bible salesmen!) that came to Guatemala early in the 19th century were mostly Anglicans; German Lutherans invested heavily in growing coffee in the second half of the century. But the churches that accompanied these immigrants did not extend beyond their ethnic communities; generally they did not invite native Guatemalans to join their churches. The exception was the Moravian Church; when Moravian refugees settled on the Atlantic Coast of Central America in the mid-19th century they engaged with the indigenous population and established what would become the majority church in that region. The other great branch of the Christian family, Eastern Orthodoxy, has not had an historic presence in Central America. In recent decades immigrants have established a small Orthodox presence in the region.

3. **Protestant Mission Churches.** These are the daughter churches of Protestant and Evangelical denominations from the United States. These churches represent widely varying sectors of society and theological positions. Here is a partial list of Protestant Mission Churches founded in Guatemala (with the year of founding):

   • National Evangelical Presbyterian Church of Guatemala 1882

   • Friends Church (Quakers) 1902

- Church of the Nazarene 1904

- Seventh Day Adventists 1913

- Primitive Methodist Church 1921

- Baptist Church 1946

- Episcopal Church (from US) 1965

- Mennonite Church 1971

- Lutheran Church Missouri Synod 1974

4. **Evangelical Faith Missions.** Denominations established in Central America by Evangelical Faith Missions from the US. These non-denominational mission enterprises first appear in the US at the end of the 19th century. They are called "faith" missions because their missionaries, coming from many different denominations, must raise their own financial support from local churches in the US; faith missionaries do not enjoy the relative job security offered by Protestant Mission Churches. The denominations created by these missions tend to place great emphasis on "sound doctrine." The following are most notable in Central America:

- Central American Mission (founded La Iglesia Centroamericana in Guatemala) 1899

- Latin American Mission (founded La Iglesia Bíblica in Costa Rica) 1921

- Christian and Missionary Alliance (founded La Iglesia Alianza Cristiana y Misionera in Guatemala) 1969

5. **Pentecostal Mission Churches,** born out of the great Pentecostal awakening at the beginning of the 20th century, are known for their emphasis on public manifestations of the baptism of the Holy Spirit: speaking in tongues (glossolalia), divine healing and prophecy. Members tend to come from marginalized social groups that find in the Pentecostal community a space of solidarity, consolation and healing. In Central America, these churches came from the United States, including:

- Church of God (Cleveland, Tennessee) (related to La Iglesia de Dios del Evangelio Completo) 1934

- Church of God (Anderson, Indiana) 1935

- Assemblies of God (Asambleas de Dios) 1936

- Foursquare Gospel Church (La Iglesia Cuadrangular) 1945

6. **National Pentecostal Churches** are churches born in Central America and characterized by the Pentecostal emphasis on spiritual gifts. Typically, they grow out of schisms in Protestant Mission Churches or Pentecostal Mission Churches provoked by charismatic local leaders, for example:

   - La Iglesia de Dios de la Profecia 1941

   - La Iglesia Príncipe de Paz (Rev. Josué Muñoz) 1955

   - La Iglesia El Calvario (Rev. Norman Parish) 1962

   - La Iglesia Elim (Dr. Otoniel Ríos Paredes) 1962

   - La Iglesia La Puerta del Cielo 1963

   - La Iglesia Monte Basán 1973

7. **Neopentecostal Churches** add to the doctrines and practices of the Pentecostals an emphasis on Prosperity Theology and on the public manifestation of exotic spiritual gifts such as exorcism, holy laughter or dancing in the Spirit. They often identify themselves as "Christians" instead of "evangelicals." They tend to establish self-sustaining denominations, rooted in the middle and professional classes, with close ideological ties to similar groups in the US and other countries. Leaders of these denominations often proclaim themselves "apostles." They organize mega-churches and invest heavily in radio and television. Many sponsor missionary efforts to South and North America and Europe. In Guatemala, they include:

   - Iglesia Cristiana El Verbo (related to Gospel Outreach, California) 1978

   - Fraternidad Cristiana de Guatemala (Rev. Jorge H. López) 1978

   - Iglesia El Shaddai (Rev. Harold Caballeros) 1983

   - Iglesia La Familia de Dios (Rev. Fernando Solares) 1990

   - Iglesia Evangélica Lluvias de Gracia (Rev. Edmundo Madrid)

   - Iglesia Casa de Dios (Rev. Carlos "Cash" Luna) 1994

   - Iglesia Evangélica Rey de Reyes (Rev. Alex González)

   - Iglesia Evangélica Betania (Rev. Efraín Avelar)

   - Iglesia Evangélica Ebenezer (Rev. Sergio Enríquez)

WOMEN'S PASTORAL PROGRAM

The Women's Pastoral Program offers women in Central America holistic training to confront the challenges of daily life. Women emerge from our training events ready to confront the real world, committed to reimagine their own selves, contributing to the development of their families, churches and communities, struggling to eradicate violence, to promote justice and live in equality. Participants also discover that they are part of an international network of like-minded women. In 2005 a total of **3007** women benefited from our program: **1897** in our courses and workshops, **601** in special celebrations, and **509** in awareness-raising events. 12% or 371 participants were Catholics, 38% or 1123 from Protestant Mission Churches, 19% or 576 from Pentecostal Mission Churches, 24% or 724 from National Pentecostal Churches, 3% or 89 from Neopentecostal Churches, and 4% or 123 had no affiliation.

The Women's Pastoral Program offers the following services:

A. **Courses and Workshops** are formal spaces for study and reflection. In 2005 1897 women participated in one or more of the following courses: *It's Marvelous to Be a Woman!, Women's Theology, Healthy Relationships, Alternatives to Violence, Naming our Pain, Holistic Health, Broken Vows, Walking Together.* Here are two samples:

- *It's Marvelous to Be a Woman!* is a course that explains how society educates women to be submissive and how women are denied the right to be persons. It emphasizes the role played by strong and creative women in the Bible and their impact on history. The course lasts two months and covers the following themes: *I Want to Be a Person, Educated to Suffer, Women Are Persons Too, Women Who Struggled Against Death, A New Way to Live, I Want to Change my Destiny but How?* One participant wrote: "In a group studying *It's Marvelous to Be a Woman!*, located in a poor, urban neighborhood, most of the women suffered from serious depression. This class came to these women at just the right time; the change in them was radical!"

- *Walking Together* is a two-day workshop that trains women how to accompany other women who have suffered from domestic violence. It offers biblical, legal and psychological resources. In 2005 we presented *Walking Together* to a total of 611 women in 9 locations in Guatemala, Nicaragua, Honduras, Costa Rica, and Mexico. A participant wrote: "We experienced *Walking Together* as a retreat where we learned about violence, how to overcome it, and how to eradicate it in our lives. It was quite an experience! On the one hand, it reaffirmed for us how important the issue is; on the other hand, it provided us with a healing, renewing alternative and lots of hope for the future."

B. **Special Celebrations:** In 2005 we held 6 Special Celebrations that attracted 601 women: International Women's Day, Women's World Day of Prayer, International Day of Non-Violence Toward Women, The "Women and Theology" Lectures, The Central American Women's Exchange, The Annual Coordinators' Encounter.

C. **Awareness-Raising Events:** Each year we hold a number of awareness-raising events with churches, theological seminaries and community groups to promote the Women's Pastoral Program and get people thinking about the issues we address. These are usually talks or mini-workshops of one day or less. In 2005 a total of 509 persons participated in awareness-raising events such as: a workshop on understanding anger held in Nicaragua, a conference on "Gender Perspectives in Television Programs" held in Guatemala, a workshop on "Using All Five Senses in Liturgical Celebrations" in Mexico, a talk on Mothers' Day in Costa Rica.

D. **The Women's Clinic** offers psychological counseling in Guatemala and Costa Rica as well as legal aid in Guatemala, especially for women who have been victims of violence. The Women's Pastoral Program is affiliated with the Society for Intercultural Pastoral Care and Counseling.

E. **Temas** (Themes) is a bi-monthly bulletin of the Women's Pastoral Program. Issues with the following themes were published during 2005: "Reimagining Our Journey," "The First Witnesses," "My Headache Was My Teacher," "Sorority—Friendship among Women," "Women in the Movement of Jesus," "In God's Name."

BIBLICAL, THEOLOGICAL AND PASTORAL TRAINING

CEDEPCA's Biblical, Theological and Pastoral Training offers Central American church leaders a unique continuing education program at three levels:

- **Congregational Studies:** A basic level course that offers an overview of the Bible appropriate for local congregations. This series of eight books leads to a Certificate in Bible Studies.

- **Pastoral Institute:** A secondary-level cycle of 30 courses, divided into 6 areas: *Administration, Christian Education, Ministry of the Word, Spirituality, Evangelism, Pastoral Accompaniment.* Students who finish 15 courses receive a **Certificate**, and those who complete the 30 courses receive a secondary level **Diploma in Pastoral Ministry.**

- **University Studies**: A degree program in Bible and Theology at Bachelor, Licentiate and Masters levels. For this program CEDEPCA has established 5 core courses that reflect our philosophical and theological commitments: *Fundamentals of Ministry, Latin American Reality, The Theological Task, Study and Interpretation of the Bible, Gender, Identity and Theology.*

This variety of study options reflects the diversity of people who are ministering in our region, many of whom are seeking academic credits and others who are not. These programs are related to the Latin American Biblical University (UBL) in San José, Costa Rica and the Inter-Ecclesial Center of Theological and Social Studies (CIEETS) in Managua, Nicaragua. CEDEPCA is a member of the Fraternity of Theological Institutions in Abya-Yala.

Enrollments during 2005:

Women	137	University level courses	25
Men	167	Secondary level courses	19
TOTAL	304		

Neopentecostal	7 students from 4 denominations
National Pentecostal	66 students from 25 denominations
Pentecostal Mission	58 students from 3 denominations
Protestant Mission	135 students from 9 denominations
Catholics	38 students

University Level Courses Offered in 2005

1. An Exegetical Look at 1 Timothy

2. Theological Ethics

3. A Biblical Theology of Grace

4. Ethics and the Environment

5. Study and Interpretation of the Bible

6. Gender, Identity and Theology

7. Church History I

8. Mission of the Church I

9. Methodology of Investigation

10. Christology

11. Holistic Evangelism

12. Liturgy 1

13. Written Communication

14. Latin American History and Reality

15. History and Theology of Salvation

16. Greek I

17. Greek II

18. English I

19. English II

PASTORAL INSTITUTE COURSES OFFERED IN 2005 (SECONDARY LEVEL)

1. Naming the Pain

2. Introduction to the Bible

3. It's Marvelous to Be a Woman

4. Church, Community and Mission

5. John Wesley: His Theology and Ours

6. Great and Wonderful Are Your Works

7. Good News to the Poor

8. Liberation for All

9. Biblical Interpretation

10. Christology

11. Of Such Is the Reign of God

12. Evangelization in Urban Settlements

A former student, now professor, gives his testimony: "A decade ago I joined CEDEPCA's Biblical, Theological and Pastoral Training program as a student. Previously I had had the opportunity to begin my undergraduate degree in theology at a prestigious private local university, but I did not have the financial resources to complete the program. In 1995, as I sought ways to fulfill my academic dream, I discovered that CEDEPCA offered excellent courses that had the academic backing of the Latin American Biblical University. Thus CEDEPCA became the place where I could fulfill my dreams. In this process, CEDEPCA has been for me an academic challenge, a personal commitment, a source of renewal and consciousness-raising, a space for humanization and personal fulfillment. I never cease giving God thanks for allowing me to become part of CEDEPCA. Being a teacher has also been a marvelous experience. I have had the opportunity to teach Pastoral Institute courses in Jutiapa and Cuilapa. In this process I have seen my students change; I truly have seen them come to see reality from another perspective. Many men and women have told me how, through these courses, their work in the church and community has become more meaningful. They note how they have come to feel themselves part of an institution that is committed to the poor. Finally, I can affirm that both students and teachers have been deeply blessed by our relationship with CEDEPCA."

Hugo R. Padilla Silva
CEDEPCA Professor
Minister of the Episcopal Church of Guatemala

Intercultural Encounters

Intercultural Encounters offers churches, universities and community groups the opportunity to discover Guatemala in all its diversity, complexity and beauty. Through immersion experiences and work projects, people from the North are able to experience everyday life in Guatemala and work alongside local communities. We also organize conversations with representatives of a broad spectrum of religious, social and economic groups, as well as local politicians.

In 2005 we received 18 delegations totaling 200 persons; most of them combined immersion in Guatemalan reality with a community work experience that allowed participants to establish direct relationships with people in local communities.

Some of the themes covered with the groups included: the role of the church in local society, free trade agreements and their impact on the national economy and the lives of the poor, the situation of women in Guatemala (with a special focus on the rise of violence against women in recent years), Mayan spirituality and the role of local organizations in community development.

Work projects focused on improvement of community and family infrastructure, reforestation, planting family gardens and assisting with vegetable planting and domestic animals.

PUBLICATIONS AND COMMUNICATION TRAINING

This department tells CEDEPCA's story and the story of Central America's churches, does research on communication, culture and spirituality in Latin America, offers training in communication to theological seminaries, Bible institutes and universities, and offers church groups, academics and journalists current information and analysis of the history of the churches in Latin America, the churches' relation to the media, and the current religious, cultural and political situation in Latin America.

Publications and Communications Training is a member of the World Association for Christian Communication (WACC). In addition, CEDEPCA coordinates communication research and training activities with the Instituto de Estudios de la Comunicatión (IEC) in Lima, Perú.

How To Contact CEDEPCA

Correspondence: CEDEPCA, Apartado 2834, Guatemala 01901, Guatemala

Telephone & fax: (502) 2254 1093

E-mail: cedepca@cedepca.org

Internet: www.cedepca.org

QUESTIONS FOR REFLECTION AND DISCUSSION

1. *Take note of the various ways in which this case study identifies and analyzes its socio-economic and spiritual context. How does your theological education program identify and analyze its socio-economic and spiritual context?*

2. *Consider how CEDEPCA includes the conscientization of women, intercultural encounters, and publications and communications training along with biblical-theological-pastoral training as essential dimensions of theological education. Does your theological education program include these dimensions? If so, how? If not, why not?*

3. *In 2005 CEDEPCA's Women's Pastoral Program engaged 3007 women throughout Central America in holistic training to confront the real world, re-imagine their own lives, contribute to the development of*

their families, churches and communities, struggle to eradicate violence, promote justice and live in equality. How does this work take place in your context? How does theological education promote these objectives in your context?

4. *What "levels" of biblical-theological-pastoral training does CEDEPCA offer? What "levels" does your biblical-theological-pastoral training program offer?*

5. *What range of church traditions do CEDEPCA's students represent? What range of church traditions does your theological education program serve?*

Chapter 11: Latin America

Latin American Doctoral Program

by Charles Van Engen

I n a recent article in *Evangelical Missions Quarterly* (P. 206-207, Vol. 42, No. 2, 2006), Rich Starcher writes of the need in Africa for "a really useful theological doctoral program." Starcher observes that,

> *Given the evident need for thousands of church leaders to be trained at the grassroots level, some strategists might consider a theological doctoral program in Africa for Africans an extravagant luxury. However, many African church leaders see it as imperative. African Bible schools, colleges, and training programs are multiplying to supply leaders for the burgeoning Africa church. This is resulting in a corresponding demand for high-level theological educators who will staff these institutions and programs. Inadequate opportunity for higher studies in sub-Saharan Africa often drives Africa's best teachers and theologians to Europe or North America. Many never return to a continent desperate for their expertise and critical thinking skills. Others return only to leave again as a result of re-adaptation struggles. High costs prevent many more from ever pursuing their dream of doctoral study. Further, many African students find their overseas doctoral programs lack relevance in light of African realities.*
>
> *For reasons similar to those mentioned above, seminaries all over the non-Western world are launching theological doctoral programs. Unfortunately, many are merely adopting (with little adapting) a Western doctoral program design. Western seminaries are exporting their programs (and faculty) to Africa, Asia and Latin America.*

The situation in Latin America is similar to Starcher's description of the African context.

The Need

The phenomenal growth and increasing maturity of the Protestant church in Latin America requires that its leaders articulate the faith with relevance, diffuse their ideas clearly, reflect deeply on the new challenges, and assist the People of God to respond constructively to the new realities facing them. In addition, it is necessary to formulate new strategies in order to penetrate with the Gospel the academic and cultural centers of information, opinion, and socio-economic and political perspectives arising on the continent. A generation of leaders is arising in Latin America that has the necessary background to carry out academic studies at a Ph.D. level. However, every day it is more difficult and costly for these persons to do doctoral-level studies outside the context of Latin America. The Latin American Doctoral Program (PRODOLA) seeks to respond to this need.

Churches in Latin America are experiencing a critical shortage of leaders. The focus of Protestant churches and missions on personal salvation and church attendance during the past century has produced an unprecedented growth of Protestant churches in Latin America. This growth has created an urgent need for qualified leaders capable of mentoring others and reproducing themselves. The need for a new generation of leaders is especially striking in relation to discipleship of new believers, involvement in transforming society, and cross-cultural mission sending.

The Present Reality

Hundreds of seminaries, Bible schools, and ministry formation programs have been established in Latin America, giving rise to a dire shortage of qualified teachers. In years past, many expatriate missionaries from Europe and North America served as Bible school and seminary professors. Because fewer of them are being sent, there is a shortage of those who will shape the next generation of pastoral leaders in Latin America. Today, over 240 Latin American mission agencies send more than 4000 cross-cultural missionaries for world evangelization. Yet many are sent into difficult cross-cultural mission situations with little or no training because there are few leaders capable of training them.

Many of today's teachers in Latin American Bible schools and seminaries lack adequate training, with most having only the equivalent of a bachelor's and some a master's degree. In many cases, courses are being taught by persons who have the same or lower degree than the candidates. This situation would be like high school teachers having only a high school education or teachers with only a Bachelor's degree teaching at the university level. Meanwhile, the educational level of the young people in the churches has risen dramatically, raising expectations for the educational level of the pastors and church leaders. Daily it becomes increasingly more costly and difficult for Latin American leaders to do graduate-level studies outside of their contexts. In addition to the increasingly prohibitive cost of doctoral-level studies in Europe and North America, Bible schools, seminaries, and leadership formation programs in Latin America cannot afford to have one of their faculty members absent from their institutions for four to six years to study abroad. Besides these difficulties, it is the matter of the brain-drain out of Latin America, evident over many years, due to the tendency for many scholars from Latin America, Asia and Africa to remain in Europe and North America after completing their doctoral studies there. Yet there are few opportunities for Latin American Protestant church leaders to pursue upper-level theological studies in their continent.

The Latin American Doctoral Program seeks to address these extraordinary needs by preparing exceptional Christian leaders. The need is urgent for graduate level studies to be offered in Latin America, by Latin Americans, in the languages of Latin America.

Latin American Christian Ministries

To meet this need, Latin American Christian Ministries, Inc. (LACM) was formed as a nonprofit corporation. At the beginning of 2000, Professors Pablo Deiros and Chuck Van Engen shared together their concerns regarding the need to provide additional theological and missiological formation for those serving as faculty members in Bible schools and seminaries throughout Latin America. As a result of this initial conversation, and in consultation with other colleagues and through much prayer, LACM was founded in 2000 with its stated purpose being "to provide teaching and church leadership mentoring skills, programs and resources for Christian ministries and pastors in Latin America." This non-profit organization would be the initiator and foundational support for the Latin American Doctoral Program.

The UNELA Connection

In September of 2000, Chuck Van Engen attended the Fourth Consultation of the Latin American Congress of Evangelization (CLADE IV), held in Quito, Ecuador. During his time there, Chuck renewed his friendship with Dr. Enrique Guang, President of the Evangelical University of the Americas (UNELA), located in San José, Costa Rica. A former president of several Nazarene seminaries in Ecuador and Costa Rica, professor of psychology in the National University of Costa Rica, and founding Rector of UNELA, Dr. Guang was very interested in the idea of PRODOLA. However, in those early conversations, Dr. Guang made it clear to Chuck that the only viable pathway to addressing the need expressed above was by means of a university-level, government accredited doctoral program. Dr. Guang offered his personal expertise and support to create the program and suggested that it could be placed under the umbrella of UNELA, a Christian university accredited by the government of Costa Rica. This is the direction that the Latin American Doctoral Program subsequently took, becoming a doctoral program of UNELA.

Initial Exploratory Gathering

In March of 2001, with the funding assistance of a Christian foundation, LACM convened thirty-five Latin American Protestant professors in Miami, Florida. The professors came from twelve countries and represented twenty-three denominations, mission agencies and theological education institutions. Together they prayed, dialogued and dreamed as to how an advanced theological education program might be created. A vision for a Ph.D.-level study program began to emerge. Known in Latin America as PRODOLA (**PRO**grama **DO**ctoral **LA**tinoamericano), the program is designed to prepare scholars and professors to shape the next generation of leaders for Latin American churches and mission agencies. It seeks to mentor the mentors who in turn will form the next generation of pastoral and mission leaders for the church in Latin America.

The Miami Consultation named an Administrative Council consisting of ten professors representing the continent. These persons have many years of experience in leadership formation in Latin America. They come from Argentina, Brazil, Bolivia, Costa Rica, Ecuador, Mexico, Peru, and the United States. All are professors involved in leadership formation in Latin America, and six of them head up their own theological education institutions at a Bachelor's and Master's level. Together, they represent more than 300 years of experience in theological education and leadership formation. Since May of 2001, the Administrative Council has met at least twice each year in order to develop the infrastructure for PRODOLA, to formulate the program of study and to extend the networks of personal, institutional and financial cooperation.

The PRODOLA Program

The Administrative Council has been the primary architect of the Latin American Doctoral Program. PRODOLA is an educational project leading to an academic doctorate in theology (Ph.D.) in Latin America. PRODOLA is organized as a multi-site and multi-denominational community of Latin American scholars working together in a School of Doctoral Studies, academically linked to the Evangelical University of Latin America (UNELA) in San José, Costa Rica and accredited by the government of Costa Rica. PRODOLA is directed by

Latin Americans, taught by Latin Americans, and offered to leaders of Latin American churches, missions, seminaries, and Bible schools. Applicants must hold a master's degree or equivalent and fulfill strict entrance requirements. A foundational value of the PRODOLA program is that *students in PRODOLA will not need to leave for any extended time the Bible schools, seminaries, churches, or mission agencies where they are ministering, in order to carry out upper-level theological and missiological studies.*

The Latin American Doctoral Program serves as a bridge between all the various Protestant groups in Latin America. Lecture series are offered by Latin American professors, and courses are taught in one-week intensive modules. (See Appendix A for a list of the core faculty.) A system of local collegial seminars is being created so that candidates in the program can interact with a professor and with each other for encouragement and mutual enrichment. Each candidates will have a Latin American scholar mentoring him/her in a particular area of concentration. Over forty Latin American professors in more than ten different locations throughout the continent are partnering together to make the PRODOLA program possible.

The Inauguration

The PRODOLA program was officially launched in Londrina, Brazil, in February of 2004, and the first two course modules were offered there, with 21 doctoral candidates from 14 countries and 18 denominations present. They were joined by 18 others in February, 2005. An additional 8 candidates began their studies in PRODOLA in February, 2006. All of these women and men are involved in their own personal ministries as well as in the formation of church and mission leaders in their countries. This program appears to be one of the first Protestant Ph. D.-level multi-site programs of its kind to be approved and accredited at a university level by a Latin American government. (See Appendix B for a description of the core courses which the candidates take during the first two years of the program.)

Philosophy of Education

The Church of Jesus Christ has the fundamental responsibility for the development of Christian leaders. The Church must train those called to this leadership and follow in a manner that seeks to be clearly faithful to the biblical models. As educators and Christian mentors we are at the service of the churches and mission agencies to help them fulfill their responsibility in the formation of leaders at the highest level. Our desire is that the theoretical content of the Christian faith be in tune with the church's practice in ministry. Thus, we cooperate together in forming the kind of leaders that the

Church needs, persons who possess a biblical pastoral vision and demonstrate a high level of expertise in the fulfillment of its mission. The pastoral vision of PRODOLA is anchored in an integrated understanding of the Gospel and in a clear commitment to Kingdom values. Emphasis is given both to the content of the faith as well as to its practice, giving special emphasis to pastoral praxis in the Latin American context.

Within this frame of reference, the relationship between teachers and candidates is characterized by collegiality, teaching by example, and participation in collaborative efforts, in an environment of mutual accountability and discipline. Both teachers and their disciples are active agents in the formative process of the construction of knowledge. It is hoped that both will experience substantive changes as a result of their life together; that is to say, that both will work for the integration of content with daily life. This means that the program aspires to that type of learning that gives priority to the formation of persons over and above the creation of programs and activities. These are the fundamental factors that guide evaluation throughout the entire educational process.

The Vision, the Mission, and the Theological Foundation

The vision of PRODOLA is a Church equipped to participate in the mission of God in the redemption and transformation of Latin America.

The Mission of PRODOLA is to offer contextual theological education at a Ph.D. level with a creative methodology in order to equip the leaders of the Church.

Latin American Christian Ministries, along with the Administration and Faculty of PRODOLA, adopted the Lausanne Covenant as their theological foundation.

Objectives

The PRODOLA program is not in itself the goal. The goal is the development, growth and transformation of those who lead the churches, seminaries, Bible schools, mission agencies and relief organizations in Latin America. The stated objectives of the PRODOLA program are as follows:

1. To form teachers who are dedicated to the mission of the Church so that the body of Christ might be built up (Eph. 4:12).

2. To accompany each candidate in the development of his/her abilities and spiritual gifts.

3. To motivate each candidate to disciple other leaders that the Church needs.

4. To promote theological and biblical maturity in each candidate in order that he/she might articulate the Christian faith and practice.

5. To train the candidate in order that his/her ministry might be extended through the production and publication of materials.

6. To prepare each candidate for reflection upon, and the development of, ecclesial and missiological strategies.

7. To stimulate the candidate to be a creator of initiatives that will impact with the Gospel the various segments of society.

8. To equip the candidate to mobilize the Church for cross-cultural missions.

THE STUDY PROGRAM

The PRODOLA doctoral program is designed to wed face-to-face classroom experiences with personal on-location and in-ministry research. The reader can visit our web-site at *www.prodola.org* for more detailed information.

General Description

During the first two years students participate in eight intensive seminars involving in-depth analysis of a subject, with an expert in the field as professor/presenter. Each seminar involves ten weeks of pre-reading and research, one forty-hour week of face-to-face classroom time, and ten weeks of individualized reading, additional research, and writing after the classroom experience. Meeting in February and August each year for two weeks, the intensive seminars are designed to help the students learn how to study, research, and write at a doctoral level. Because the seminars are offered in a different location each time, the candidates are able to have their horizons broadened and their knowledge deepened by visiting each other's countries and seeing first hand a wide variety of ministries and church forms. Thus far, courses have been offered in Londrina, Brazil; Buenos Aires, Argentina; Quito, Ecuador; Santa Cruz, Bolivia; and Caracas, Venezuela. Our desire is to see the PRODOLA candidates transformed from being predominantly leaders in their individual nations to becoming continent-wide leaders.

During their third year, students complete three personal learning units called "tutorials." Each of these involves about 350 hours of individualized reading, research, and writing which the candidates do in their places of residence and ministry. Latin American scholars supervise the individualized tutorials in the areas of their expertise. During the third and fourth years, groups of students in the same county gather twice a year with a professor in order to give candidates the academic, personal, relational, and pastoral support they need. Each professor commits to mentoring and supporting a candidate's study program and accepts responsibility for the candidate's formation. CD-ROM and internet technology along with access to libraries in Latin America and elsewhere in the world support each candidate's research.

PRODOLA is fast becoming a community of scholars willing to learn from one another and reflect together on the implications of the Gospel for this century in Latin America. As the candidates study together and learn from their mentors and from each other, our hope is that much of their research and writing will become new textbooks that can be used in Bible schools and seminaries throughout Latin America.

The government of Costa Rica requires all Ph.D.-level study programs to include an empirical, field-based research component in addition to the library-based research of a topic. Following the auto-didactic pedagogical philosophy of educators like Paulo Freire, doctoral candidates in PRODOLA are actively involved in designing, shaping, modifying, and guiding their own program of study. Within the general PRODOLA program, candidates choose between two specializations: Ecclesiology (matters dealing with issues internal to the life of the church) and Missiology (matters having to do with the church's relationship to society and the world external to the life of the church).

The Didactic Process

The educational process of PRODOLA consists of the following components:

- **A Proposal:** The candidate submits a research proposal as a prerequisite for admission to the program. This individualized research-design proposal undergoes significant modification throughout the doctoral candidate's study program. Having studied research methodologies with Dr. Enrique Guang, the Rector of UNELA, the candidate re-writes the original proposal, and it becomes the candidate's Research Project that guides the candidate's entire study program. At this point, the approval of the project is required for continuation of studies in the program. Subsequently, having completed the first two years of foundational, course-based study, the candidate re-writes the Research Project a second time, with a view to the design and focus of the research to be done in the third-year tutorials and the fourth-year dissertation-writing.

- **Attendance at Intensive Courses:** Each candidate completes eight face-to-face courses (2 in methodology, 3 core courses, and 3 courses in the candidate's specialization) in the form of intensive classroom study with a professor.

- **Mentors:** Beginning in the third year of the program, each candidate has a personal mentor who will guide the candidate throughout the rest of the candidate's study program. It is the responsibility of the mentor to guide the candidate in the special focus of his/her program and in the elaboration of his/her dissertation.

- **Participation in Collegial Integration Seminars.** Candidates located near each other are expected to create an interdisciplinary collegial group to share the progress of their research and to serve one another through personal and spiritual encouragement. These groups are to meet at least twice each year, convened by a professor/coordinator.

- **Tutorials:** During the third year of the program, and with the approval of the candidate's personal mentor, the candidate takes three self-designed tutorials corresponding to the area of the candidate's specialization. A professor who is a specialist in the area directs the individualized research in each tutorial.

- **Preparation and Defense of the Doctoral Dissertation.** During the fourth year of the program, the candidate prepares and defends his/her doctoral dissertation under the guidance of his/her personal mentor, following the guidelines provided by UNELA/PRODOLA.

The Curricular Design

The program of study in PRODOLA consists of 84 credits distributed in the following manner:

Two Courses in Methodology (6 credits each):

> 1. Research Methodology
> 2. Pedagogy in Latin America

Three Core Courses (6 credits each):

> 1. Theological and Social Hermeneutics
> 2. Biblical Perspectives of the *missio Dei* and the Role of the People of God.
> 3. A Socio-Historical Analysis of the Church and the Latin American Context.

Three courses in the area of the candidate's specialization (6 credits each):

Ecclesiology (select three)

a. Contextual Pastoral Issues
b. Leadership
c. Latin American Theology and the Church
d. Psychology of Religious Experience
e. Theology of Social Development

Missiology (Select three)

a. Mission in and from Latin America
b. Cross Cultural Communication
c. Culture, Spirituality and Mission
d. Phenomenology of the Religious Experience

Three Tutorials (6 credits each)

a. Religion (or Mission) and Society
b. Religion (or Mission) and Theology
c. Religion (or Mission) and Culture

The Dissertation (18 credits)

OBSERVATIONS

It has now been five years since we began this initiative, and two years since we launched the PRODOLA program. Some observations are in order.

Recruitment

The Academic Council has wanted to make the resources of PRODOLA available to the best and the brightest emerging leaders in Latin America. Thus far this has meant that the PRODOLA program has done very little active recruitment. In early 2003 an announcement went out via e-mail to major Bible schools, seminaries, and mission organizations to let them know that PRODOLA would begin in February of 2004. Since then, the candidates who have become part of PRODOLA have come to us by way of personal recommendations from other Latin American scholars, heads of Latin American denominational and mission agencies, and others involved in Protestant leadership formation throughout the continent. The requirement that applicants must have completed the master's degree reduces the number of eligible candidates. Further, the fact that this is a decentralized, individualized, and auto-didactic program means that we accept only those leaders who have demonstrated that they are self-starters, disciplined students, life-long learners, and committed to this kind of study program. When the candidates begin their studies in PRODOLA they sign a "COVENANT OF PRODOLA" in which they commit themselves to the energy, time, dedication, and discipline that the program entails. We also request that the Bible school, seminary, mission organization or church in which the candidate ministers be committed to supporting the candidate with the finances, time, and other resources necessary to make the candidate's course of study possible.

Affordability

Financing a continent-wide educational program is complex, due in part to the constant flux of currency-exchange rates, the ever-changing rates of inflation of the national economies, and the economic instability of most of the countries of the continent. Given that reality, PRODOLA has created a financial support system that seems to be working well at this time. Including all costs the program is calculated to cost $7,000.00 per candidate per year. Professors are contracted and paid a substantial honorarium for teaching or mentoring. The candidate's travel and all other costs associated with the intensive courses are included in this total. In order to avoid dependencies, all candidates are expected to cover forty per-cent of the total, drawing from their educational institutions, denominations, mission agencies, churches, families and friends for their portion. On a need basis, PRODOLA grants some scholarship assistance. A number of the candidates receive scholarship help from other foundations or international organizations in order to cover part or all of the cost of their program. The cost is very low when compared to what it costs for someone from Latin America to study in Europe or North America. Latin American Christian Ministries raises funds from individuals, churches, mission agencies, denominations and Christian foundations to cover the remainder of the cost of the program. Many of those involved in the administration of PRODOLA donate their time to run the program. Thus far, the program has been affordable, though it represents a very real financial burden for the candidates themselves, since many of them have annual salaries equal to the annual cost of their study in PRODOLA.

Retention

After two years of operation, the rate of retention of the doctoral candidates has been quite good. Out of a total of 47 candidates, one person was forced to drop out because of change of location and ministry responsibilities. Six candidates have asked to slow down in their study program during 2006, due to health difficulties or overload in their ministry responsibilities. They will continue their studies, but will take a little longer than anticipated. As the first group moves into the tutorial and dissertation phases of their study programs, time will tell how many are able to complete their program. PRODOLA is committed to encouraging and empowering the doctoral candidates to be able to complete their study programs.

CONCLUSION

We think of the existence of PRODOLA as nothing short of miraculous. Thus far, we are on target with the projections and program goals set five years ago. Miraculously, the Lord has provided the people, the financial resources, and the growing infrastructure necessary for the program. The caliber of doctoral candidates is truly impressive. But we also face some major challenges in guiding a Ph.D.-level study program across an entire continent. One of the challenges we now face has to do with the growth of the program that is stretching the available resources in terms of time, personnel, infrastructure and financial support. We need to add more staff persons, broaden the structural support, and increase the financial under girding of the program. A second challenge has to do with communication. Although e-mail and the Internet have made the program possible, it is quite difficult to keep in touch with all 47 doctoral candidates and all the professors and supporting personnel involved in the program to the extent needed. A third challenge has to do with the contingencies of holding the intensive seminars in a different country every six months. Although this is a non-negotiable aspect of the program, it substantially raises the cost, time, and administrative energy needed to run the program.

The most amazing—and nearly miraculous—aspect of the past five years is that there have been no major surprises. The program has developed exactly as it was envisioned five years ago. We praise God for this! As our motto says, Latin American Christian Ministries, the Evangelical University of Latin America (UNELA), and the PRODOLA program continue to seek innovative and effective means for "Preparing Leaders in God's Service— Eph. 4:12." May the Holy Spirit continue to guide us all to find contextually appropriate means of forming a new generation of leaders for church and mission, in Latin American, in the twenty-first century.

Appendix A
The Core Faculty of PRODOLA

ABARCA, Sonia, Ph.D.
Costa Rican; educational psychologist; Ph.D. in Education from the Universidad Estatal a Distancia, San José, Costa Rica; professor in the School of Psychology of the National University of Costa Rica; director of the Department of Psychology of the National University for 11 years; professor of psychology at the University of Costa Rica for 4 years; lives in Costa Rica. Selected Publications: *Psicología del niño en edad escolar; Psicología de la motivación.*

ÁVILA, Mariano, Ph.D.
Mexican; Professor of New Testament at Calvin Theological Seminary, Grand Rapids, Mich.; received his doctorate in Hermeneutics from Westminster Theological Seminary in Philadelphia, Pennsylvania; pastor of churches in his country of birth, Bible professor and advisor in theological institutions in Mexico and other countries; member of the translation team for the *Spanish Version of the New International Version* of the Bible and *The Bible in Simple Language*; research fellow and candidate for doctorate in social sciences. Selected Publications: *La comunidad en que vivo; Historia social y política de la iglesia evangélica en México.*

BARRO, Antonio Carlos, Ph.D.
Brazilian, missiologist, professor of missiology in the South American Theological Faculty in Londrina, Paraná, Brazil; pastor of the 8th Presbyterian Church in Londrina; Ph.D. of missiology from the School of World Missions, Fuller Theological Seminary, Pasadena, California; lives in Londrina, Brazil. Selected Publications: *Orlando Enrique Costas: a Mission Theologian at the Crossroads and on the Way; Missão Integral Transformadora* (with Manfred Kohl); *Liderança para um novo século* (with Manfred Kohl).

BERGSMA, Pablo, Ph.D.
American; professor of Bible, theology and missions; Ph.D. in Philosophy from Southwestern Baptist Seminary, Fort Worth, Texas; Assistant Academic Dean and professor of Bible, theology and missions at the Evangelical University of the Americas, Costa Rica. Selected Publications: *The Compulsion of the Spirit; Misión transcultural: Iglesia en misión.*

BULLÓN, H. Fernando, Ph.D.
Peruvian-Costa Rican; professor of Ethics and Social Sciences at the Nazarene Seminary of the Americas and the Evangelical University of the Americas, both in Costa Rica; visiting professor of the post-graduate program of the Nazarene Seminary and the Evangelical University of the Americas in Latin American

countries of Mexico, Guatemala, Cuba, Ecuador, Peru, Brazil; postgraduate studies in Anthropology, Economics and Educational Administration; Ph.D. from the School of Economic and Social Studies of the University of Manchester, Great Britain; specialized studies in Theology and Development at the Oxford Center for Mission Studies, Great Britain; consultant in Development; lives in Costa Rica. Selected Publications: *Enfoques Teológicos y Técnicos en torno al Desarrollo en América Latina; Misión y desarrollo en América Latina: Desafíos en el umbral del Siglo 21.*

DEIROS, Pablo Alberto, Ph.D.

Argentine; historian and theologian; professor of Christian History at the International Baptist Theological Seminary in Buenos Aires; professor of history of mission in the School of World Mission, Fuller Theological Seminary, Pasadena, California; Ph.D. in Church History from Southwestern Baptist Seminary, Forth Worth, Texas; pastor and counselor; lives in Argentina. Selected Publications: *Historia del cristianismo en América Latina; Latinoamérica en llamas; Protestantismo en América Latina.*

GUANG, Enrique, Ph.D.

Ecuadorian; psychologist, professor of psychology and theology; pastor; President of the Evangelical University of the Americas (UNELA); dedicated to family therapy practice; lives in Costa Rica. Selected Publications: *El enfoque sistémico-comunicacional de la familia; Tecnología educativa y educación teológica popular.*

PAREDES Alfaro, Rubén, Ph.D.

Peruvian; anthropologist; professor of anthropology and mission; director of the "Orlando Costas" Faculty of the CEMAA in Lima, Peru; Ph.D. in Anthropology from the University of California, Los Angeles; lives in Peru. Selected Publications: *El evangelio: un tesoro en vasijas de barro; "Cambio social y conversión" in Misión #9, junio 1984; "Evangelio y cultura" en CLADE III: Quito, 1992.*

ROLDÁN, Alberto, Ph.D.

Argentine; professor of theology in seminaries in Guatemala, Brazil and Argentina; pastor; Ph.D. in Theology from the Superior Evangelical Institute of Theological Studies (ISEDET), Buenos Aires, Argentina; lives in Buenos Aires. Selected Publications: *El Dios que adoramos; El mundo al que Dios me ha enviado; La ética cristiana en un mundo en cambio; Señor total; ¿Para qué sirve la teología? Una respuesta crítica con horizonte abierto.*

SARACCO, Norberto, Ph.D.

Argentine; pastor of the Good News Church, Buenos Aires; co-founder of the Pastoral Council of Buenos Aires and vice president of the National Evangelical Council; founder and director of the International Faculty for Theological Studies (FIET) in Buenos Aires, Argentina; Ph.D. in Theology from the University of Birmingham, England; specialist in Pentecostal Studies and Latin American Theology; lives in Buenos Aires. Selected Publications: "El evangelio de poder" en *CLADE III: Quito, 1992; History and Theology of the Argentine Pentecostal Movement; Palabra y Espíritu en la comunidad evangelizadora; Las opciones liberadoras de Jesús.*

THOMAS, Nancy J., Ph.D.

American; professor of missiology; pastor; co-director of the Center for Intercultural Studies in the Evangelical Bolivian University in Santa Cruz, Bolivia; Ph.D. in Missiology from the School of World Missions, Fuller Theological Seminary, Pasadena, California; has a vocation as a writer and trains writers; lives in Bolivia. Selected publications: *Of Deity and Bones* (poetry); *El hogar que Dios bendice; Footprints of God* (co-editor); articles and poetry in many journals.

VAN ENGEN, Charles E., Ph.D.

Mexican; missionary to Chiapas, Mexico; professor of Biblical Theology of Mission in the School of World Missions in Fuller Theological Seminary, Pasadena, California; Ph.D. in Missiology and Theology from the Free University in Amsterdam, the Netherlands; lives in California. Selected Publications: *The Growth of the True Church; You are My Witnesses; Hijos del Pacto; Pueblo Misionero de Dios; Mission on the Way; Evangelical Dictionary of World Missions* (co-editor).

Appendix B

The PRODOLA Courses—First Two Years of the Program

Course Descriptions

A. Two Methodology Courses (6 credits each)

1. **RESEARCH METHODOLOGY (Six credits) Enrique Guang Tapia**

   In this course the student will develop his/her abilities in research methodology and the writing of the dissertation. The focus is refined, the problem and hypothesis stated, the objectives elaborated, the variables identified and the research methodology determined. The student works toward defining his/her theoretical frame of reference, both contextual and institutional. Finally, this course offers the student insight into the total process of research, including the heuristic process, critical descriptive analysis, and synthesis. Based on the proposal submitted earlier by the student, the course culminates in the elaboration of his/her research project.

2. **PEDAGOGICAL METHODOLOGY** (Six credits) **Sonia Abarca**

This course will enable the student to recognize the different philosophies of education in Latin America and to articulate a theory of education applicable to, and effective in, the context in which he/she serves. The principle objective is that the student develop teaching abilities that contribute to an effective teaching ministry.

B. *Three Core Courses (6 credits each)*

1. **BIBLICAL AND SOCIAL HERMENEUTICS** (Six credits) **Mariano Ávila**

This course updates the student with reference to the centrality that hermeneutics has acquired in recent decades in the academic world (philosophy, literature, history, biblical studies and theology). After establishing the advances and discoveries in the field of interpretation, the course examines two fundamental areas: the biblical-theological and the sociocultural reality. It offers the student tools for the interpretation of biblical and theological texts. It familiarizes the student with resources to interpret social and culture phenomena with utmost academic seriousness.

2. **BIBLICAL PERSPECTIVES OF THE *MISSIO DEI* AND THE ROLE OF THE PEOPLE OF GOD** (Six credits) **Charles Van Engen**

In this course the student studies the Bible from the perspectives of the mission of God, from the dawn of history to its culmination. This study will provide the student an ecclesiological and missiological foundation for reflection and action in the Church and Society.

3. **A SOCIO-HISTORICAL ANALYSIS OF THE CHURCH AND THE LATIN AMERICAN REALITY** (Six credits) **Pablo Deiros**

In this course the history of Christian witness is related to the social sciences. Drawing from the basis of knowledge of Christian history that the student brings, a second reading of that knowledge is done through the ecclesiological and missiological perspective of the Latin American reality. In this way the course will provide necessary tools to understand, interpret, and transform the student's spheres of ministry.

C. *Three Courses in the Area of Specialization (Six credits each)*

1. Ecclesiological Area (select three)

a. **CONTEXTUAL PASTORAL MINISTRY** (Six credits) **Norberto Saracco**

This course develops expertise in the exercise of an integrated, contextually appropriate pastoral ministry. Under consideration are aspects of a wholistic pastoral ministry that is informed by creation, by various stages of life and relationships, and by the conflictive circumstances of the societies in which we live. These situations are examined in light of the biblical concepts of shalom, justice, reconciliation and the kingdom of God.

b. LEADERSHIP (Six credits) Antonio Carlos Barro

This course deepens the student's understanding of, and develops models for, leadership according to biblical principles. It seeks to interrelate what we are with what we do. Contemporary models of leadership are analyzed in terms of their influence, limitations and contributions for differing Christian ministries. Special emphasis is given to the principles, values and perspectives of the Kingdom of God essential for the transformation of society.

c. LATIN AMERICAN THEOLOGY OF THE CHURCH (Six credits) Alberto Roldan

This course considers the contribution of systematic ecclesiology in relation to the reflection that emerges from the student's context. The final objective of the course is to enable the student to develop appropriate goals for the life and mission of the Church in his/her own context.

d. THE PSYCHOLOGY OF RELIGIOUS EXPERIENCE (Six credits) Enrique Guang Tapia

This course analyses the practice of different religious expressions and their impact upon the person, the community of faith and the society. Study is done regarding change and crisis, emotional understanding and other factors. Attention is given to the development of a critical reading concerning emotional dimensions, experience with the supernatural and other elements of religious life.

e. THEOLOGY AND SOCIAL DEVELOPMENT (Fernando Bullón)

This course examines the theological and missiological foundations of the ministry of the church and its members in social development in the context of Latin America.

2. Missiological Area (Select three)

a. MISSION IN AND FROM LATIN AMERICA (Six credits) Pablo Bergsma

This course has three central foci of mission: historical, theological and strategic. A critical study is offered of paradigms of the mission of the Church throughout history and the way in which the Church has developed these paradigms over time. Attention is given to present mission problems, and guidance is offered so that the student will be able to formulate a missionary model that is relevant to his/her reality and context.

b. CROSS-CULTURAL COMMUNICATION (Six credits)
Rubén Paredes

The transmission of the Gospel demands better use of the tools of the social sciences. Thus, in this course special attention is given to culture as a dynamic reality and to cross-cultural communication as essential for the missionary task. At the end of this course, the student will understand and be able to apply a holistic Gospel in relation to a world in need of redemption and transformation.

c. CULTURE, SPIRITUALITY AND MISSION (Six credits)
Nancy Thomas

This course explores the dynamic relationship between culture, spirituality and mission. It emphasizes the work of the Trinity in the development of mission and considers different models of spirituality. Tools are developed in order to discover the spirituality of the context and its implications for mission in that context. Included is an intercultural and missiological examination of worship, prayer, spiritual disciplines, spiritual gifts, the fruit of the Spirit and spiritual conflict.

d. PHENOMENOLOGY OF RELIGIOUS EXPERIENCE
(Six credits) Fernando Bullón

This course looks at the phenomena of religious experience from a socio-cultural perspective. It attempts to discover, understand and explain the observable aspects of diverse religious experiences in Latin America and considers the missiological and ecclesiological implications of these phenomena.

Charles Van Engen, administracion@prodola.org

PRODOLA, www.prodola.org

QUESTIONS FOR REFLECTION AND DISCUSSION

1. *What is the mission of PRODOLA in relation to the mission of the church and in relation to the urgent needs of the peoples of Latin America?*

2. *Why does PRODOLA dedicate all its resources to a program for Ph.D. studies in theology for Latin America?*

3. *What are the main components of this educational model? How can Ph.D. candidates be expected to carry out their studies on a part-time basis in just four years?*

4. *Who make up the faculty in this model of doctoral studies? How can they dedicate the necessary time to provide the guidance and input for this program?*

5. *How does the cost of this model compare with other doctoral programs?*

Chapter 12: North America and Europe

TEE in First Nations Communities

by John A. (Ian) MacKenzie

On Thursday, July 20th, 2006 at the morning service of Holy Communion during the Native Ministries Consortium summer school I heard the preacher, the Reverend Verna Jebb, observe how great it was to see so many familiar faces again. One might say how like a congregational morning service. Except that Verna had not attended summer school for five years. Further, she went on to note that some of the familiar faces were from winter school at the Charles Cook Theological School in Phoenix. Verna herself comes from The Pas, Manitoba. The community gathered for this particular worship service consisted of First Nations[1] and others from many denominations and from many tribes in both Canada and the United States. Present at this service were people from almost all of the main institutions involved in extension education for First Nations in North America. They included people from the now closed TEE Centre and Caledonia School of Mutual Ministry, Vancouver School of Theology, the Episcopal Diocese of Alaska, the Henry Budd School of Ministry, Manitoba, the Diocese of Navaho land, the Charles Cook Theological School, the Diocese of South Dakota (leadership programs), the Diocese of Rupertsland, and representatives from the United Church of Christ, Hawaii. Missing from this gathering for the first time in many years were people from the Maori, New Zealand.

The story of how it came to be that this diverse group of people came together in a worshipping community in 2006 is what this case study will explore. But what struck me as I reflected on Verna's words was the immense impact that the extension movement continues to have among First Nations congregations and communities throughout North America. While those of us who are educators focus on the curriculum, classes and extension programmes, the greater significance is in the liberating power brought about through the interaction of these diverse First Nations people with each other. If we use Rolland Allen's criteria for the ideal indigenous church whereby such a church would be self-governing, with its own ministers, developing their own theology and financially self-supporting, then the community gathered at Vancouver in 2006 reflects a nascent indigenous church. All of the First Nations participants were either ordained or were active lay leaders. While the people there might not have been consciously aware of the growth of an indigenous theology, it was clearly happening at many levels. Many of the participants were financially supported by their tribal governments. While self-government within traditional church structures was not obvious, self-government at the local and congregational levels was quite clear. Even though Bishops, presbyteries and judicatories still operated as though they were in charge, religious life at the local level continues for the most part controlled by the local communities. While the extension movement over the years in North America has received set backs by mainstream institutions, it has in fact in many areas reversed the colonial churches, control over First Nations congregations, and the congregations in those areas will not return to the Victorian model taught them by the missionaries.[2]

The Anglican Church of Canada consists of 28 dioceses. It is governed by a General Synod consisting of all of the diocesan bishops and elected clergy and laity from each diocese. Policies of General Synod must be approved by each of the three houses, that is, bishops, clergy and laity. Within this structure there also exist four smaller units or ecclesiastical provinces made up of the bishops, elected clergy and laity of the dioceses which exist within those provincial boundaries. When the Anglican Church of Canada was formed, the four provinces transferred most of their responsibilities to General Synod. Canada is geographically the second largest country in the world with an estimated population 32,547,200[3] in 2006. The majority of the one million Anglicans live in cities or large towns within one hundred miles of the U.S. border. It is estimated that about 100,000 Anglicans are First Nations, spread across the north of Canada. For example, 90% of the Inuit population is Anglican living in the Diocese of the Artic in small villages in a territory which is 950,000 square miles in sise. The estimated 15,000 First Nations (Haida, Nisga'a, Tsimsian, Gitsan, and Tahltan) in the Diocese of Caledonia live in a Diocese which originally was 450,000 square miles.[4] When one considers the huge distances, the concentration of the population in cities in the south, the complex decision making structures of the Anglican Church, one realises how difficult it would be at the best of times for First Nations Christians to have a real influence on decision making. Nevertheless, within the Anglican Church of Canada there is at present an attempt to create an indigenous bishop![5]

The conversion of native peoples is a story which can be characterised as magnificent in terms of the personal sacrifices of the early missionaries and their families yet tragic in its effect on First Nations peoples. With few exceptions the missionary process of the Anglican Church regarded native people as pagan and uncivilised. The goal was to bring them civilization, which meant to make them into Victorian-like English congregations.[6] This activity paralleled the policies of the government of Canada, whose policy was fundamentally genocidal. In the early 1900s they hoped to eliminate "Indians" through assimilation by education or by not supplying services to outlying areas so Indians would die off. The churches established residential schools, which were partly supported through government funding. They punished children for speaking their own language, denigrated native culture, made sure they attended church and brought them up as Christians. In the last thirty years it has been brought to light that, as well as fostering the destruction of language and culture, there was also a preponderance of sexual abuse. Several generations of First Nations were not only deprived of good parenting but many carried the pain of sexual abuse which they themselves often practiced on their own children.[7]

The theft of the First Nations land base in Canada took two forms. First, there was a treaty process whereby the government received ownership of vast amounts of territory and placed native people on small reserves with the additional promise that they would provide food, housing, education and health services. But they also simply declared two-thirds of Canada as theirs without such treaties.[8] Indeed in the Province of British Columbia some white people convinced themselves that native people did not come to British Columbia until after whites had arrived. In 1927 the Federal Government passed an amendment to the Indian Act which made it illegal for more than two people to gather to discuss the land issue. This act was not repealed until 1950 and almost immediately thereafter Frank Calder, a Nisga'a activist, began to organise the Nisga'a Tribal Council to take up the land question. The Nisga'a finally went to court and achieved a decision at the Supreme Court of Canada which forced the Government of Canada in 1973 to begin to negotiate the land question. However, it was not until 2000 A.D. that a Nisga'a treaty was achieved.[9]

It is against this background of hundreds of years of colonial rule, first by the French and then the English and for the last 119 years the government of Canada, that the churches in the early sixties began to re-evaluate their policies. The major impetus for change within both the Anglican and the Roman Catholic Churches began with the cumulative complaints about the treatment of native people in the residential schools. The Anglican Church of Canada commissioned a study which resulted in the Hendry Report. This report made far reaching recommendations to the Church in terms of justice issues and called for a reformation of its internal mission policies. General Synod of 1968 adopted these recommendations which quickly were picked up by the United Church of Canada and the Roman Catholic Church. The main line denominations soon formed an alliance to support First Nations attempts to achieve justice by challenging government policies, working for First Nations self-government and supporting a just settlement of the land issues. At the same time the Anglican Church began to take steps to challenge and change the way in which ministry takes place in those northern dioceses in which a majority of the parishioners were First Nations but with few Native clergy.

Several dioceses began to implement the Hendry report recommendations to begin recruiting and training First Nations clergy and lay leaders. The Diocese of Caledonia initiated such a process and a few years ago I wrote an article entitled "Thirty Years of Change and Development" in the Diocese of Caledonia.[10] In December of 2004 the newly elected Bishop, the Rt. Rev. William Anderson, supported by his executive, brought to an end the process of Theological Education by Extension in the Diocese, broke off relationships with the extension programme of the Vancouver School of Theology and declared that in future men and women studying for ordination would be required to attend a traditional residential seminary. He indicated on several occasions that he believed the previous bishops' attempts to take seriously the cultural context of First Nations peoples in Caledonia had gone too far. His vision for the future in Caledonia was to phase out non-stipendiary ordained ministry and return to the fully stipendiary policies of the Diocese which had characterised it up to the 1960s. This case study is contained within a clear time frame, and I will try and identify the characteristic which impelled us to move in the direction of extension and alternative models of ministry and the factors which killed it. In one of the evaluations of the programme we identified our vision and ideas for the future and characterised the challenges to the programme by visually depicting them as "sharks". We will look at both aspects in this case study in the hope that it might be helpful to others around the globe who are engaged in similar activities.

The initial impetus for change and action in the Diocese of Caledonia was the placement of progressive activist clergy in most of the First Nations congregations in the Diocese. Amongst the Nisga'a this resulted in the ordination of two Nisga'a clergy. But the diocesan wide revival began with the introduction of the SEAN Bible study (*Seminario por Extensión a las Naciones*) brought by the Bishop from Argentina.[11] This first Theological Education by Extension programme caught on in congregation after congregation resulting in the emergence of lay leaders as well as people feeling called to the ordained ministry.

I think that one of the fundamental lessons from this experience is the necessity of basing one's work through listening to the Word of God through the study of Holy Scripture. There is no question in my mind that the initial success of our exploration of ways of responding to the many crises we faced in parishes throughout the Diocese came from this corporate study of Scripture. It has often been the experience of churches throughout the globe that they explore alternate forms of ministry when faced with financial or other crisis. The development of new forms of ministry was most successful in those congregations that took the time to study and listen to Holy Scripture.

As the Diocese began to take seriously this emergent leadership, it became apparent that we needed more educational tools than were provided with the SEAN curriculum.

At this point the Diocese began to negotiate with the Charles Cook Theological School in Arizona. As our programme expanded, it became apparent that we needed a full time person to coordinate the training activities. By 1982 extension programmes were active in about 80% of the 26 congregations in the Diocese. Between 1970 and 1982 over 12 people in the Diocese were prepared locally for ordination and most of the First Nations congregations had First Nations clergy. In order to continue this expansion the TEE Centre was established with a half time staff person to assist the coordinator.

In 1984 the Diocese was invited to attend the Pacific Rim Conference in Hawaii in memory of Rolland Allen. Three of us attended and we had hoped to find answers to a number of questions which had arisen during the first 15 years of our programme. For example, in consulting congregations about the readiness of identifying local candidates for ordination, the Bishop had qualified his traditional authority in selection by sharing it with the congregation. However, when a few years later some form of disciplinary or corrective action was needed to apply to the candidate, congregations expected the Bishop alone to act. Since part of the congregational reluctance to participate in this is a cultural issue in tribal societies, we had hoped to receive some guidance from the Pacific Rim Conference. In any case, the Pacific Rim Conference was the catalyst for the Diocese of Caledonia, the Episcopal Diocese of Alaska and Cook School to open discussions with our provincial seminary[12], the Vancouver School of Theology.[13] As a direct result the group which later became known as the Native Ministries Consortium was formed.[14]

The Pacific Rim Conference made possible a new connection between Caledonia First Nations peoples, Alaska Natives and the Maori in New Zealand. Following the conference the Bishops of Alaska and Caledonia asked John A. (Ian) MacKenzie, Archdeacon of Caledonia, to arrange a meeting between themselves and representatives of the Vancouver School of Theology and the Charles Cook Theological School. They wanted to explore ways to cooperatively establish Theological Education by Extension programmes for this part of the Pacific Rim and if possible to find ways of including other Pacific Rim aboriginal groups in this endeavour.

A meeting was held at Vancouver School of Theology in 1985, and it was agreed that these four groups and the British Colombia First Nations section of the United Church of Canada should establish a task force to explore the implementation of these ideas. Gordon Pokorny, the Executive Director of the Native Ministries Consortium and Presbytery Officer for the Prince Rupert Presbytery, summarised this development in his report to the Consultation on Theological Education by Extension and Technology.

The Native Ministries Consortium was formed in 1985 in response to a challenge by Native Christians. They called upon the churches to create a new, effective way of developing and equipping Native leadership for ministry in Native congregations both ordered and lay.

Initially, the members of that Consortium were the Charles Cook Theological School, the Diocese of Caledonia of the Anglican Church of Canada, the British Columbia Conference Native Ministries Division of the United Church of Canada, and the Vancouver School of Theology. After a few years, because of financial constraints, Charles Cook College withdrew; however, in 2005 they rejoined the Consortium. At the time Cook withdrew the Episcopal Diocese of Alaska renewed its participation, which had been limited since 1985 because of lack of finances. The Henry Budd College for Ministry in Manitoba and the Episcopal Church in Navajoland have also joined the Consortium. Since 1985 the Consortium has had a continuing relationship with the staff and faculty of Te Rau Kahikatea, the Maori seminary in Auckland, New Zealand.

The original mandate of the Consortium was:

- To refine and expand lay education programmes in Native villages on the West Coast of Canada and Alaska;

- To develop an appropriate curriculum for Native people entering the ordained ministry, with a particular emphasis on the establishment of an extension or community-based degree programme;

- To establish appropriate cross-cultural courses to assist the church as a whole in its ministry with Aboriginal peoples, with a particular attention to the infusion of Aboriginal thought into the dominant Christian theological world (that mandate includes the establishment of opportunities for dialogue and discussion between Aboriginal Christians in Canada and with Aboriginal peoples of other parts of the Pacific Rim);

- To commend to its founding institutions ways in which Native people might gain a permanent and significant role and involvement in the educational decision-making at all levels of the Church and seminary.

The Consortium decided to implement its ideas by sponsoring a two-week summer school at Vancouver School of Theology in Vancouver, which it began in 1985. It has run such schools every summer since then and has also established these schools in cooperation with other institutions in South Dakota and Alaska. The schools student body and faculties have included people from New Zealand, Australia, Hawaii, Europe, Great Britain, Latin America, six Canadian Provinces and the two Territories, and at least ten U.S. states, representing approximately 30 different First Nations.

From the ecumenical emphasis in the Consortium emerged discussions between Caledonia and the Prince Rupert Presbytery that resulted in the expansion of the TEE Centre in Terrace as a joint project of both denominations. The Consortium began in 1986 to explore the possibility of the Vancouver School of Theology offering a degree programme to facilitate the development of Native Ministries both lay and ordained. After two years of discussion and consultation it became apparent that First Nations communities in this region insisted on a programme which provided credentialing equal to that of non-native ministers but one which took seriously the social, political cultural and religious traditions of each First Nation. In 1988 the faculty of VST accepted the idea of transforming their fully accredited M.Div. Programme into an extension programme for delivery in the communities in which the candidate resided. This decision was confirmed by the Senate and Board, and in 1989, supported by major grants from the Trinity Grants Programme in New York City and the Maple Leaf Fund in Great Britain, the programme began by engaging Ian MacKenzie as the part time Director.

The programme was a response to the work of the Native Ministries Consortium—and particularly the First Nations constituencies that make up the Consortium—to deliver a Master of Divinity degree programme which would be identical in standards and quality to the M.Div. that any other ordained minister in our churches might receive in this country. (Because part of our constituency includes parts of the United States, it had to be appropriate for them as well.) More significantly the degree programme needed to be delivered by extension and to be culturally sensitive, taking seriously the socio-cultural and religious environment of First Nations peoples. (I emphasise "peoples" because there are one hundred and fifty different native nations on this continent.)

We took the residential theological education programme and examined how that programme could be transformed into a programme for the field. We decided to use a combination of programme materials, including print, video and audio, and to use tutors who would be appropriately accredited by the Vancouver School of Theology in partnership with the constituencies that put forward the candidates. In this programme, a student cannot simply apply to VST to enter into the Native Ministries Programme by extension. The diocese, presbytery or other ecclesiastical authority must apply on behalf of the students and enter into a relationship with VST where they are responsible for the delivery infrastructure. The diocese, presbytery, conference or congregation handles the cost for tutors, travel, and students, which is a major departure from what we usually see in programmes offered by seminaries.

We had to deal early on with the question of admission. We discovered a number of our potential candidates needed to acquire the equivalent of two years of college transfer credits. The development of the Native Ministries summer school was a major thrust to make it possible for students to meet the admission requirements, as their courses are recognised as carrying college transfer credit.

We decided at the beginning of the programme not to wait until we had it all in place before we admitted students. We graduated three students in 1996 who began the programme in 1989—it took them seven years to complete the programme, but part of that was because they were often waiting for the materials to come to them. Since then we are delivering or have delivered the programme to 40 plus students in British Columbia, Alberta, Saskatchewan, Manitoba, Yukon, Alaska, South Dakota, Northern California, Oregon, Arizona, Georgia and Hawaii. While the largest number of students and tutors have been Anglican or Episcopalian, we have graduated people from the United Church of Canada and the Presbyterian Church in both Canada and the United States. At the time of writing Vancouver School of Theology is exploring delivery of the programme to 10 or more possible candidates from the United Church of Christ in Hawaii and two from the United Methodist Church in the same state.

Some Analysis

I became involved in training Christian leadership for First Nations communities when I became the Rector of St. John's Church, Old Massett. After thirty-one years of working at these issues of alternative ministry and alternate training, what have we learned?

First, we have to recognise that as we move to choose older men and women for ministry, ordained and lay, that what we get at the end of the process will pretty much be what we have at the beginning. Despite lots of training and education, mature men and women have been largely formed before they enter the training process. Our expectation of their abilities and performance needs to recognise that they will not change very much through our training. This means much greater reflection should be given to the selection process.

Secondly, the most successful developments in our Diocese have emerged from congregations where there has been some serious Bible study. Where there is not Bible study, there are usually problems. It is my firmly held belief that, while economic, social and other factors may be part of the impetus for change, these alternative programmes must also be firmly related to the study of the Bible or they will eventually fail. The mission of the church must be the overriding principle.

Thirdly, there is a question in my mind as to how effective the process of community selected and trained ordained ministries will be in non-native parishes in the long run. In native congregations there is a permanent, closely-knit, congregation and community of kinfolk. These are communities who know who they are! They do not have to search for community or continually evaluate the nature of the community. It is a given. Our urban and even now our rural congregations are characterised by rapid change in membership and continuing struggles to re-create community. While the characteristics of native communities also bring into play a whole new series of problems for their congregations, the tentative nature of "community" in North American urban congregations may be a serious problem for the permanency of many of the current experimental models of ministry.

Fourthly, the most difficult question for First Nations congregations and their ecclesiastical authorities is the question of discipline and accountability. While First Nations congregations have played a significant part in the selection of candidates, they are not so far able to develop appropriate accountability practices to deal with their concerns about their own ministers or priests.

Finally, as I reflect on my own experience during the last thirty-one years, I have begun to realise that when we began to focus on the training for ordained ministry to the detriment of emphasis on the ministry of the whole church we began to move off the track. I think this was true in the Caledonia programme, and it may also be the case with the Native Ministries Consortium summer school. In the eighties the summer school was primarily attended by lay people expanding their calling to minister in their communities. Now almost 50 % of the participants are candidates for ordination. This also leads to more emphasis on "theology" and less and less concern with the social justice issues of poverty, HIV/AIDS, the deterioration of the environment, the situation of women in most of the globe, etc.

Concluding Comments

First, for most First Nations peoples in North America who have participated in the extension movement there has been a considerable change.

- More and more congregations are led by First Nations clergy.

- Because of institutions like the Charles Cook winter school and the Native Ministries Consortium summer school there is a nascent indigenous Church.

- The model of dependence inculcated by the colonisers is rapidly disappearing.

- In many areas there is a growing inclusion of First Nations religious practices into Christian worship in First Nations congregations.[15]

- There is an increasingly strident call by First Nations Christians for the development of aboriginal theology.

- Extension education empowers local congregations/communities and develops local community theology which will usually pose a challenge to the established church leadership.

Sharks

In the visioning and/or evaluation processes our programmes have pursued we have often called the barriers to moving forward "sharks". While at least two global TEE conferences concluded that TEE and traditional residential training programmes were not mutually exclusive, I would need to note that a major shark continues to be the power of traditional educational institutions to eliminate extension programmes. People today often talk about systemic racism in our institutions. There is a systemic element in academic institutions which often makes it difficult to grasp the significance of local community theology.

Other sharks lurking everywhere include:

- The lack of financial support, which usually means choosing to spend money on shoring up the existing church infrastructure.

- Resistance to change of any kind (for extension education causes change).

- The need of church leaders, particularly clergy, to control things.

- The fragility of extension programmes—"when the champion departs the programme disappears".

- Cultural imperialism of the mainstream church and educational leaders.

CONCLUSION

Where TEE has interfaced over time with First Nations communities and fostered the growth of an indigenous church, I am confident such churches will continue to grow even if it requires a kind of separation from the main stream church structures and the establishment of new infrastructure.

The TEE movement itself will continue to struggle and be challenged by the traditional models of education despite the good will of many people to recognise that they are complementary, because a continuing result of TEE is that it challenges the mainstream. While the Dakota Leadership programme and Caledonia programmes fell to this conservative pressure, similar programmes will continue to arise elsewhere. TEE continues to be a global movement, and wherever it operates in ways in which the programmes are rooted in the Biblical materials, it cannot help but be revolutionary.

During the 1997 TEE and Technology conference there was an expressed feeling that we had developed a bridge between TEE and residential seminaries, that is, that both methods were important and complementary. Ross Kinsler concluded that meeting by reminding us of the following definition of TEE.

All God's people are called to minister. Churches all around the world have devised new programmes of TEE to equip people for ministry in the context of their varied life, work, and social-cultural settings. TEE offers new possibilities: it provides essential theological tools and opens doors to ministry for people previously excluded by age, educational level, family situation, social position, language, race, sex or occupation. It establishes new relationships between theological education and the church, teachers and students, theory and practice, theology and context, clergy and laity. It not only equips many more people for ministry, but it also engages those who's gifts and service most qualify them for leadership.

The simple statement that all God's people are called to minister still poses a challenge to the churches' institutional structures. Yet it remains a principle at the core of the biblical message. We ignore it at our peril.

John A. (Ian) MacKenzie

ianmackenzie@telus.net

Endnotes

1 The term "First Nations" in Canada denotes Indians, or native peoples. It has become the politically correct way to refer to native peoples in a country which up until recently described itself as the result of the two founding nations, that is, the English and the French. As native people began to shed the burden of colonialism during the past forty years they began to remind Canadians that they were already here when the colonisers arrived and that indeed they consisted, then as well as now, many nations. So the plural for "nations" also challenges the North American stereotype explicit in the term "Indians" which suggests all native people are the same. As an Odawa poet wrote as he began his presentation on Indian poetry, "There is no Indian poetry because there are no Indians".

2 A few years ago the present Bishop of Caledonia threatened to close the Anglican Church in the Nisga'a village of Lakalzap. When he met with the congregation a large turn out of elders made very clear to him that this church was their church and he could not close it. One elder, Simogit (Chief) Jacob McKay said to me later that the past thirty years of development led by previous bishops and clergy had broken the Nisga'a dependence on a Victorian model of the church and there was no way that they would return to it.

3 For information about Canada look up http://en.wikipedia.org/wiki/Canada.

4 These figures have changed in modern times—for example, the far northern congregations in Caledonia have been transferred to the Diocese of the Yukon.

5 While there is mixed feeling about how effective such a position might be, it is regarded by many as at least a beginning! The reader can find a discussion of this online at (http://www.anglican.ca/about/committees/acip/documents/acip-nib.pdf). In January the Primate of Canada announced the appointment of the Rt. Rev. Mark MacDonald, Bishop of Alaska. (http://www.anglican.ca/about/committees/acip/)

6 Robert K. Thomas and I have argued elsewhere that the Roman Catholic process made Indian villages into French peasant communities through the Oblate missionaries.

7 The National Chief as such a few years ago indicated this about himself. The reader can follow the tragic story of the church residential school era online at http://archives.cbc.ca/IDD-1-70-692/disasters_tragedies/residential_schools/

8 The history of land theft and the contemporary land claims process can be reviewed at http://cccm.nrcan.gc.ca/english/comprehensive_claims_e.asp. Follow the links. In British Columbia. The issue has always been described by the Nisga'a and others as the "land question" because the "land claims" language used by government suggests the First Nations are making a claim when, in fact, it is the government who are claiming ownership of land which is in fact owned by First Nations.

9 A quick summary of this can be found at http://www.ainc-inac.gc.ca/pr/info/nit_e.html as well as lots of references for a more detailed look at Canadian land question issues. For a Nisga'a perspective go to http://www.nisgaalisims.ca/?page=treaty/treaty.

10 The article has been rewritten and edited several times. The most recent version was published in *All who minister: New ways of serving God's people*, by Maylanne Maybee (Editor), Anglican Book Centre, 2003.

11 We had to translate the material from the Spanish.

12 The ecclesiastical Province consisted of all the Anglican Dioceses in British Columbia and the Yukon.

13 http://www.vst.edu/.

14 http://www.vst.edu/nativemin/index.php.

15 Examples would include the wearing of blankets in many North Coast communion services, the use of sweet grass and smudging in many services, the use of dried salmon at the Eucharist instead of or along with bread.

QUESTIONS FOR REFLECTION AND DISCUSSION

1. *What are the geographical and cultural reasons for adopting TEE among "First Nations" church leaders?*

2. *What are the biblical and theological reasons for adopting TEE among "First Nations" church leaders?*

3. *What are the historical and ideological reasons for adopting TEE among "First Nations" church leaders?*

4. *What are the educational components of this case study?*

5. *What kinds of resistance to this program have emerged over the years?*

Master of Arts in Global Leadership, Fuller Theological Seminary

by Robert Freeman

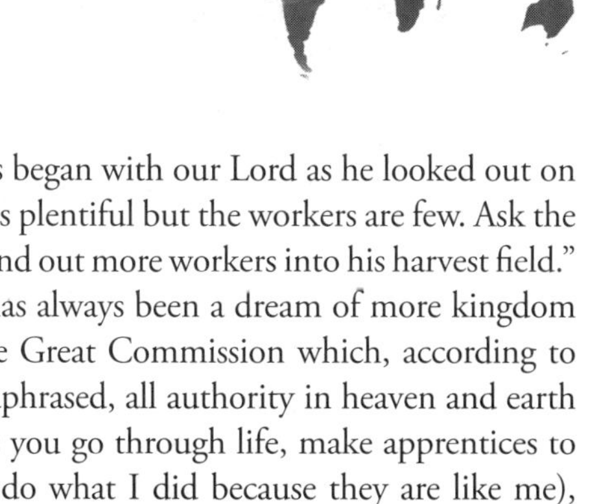

You might say that the dreams began with our Lord as he looked out on the crowds and said, "The harvest is plentiful but the workers are few. Ask the Lord of the harvest, therefore, to send out more workers into his harvest field." (Mt 9:37 8 NIV (1978)). There has always been a dream of more kingdom workers. Or when Jesus spoke the Great Commission which, according to Dallas Willard, might best be paraphrased, all authority in heaven and earth has been given to me, therefore as you go through life, make apprentices to me of all peoples (ones who will do what I did because they are like me), immersing them in the Trinitarian presence, and guiding them to obey all the things I have taught you, and surely I will be with you all day of every day (Willard 2002). There has always been a dream of better disciples who are apprentices of Jesus. More and better workers and disciples requires more and better leaders.

These dreams of more and better leaders led several who were associated with Fuller Seminary's School of World Mission (SWM), now the School of Intercultural Studies (SIS), to help develop an alternative method of leadership development known as Theological Education by Extension (TEE), beginning in the 1960s. They sought to help leaders who were already leading to stay in their positions while they trained. Primarily this included Ralph Winter, former missionary in Guatemala, and his colleague Fred Holland who worked in TEE in Zimbabwe and Zambia, along with Winter's colleagues in Guatemala, James Emery and Ross Kinsler. Peter Wagner also helped implement TEE in Bolivia, Paul Pierson in Portugal and Jehu Hanciles in Sierra Leone (Kraft 2005). Chuck Van Engen is currently working with a TEE doctoral program throughout Latin America. Thus, people associated with Fuller had a large voice in establishing and defining what became know as the TEE movement.

In recent decades, these dreams have been well voiced by what has come to be known as the missional church movement which calls for a new way of "doing" church and has profound implications for leadership development. Roxburgh and Romanuk in *The Missional Leader* describe the missional church with the following words: "Mission is not about a project or a budget, or a one-off event somewhere; it's not even about sending missionaries. A missional church is a community of God's people who live into the imagination that they are, by their very nature, God's missionary people living as a demonstration of what God plans to do in and for all creation in Jesus Christ" (Alan J. Roxburgh 2006). This calls for a dream of new types of leaders.

In addition to these dreams are the very specific dreams of thousands of leaders currently in ministry throughout the world who find themselves serving in leadership because their calling and gifting has been confirmed by their congregations, but they have had no opportunity for theological education. For instance, here are the stories of just two leaders newly enrolled in the Master of Arts in Global Leadership (MAGL) at Fuller.

> *After being a full-time teacher for the Department of Education in Hawaii for 12 years and a part-time pastor for eight of those 12 years, God has given me the green light to be a full-time pastor at my home church. In truth, the MAGL program seems tailor-made for what I believe God is calling me to do in my church, my community, and beyond. First, I hope to gain a better and deeper biblical perspective of the world and develop practical ways to share, teach, and encourage people within the church and my community about God's purpose for their lives. Second, our own church conference has been talking about employing missional teams within the local churches to help bring about needed changes in the way the Good News is being presented. I am looking forward to learning more about how the MAGL program can help me to understand how the missional teams may be able to accomplish their goals. Last, I live in one of the most culturally diverse areas in our nation. I have always worked well with everyone, no matter a person's ethnicity; I always look for what's in a person's heart. Therefore, I hope to achieve a better understanding of how people with diverse cultural views can contribute to a more global view of Christ.*
>
> *My husband, Jerry, and I have been missionaries since 1979. In 1985, we came to Guayaquil, Ecuador, where we founded a school and became pastors of a small two-year-old house church. Since then, the church and the school have grown. I'm currently leading our church's Sunday program for the children.*

We have over 1000 children attending on a given Sunday, and almost 400 volunteers are involved in this ministry. Most of the time I don't feel like I know what I'm doing. I need God's wisdom and skills to help me care for and prepare these volunteers. I am hoping this program gives me the tools to lead my staff, the volunteers and the children in an effective manner. I want to grow as a person to be everything God has for me. The job is bigger than I am.

For Janice and Brian and many like them, along with many leaders of the TEE and missional church movements, the MAGL is a dream coming true.

PRESENT REALITIES IN FULLER'S CONTEXT

The present need for an alternative leadership development method, at least in Fuller's primary context of the U.S. church, is found in a diagnosis of the current state of that church. Dr. Greg Ogden, former Director of Fuller's Doctor of Ministry program and current pastor, describes the situation in an issue of Fuller's audio subscription series, *The Pastor's Update* (Ogden 1988). What is it that underlies the changing landscape of ministry in the local U.S. church? His presentation is summarized below.

The Collapse of Christendom

There is a growing consensus among church observers that the church in Western culture is on an entirely different footing than it was even a generation ago. What we are witnessing in the changing forms of the church is a fundamental shift of the church's purpose from maintenance to mission. This changing purpose parallels the downfall of the Christendom context for the church (4th century through the 1950s) and the rise of a new paradigm of church in a Post-Christian era.

Loren Mead's seminal work, *The Once and Future Church* (Mead 1991), outlines the common characteristics of the church in the Christendom paradigm.

The sacred and secular were intertwined

The basic assumption was that for a stable social order to exist there must be shared moral underpinnings among the populace. To ensure this, the state backed the church as the arm through which religion and morality would be taught. Even in a country like the United States, which officially separated church and state, the church still was to play a stabilizing role in order for there to be a "functional Christendom" (Guder 1998).

Mission was a far-off enterprise

Since the nation was Christian, mission existed beyond the borders of the empire. The church sent and supported its missionaries to take Christianity to where it did not reign. Consequently, mission ceased to be the vocation of the ordinary Christian.

The congregation acted as a parish

Instead of the church being a "called-out" community with a distinct sub-culture, the church was a sub-set of the dominant culture. It was the center around which many Christian activities in the community emanated and were preserved. People were born into the church, rather than converted into it. People identified with a church in their region, even if they were not a part of a tight-knit community.

The role of the laity was to support the ministry of the clergy

The laity served to uphold the institution of the church by taking various organizational roles in the maintenance structure. This, in turn, created the context for the professionals to provide the ministry.

The role of the pastor under Christendom was to do the ministry

Four roles were honed and shaped over time that dominated the identity of the clergy. (1) The clergy preserved the theological and worship tradition of the denomination by presiding at worship, offering the sacraments, and teaching and preaching God's word. (2) They provided care for the ill, those who were grieving, and those in crisis. (3) They served as public symbols of the sacred, representatives of the respected institution of the church. (4) They presided over rites of passage such as baptism, confirmation, marriage and burial. The pastoral call under Christendom was clear and had high status.

The Changed Climate Surrounding the Church

The church under Christendom was a highly respected institution in a friendly environment. But much of that seems to have changed. The current milieu is shifting to what some are calling Post-Christian and postmodern. This means that the church is on a very different footing than it enjoyed under the favorable treatment of Christendom. What are the signs of change from friendly to ambivalent, to even hostile, surroundings?

The church has been marginalized and/or pushed to the edge of society. Stephen Carter in *The Culture of Disbelief* (Carter 1993), chronicles how recent court decisions and faulty reasoning have made it politically incorrect to state a moral or political conviction for public consumption from the standpoint of a religious or Biblical perspective. This is substantiated by Guder,

> *Notions of public morals gave way to personal decisions of expediency, pleasure and private judgment. People no longer assumed that the church had anything relevant to say on matters beyond personal faith. Public policy became*

increasingly secularized, as public morals became increasingly personalized and privatized (Guder 1998).

We have lost the memory of Christianity in our country. At one time in our nation's history, even if you were not Christian, your education would have made you familiar with the Biblical story and its images. Today, vast numbers of people who have come from other worldviews or religions as well as those with roots in this culture have no faith background or Biblical understanding.

Since the social revolution of the 1960s, basic Christian moral tenets have lost their influence to a highly individualized morality, where tolerance of any chosen lifestyle is the prevailing philosophy. Therefore, marriage is no longer a sacred institution, and certainly not one that serves to preserve the sanctity of the sexual union; doctors are not necessarily to preserve life; the poor, near to the heart of God, are the scapegoats for society's ills, etc.

Finally, many philosophers and theologians are saying that we are in the midst of a worldview shift in Western culture from the modern or Enlightenment perspective to one that is postmodern. What the shape of this will be is still emerging, but one characteristic of which we are sure is that truth will be seen as relative. Not only will all truth be personal, but there will be no objective truth to be found. This stands in direct opposition to a faith revealed in propositional truth and based on the work of one true Savior.

The Changed Purpose of the Church

The shift in cultural context reduces the maintenance purpose of the church under Christendom almost to irrelevance. Though certainly some of the same functions of the Christendom church will carry over to a new model, what is needed is a fundamental shift in the *de facto* purpose of the church from maintenance to mission. What underlies and gives shape to the "new paradigm" churches is the return to mission as the driving force of the church. Mission is no longer a far-off enterprise to be engaged in by a few, but also needs to be seen at the doorstep of the American church. It is to this fundamental shift that the "prophets" of our day are pointing us. The need to see the church in the West rediscover its identity as a missional community has served as the impetus to form the "Gospel and Our Culture Network." The Network has helped coin the term "missional" to stress that the challenge of our day for the traditional church is to find a way to redirect its energies to become again a mission church (abroad and at home) in a culture that does not predominantly share its worldview.

The Changed Profile of Church Leaders

For those of us who are involved in the training of church leaders, we must train and support this new profile church that is emerging in order to produce missional leaders—those who embody this rediscovered purpose of the church. As Ogden concludes, it is clear that in this transitional period, which could go on for decades, we will need leaders who share some of the following characteristics:

The Pastor as Missiologist

In order for Western churches to become mission outposts, pastors need to develop the skills of the missiologist. Pastors will be leading congregations to grow with a passion for effective evangelism as well as serving their communities through ministering to the broken lives of those outside their faith community. The communities surrounding most churches today have become increasingly multi-ethnic in language and varied in religious convictions. Also, in a day where the Gospel is not immediately accessible to the average person, its timeless message must find relevant expression.

The Pastor as Organizational "Re-inventor"

Church after church will have to move from structures that have been top-heavy in program maintenance to streamlined mission structures. The goal is to have fewer people involved in running the organization and more people involved in front lines mission.

The Pastor as Team Builder

One of the characteristics of the church as a mission outpost will be the breakdown of the clergy/laity bifurcation. All of God's people are needed to carry out the mission of the church in partnership with its equipping leaders. There is not be the luxury of equating the ministry with what the pastor does. Teams composed of pastors and lay people will form around a common mission to address a felt need or a place of brokenness in humanity.

The Pastor as Visionary Leader

It will most likely be pastors who lead the charge to help move the church from its maintenance profile to a mission outpost. Since change only occurs in a climate of urgency, it will require pastors who can read the times, see where we need to go, and call God's people to go with them. Along with the visionary role, pastors will also be leading a process to refocus the church's energy and clarify the foundational ministry values. The church not only needs to be an apostolic community, but increasingly in this day it must rediscover itself as a counter-culture community that reflects the lifestyle of a follower of Jesus which is counter to the dominant culture.

The Pastor as Leadership Developer

In a culture where many of the new believers in Christ will come into the church without even a memory of Christianity, there will need to be an intentional way to help develop followers of Christ into mature disciplers, who can become the next generation of lay and pastoral leaders. This will require a shift from the reaction, responder profile of the Christendom pastor to a proactive investment in the discipling of believers to maturity (Ogden 1990).

Along with these new roles, pastors will still be called upon to be teachers and caregivers. The need for leaders to understand the historical and Biblical foundations of our faith has never been greater. But they also need much more than that. Only a lifelong learning view of preparation can equip leaders for the dramatic and fast-paced changes of this new day. We are at an awkward and confusing time in the church. What once was is no longer working. What is yet to be is still taking form. This leads to role confusion and tremendous stress upon all involved. Our call as people preparing congregational leaders is to become as clear as we can about the nature of the missional church and the profile for those who can lead in this time of change and then to provide access to training for those who show promise as those missional leaders. The most important step in the design of any training program is to train the right people. Where can we find these new missional leaders? The best place to find proven leaders is to find them already leading. Such leaders will require a new paradigm of in-ministry leadership formation which allows them to remain in their leadership role while they study.

Overview of Fuller's Response to Its Context

Over the last four decades Fuller Theological Seminary has responded to the need for lifelong, in-service education through the development of programs associated with what is now called the Horner Center for Lifelong Learning (HCLL). In addition to the Schools of Theology (SOT), Psychology (SOP) and Intercultural Studies (SIS), HCLL forms the fourth division of Fuller. It includes one of the largest Doctor of Ministry programs in the world in which approximately 900 pastors are enrolled each year for post Master of Divinity work after having at least three years of ministry experience. HCLL also includes six major extension centers throughout the western U.S. which offer Masters degrees. Approximately 800 students are enrolled in these centers each fall. Finally, in terms of credit programs, HCLL has dramatically expanded the use of distance learning courses, where teacher and students are separated by geographical distance or time constraints. These courses now enroll approximately 450 students each fall. Individualized Distance Learning (IDL) courses include audio files and text resources that can be studied at the students' own pace. Approximately 20 courses are available in this format, which can also be downloaded in electronic format (http://www.fuller.edu/cll/dl/—IDL). Fuller Online (FOL) offers approximately 8 courses per quarter in a fully interactive experience via the internet at www.fulleronline.org. Therefore, the credit programs specifically designed for in-service leaders enroll approximately 2150 of Fuller's 4000 students each fall (Wakeman 2006). The most recent degree program to be designed for these in-service leaders is the MAGL which is described in detail below.

MAGL Educational Model

While the educational model for the Master of Arts in Global Leadership uses the foundation of TEE, it attempts to correct some weaknesses of that model as previously applied. It does this by taking advantage of the convergence of several communications technologies in the internet and firmly undergirding the program with principles of adult education theory.

Foundations of TEE

In Ralph Winter's book, *Theological Education by Extension* (William Carey Library, 1969), he describes the relationship between TEE and the seminary:

> *The traditional U.S. Protestant seminary has in the past sixty or seventy years become two things, prominently: a) a community of scholars carrying on research as professional academicians, and b) a place where candidates for the ordained ministry (and Christian scholarship) are trained. The extension seminary as we will use the term here, does in no way intend to replace or play down the first crucial function, but it does intend to operate parallel to the latter by a new method which allows a wider, and perhaps superior, selection of students (as well as a larger number),* training them for ministry whether scholarly or pastoral or both *(Winter 1969).*

Winter defines an extension method as "Any method that allows a person to continue as a member of society, earning his support" (Winter 1969). Many mission leaders then go on to distinguish an extension seminary or TEE from Christian Education. Winter writes, "The Extension Seminary, as we use the term, is not primarily set up to offer a course of basic Christian training, but is not in any sense opposed to the idea" (Winter 1969). They define TEE as education of church leaders. The two important points being: it is training beyond Christian Education (necessary for all church members), and it aims to educate *church-chosen leaders* as against training *for* leadership (Winter 1969). The concern in this movement is to extend the resources of theological education in order to reach the people who are the natural leaders of the church and to encourage and enable local leaders to develop their gifts and ministries without leaving their homes, jobs, communities, and local congregations (Hill 1974).

Thus, having been developed in a part of the world where the number of young churches is growing faster than the supply of trained leaders, TEE has come to be defined not as an alternative method of teaching but as a new system of developing church leadership. The extension philosophy involves starting with the *person* rather than the *institution*. In this model, the task of the seminary is not to *make* leaders; the calling of the seminary is to *train* the leaders that God has already made (Kinsler 1978). We need an institution, but the institution should not be the starting point. Consider this as an alternative starting point: first answer the questions, "Who should be trained for the ministry, what ministries require special training, and what kinds of training will produce the needed knowledge, skills and attitudes?" Then find these people and establish institutions that conform to the needs of the students (Wagner 1974).

Weaknesses of TEE

Building on this foundation, conversations between this author and Dr. Eddie Elliston, former Associate Dean of Fuller's School of World Mission, began in 1996 about developing a TEE degree from Fuller Seminary. In these conversations we attempted to find ways of overcoming some weaknesses that had caused the TEE movement to stall, such as a poor completion rate, reliance on one technology of the programmed learning notebook, which did not facilitate much interaction, and lack of credibility with established denominations and accrediting agencies due to not having a well recognized philosophy of education undergirding the movement.

Toward Missional TEE with the MAGL

Building on the TEE foundation and early conversations, the following philosophy was put forth to undergird the MAGL:

> *Fuller's mission is "to equip men and women for the manifold ministries of Christ and his church."*

Perhaps this should be edited to say "help equip," because it is God who calls and gifts people for ministry and the church that confirms those people by observing them in ministry. Seminary education is a valuable part of the process, but it alone does not equip people for ministry. That said, important questions to ask would be, "Are seminaries enrolling people who have been called and gifted, and are we getting enough of them to meet the needs of ministries for leaders?"

There are two main reasons why Fuller's mission should be extended through distance education. First is that Pasadena and other residential seminaries *cannot* educate the number of leaders required. Second is that Pasadena and other residential seminaries *should not* educate them all even if they could! Why? While technologically enhanced distance education may have some disadvantages over residential study, it also has certain advantages, particularly in reaching proven leaders who are already in ministry. The strengths of both of these systems are needed because changes in the world are changing the nature of how the church "does business," thus requiring more and better leaders.

With this as a beginning point, then, the comments below will focus on using distance education in a complementary approach to, rather than a replacement of, the current residential model. Let us briefly list several presuppositions, then describe the elements of what might be termed "Missional" theological education and how technology can help provide the ability to accomplish it. Finally, we will address the important concerns of how formation and community can take place in this type of technology-mediated distance education. As will be seen in the program description section, all of these aspects have been important in the design of the MAGL.

Presuppositions

Technology should not be the basis of change

The reasons for us to make changes in the way we do things are not solely because we can make changes. However, a very important question is, What opportunities for better teaching and learning are offered by technology? Would not the fact that the cost of communication is becoming basically free, resulting in the death of distance as an important factor in communication, have important implications for education?

The current paradigm was not always the dominant paradigm

The ways we do theological education today are not the same ways we have always done them and, lest our modernist worldview blind us, might not always be the best ways yet discovered. Certainly, they will not always be the way we do them in the future.

Personal/spiritual formation is essential for ministry leaders

However, more interesting questions might be, "Does this require *Being There* (the title of the Association of Theological Schools President Dan Aleshire's book on the subject) (Carroll 1997) or would it be better to ask Being Where?", "What is formation and how is it done?" and "How well is it currently done?"

Community is essential for learning

Learning takes place best in community. Again, more interesting questions might be, "Which community?", "What is community and how is it formed?" and "How well is it currently done?"

Towards Missional Theological Education for all of God's People

Major aspects of missional theological education

With these presuppositions, let us attempt to describe the major aspects of what might be called Missional Theological Education for all of God's People. According to Banks,

> *The missional model of theological education places the main emphasis on theological mission, on hands-on partnership in ministry based on interpreting the traditions and reflecting on practice with a strong spiritual and communal dimension. On this view theological education is primarily, though not exclusively, concerned with actual service—informed and transforming—of the kingdom and therefore focuses on acquiring cognitive, spiritual-moral, and practical obedience (Banks 1999).*

Banks lists several implications of this model for the way we envision and undertake theological education:

- It ought to comprehend the broader **people of God**, not just an elite cadre.

- It should orient itself primarily around **"in-service"** ministry activities.

- At its center should be a living and working partnership or **mentorship** with an experienced person.

- It can be done either **in residence or in extension.**

- It should have a stronger connection between **seminary and church** and between **study and practice** (Banks 1999).

Banks also points out that "Whatever seminaries contribute to their members' theological education, it is only a part of what should be a **lifelong process** ... All this calls for closer links between theological institutions and other structured forms of Christian life (Banks 1999)."

To Banks' list of characteristics of missional education, we should add that the educational process should be **personalized** within a community. In other words, differences in worldview (whether cultural or modern/post-modern) or differences in learning styles should be taken into account. In addition, according to adult learning theory, adult students should be given a large say in what they are to study.

How technology can facilitate missional theological education

It seems easy to see how all of the characteristics mentioned above could be done well in a circumstance where the theological education was taken to the student who remained in service. Technology, especially the convergence of several technologies in the Internet, can facilitate this. In fact, technology is not only changing the way courses can be delivered and the way they can be taught, but also the nature of the educational process. Specifically, the challenges to education by the increasing sophistication and influence of information technologies are large and complex but include (a) an increase in the ways that education can be delivered to bridge both time and distance gaps between learners and teachers, thus transforming *where and when* we do education; (b) an increased ability to use various methods in teaching/learning, thus transforming the *way* we do education; and (c) a redefinition of the *why* of education away from the accumulation of knowledge to the ability to find, sort through, and think critically about the knowledge that will be bombarding people (Connick and Russo 1994).

Formation and Community or Being Where?

Let us turn to the important question of how **formation** and **community** could be accomplished in such a missional, in-service situation. As Banks argues, "It is precisely undertaking mission alongside others rather than imitating them in the abstract that provides the strongest stimulus to spiritual formation (Banks 1999)." He also reports from a 1992 survey of seminaries that less than 40 percent of students felt that their experience helped them grow spiritually. Fuller's experience as reported in the 1996 Communicorp survey seems to be better, as 70% of extension, 68% of SWM, 67% of SOT, and 58% of SOP students agreed with the statement that their experience increased their spiritual maturity (Communicorp 1996).

Banks notes a dilution of community as one of the problems facing theological institutions today and lists the increase in commuter students, in work and family obligations, and in general time pressures as some of its causes. He also points out the increased diversity of student bodies and the challenges that this poses for community. Increasing the use of small groups and house church type groups are his major suggestions for dealing with these issues (Banks 1999).

All of us would admit that it is not just the number of leaders, nor just the knowledge of leaders, but also the spiritual maturity of those leaders that counts—and how can you do that at a distance? Eddie Elliston, in a helpful presentation to the Fuller faculty (Elliston 1997), listed several key variables related to this question. In each case, the issue for formation is not location, but accessibility:

- **Instructors.** If accessibility for meaningful interaction is the concern, little difference may in fact be present between residential and distance education.

- **Existing Leaders/Mentors.** If the goal is to develop pastors and local church leaders, then learners may in fact be distanced from their important mentors in a residential program.

- **Formative/Supportive Community.** Being present in either or both church and seminary communities may provide opportunities for formation, but cannot insure it. Many see the seminary as *the* primary place and time to "form" Christian leaders. Yet, the role of the church in leadership formation in this view may be overlooked, neglected, or even in some cases depreciated.

- **Learning Community.** A residential setting may better provide a safe environment to address complex, difficult or controversial issues. An environment where diverse and perhaps contradictory opinions are expressed may be established. Interaction with fellow learners who bring a wealth of diverse experience serves to produce important aspects of a learning community. However, the community to be served still provides the primary context for the *practice* and the *longer-term formation* of the emerging leader.

- **Applicational Context.** Learning *about* leading and what to do is not the same as *practicing* in a real context. While the simulations on a campus may be analogous and useful for practice, they are not equivalent. A role-play, a simulation, preaching in a preaching lab, or the writing of a paper may all be useful. However, all these contrast significantly from the context for which students are preparing.

- **Learning Resources.** Distance learners may be distant from a significant library, faculty, staff and other students. If, on the other hand, learning resources include experience and experienced practitioners who mentor, model, empower and sponsor, then these resources may be better found in an in-service setting.

To summarize: What is distant in distance education? One can see that a number of issues may in fact generate "distance." Some of these variables generate more distance in a residential setting, while others generate more distance in an "extended" or in-service setting. Distance is not just a function of geography, but more one of accessibility for interaction with the key formative variables.

It is often said of distance education that, "The educational experience is not the same." Truly, it is not the same, but questions of quality are different from those of formal equivalence. Even the Association of Theological Schools' (ATS) standards have changed the measure to be, "Is the educational experience *appropriate to the purposes* of the program?"

In addition to allowing formation and community to happen in the context of service, Internet technologies can also facilitate community as described. People seeking commonality and shared interests can form groups and communities in order to pursue the interests that distinguish them from other groups. In the past, communities were generally considered to be place based. Today, involvement in a community is not assumed to be based on where you live or have family connections, but it does take a conscious commitment (Palloff 1999). Shaffer and Anderson (Shaffer and Anundsen 1993) define community as a dynamic whole that emerges when a group of people share common practices, are interdependent, make decisions jointly, identify themselves with something larger than the sum of their individual relationships, and make a long-term commitment to well-being (their own, one another's, and the group's). Online groups normally go through the same stages of forming, norming, storming, performing and adjourning as face-to-face groups.

Palloff and Pratt point out that in excellent online learning, just as often times on campus, the development of community becomes a parallel stream to the content being explored. Community formation is given its own equal status and is not seen as something that "mucks up" or interferes with the learning process. Social communication is an essential component of educational activity. Just as a face-to-face school provides places for students to congregate socially, an online educational environment should provide a space, such as a virtual café, for informal discourse. Online instructors usually establish minimal guidelines for participation, which differs significantly from the face-to face classroom. The ability to think before responding and to comment whenever the student wishes helps to create a level of participation and engagement that can be substantial. Some of the desired outcomes indicating that an online community has been formed, would include: active interaction involving course content and personal communication, collaborative learning evidenced by student-to-student comments, socially constructed meaning evidenced by agreement or questioning, sharing of resources among students, and expressions of support and encouragement between students (Palloff 1999).

In conclusion, the educational philosophy undergirding the MAGL focuses on finding proven leaders and then coming alongside what God is already doing in their lives through an adult-oriented, lifelong learning view of education. This education takes place in the context of their ministry and in community with other in-service leaders through the use of Internet technologies. In this way it advances Fuller's mission and helps equip more and better leaders for the manifold ministries of Christ and his church.

PROGRAM DESCRIPTION

The following section describes how the MAGL educational philosophy has been fleshed out in terms of program outcomes. It describes the MAGL mission, vision, values, goals and learning objectives.

Mission, Vision, Values

The faculty of the MAGL have articulated the following mission, vision and values for the program:

> *Our mission is to provide transformational graduate education for ministry to in-service leaders in all parts of the world.*

> *Our vision is to see more and better leaders of missional churches and ministries who are lifelong learners associated with biblically informed learning communities.*

Some values of the MAGL are:

- **Global.** Since this is a Master of Arts in Global Leadership, it is important to define what we mean by global and what we do not mean. What we mean includes: the program is to be delivered globally, students will study with other leaders from around the world, they will be exposed to global trends, they will be introduced to cultural contextual analysis. What we do not mean is that they will lead a global enterprise or that they can be deeply exposed to global trends or contextual analysis.

- **Missional.** The missional church movement influences our thinking deeply; however, we recognize that most of our students will not be coming from or going to "missional" churches.

- **In-service leaders.** We believe, according to Acts 4, that it is Christ who appoints and gifts people for leadership, not their education or position. We desire to find those people who have already been identified by their church body as having this appointment and to work with them. We believe that learning takes place most effectively by doing and then reflecting and then doing it again. Consequently, we want to work with people while they function in a leadership role.

- **Biblically informed learning communities.** Learning is a social enterprise where leaders can learn best from peers who have dealt with similar issues and where they can receive mutual support.

- **Adult and lifelong education.** We intend to begin to transform not only what is taught but how it is taught. As faculty, we desire to behave as guides on the side, rather than sages on the stage. We desire to affect the inner transformation of our students so that their leadership will flow out of who they are as gifted and called individuals.

Goals and objectives for the MAGL

Biblically Informed Practice—the Origin and Objective of Leadership

1. Graduates will integrate theology and praxis to develop biblically informed responses to situations encountered in their ministry/mission.
By the end of the program, students will have:

- Examined and critiqued a variety of contemporary and historical theological paradigms.

- Constructed plans for biblical/missional engagement with society in response to issues encountered.

Missional Church—the Goal of Leadership

2. Graduates will make plans for their church's missional engagement with their cultural context(s) to promote transformation.
By the end of the program, students will have:

- Contrasted traditional and missional forms of church life.

- Developed a biblically informed plan to engage local and global culture in indigenous ways.

- Designed a holistic framework of ministry to promote personal and social transformation.

Global Diversity—the Context of Leadership

3. Graduates will demonstrate familiarity with the diversity of theories, practices, and global contexts of missional leadership.
By the end of the program, students will have:

- Distinguished issues of modernity/postmodernity impacting their local ministry/mission.

- Identified the effects of globalization on their local contexts and churches.

- Developed missiological plans of engagement that reflect both local and global dimensions.

Lifelong Learning in a Diverse Community—the Continuing Development of Leadership

4. Graduates will employ a lifelong learning posture that values peer learning with diverse persons as well as reflection on practice.
   By the end of the program, students will have:

   - Developed and fulfilled a personal learning plan.

   - Investigated adult learning principles.

   - Participated in a diverse community of learning which incorporated peer learning and reflection on practice.

Organizational Dynamics—the Implementation of Leadership

5. Graduates will examine various organizational dynamics and apply selected administrative tools.
   By the end of the program, students will have:

   - Observed their church/organization from a variety of perspectives.

   - Evaluated their church/organization in order to diagnose health and offer prescriptives if necessary.

   - Sharpened their administrative expertise.

Leadership Development and Character—the Heart of Leadership

6. Graduates will implement a developmental perspective that prioritizes personal spiritual formation.
   By the end of the program, students will have:

   - Described and evaluated their ongoing personal leadership development.

   - Designed and implemented relationally-based plans for character development & mentoring.

   - Identified resources to facilitate lifelong development as a leader.

Study Program Details

To accomplish these outcomes, the MAGL study program is designed around three primary building blocks: a student learning plan, a cohort learning community, and core global leadership courses. These building blocks are then cemented together by technology and quality online courses.

Student Learning Plans

In implementing adult education theory, the MAGL believes that one of the most important educational resources for a program like this is the students' prior experiences. Consequently, during their first course, students create a learning plan to guide their studies. This plan begins with a personal assessment, including previous experience and learning (formal, nonformal and informal), a short autobiography, and input from a ministry colleague on what he/she might see as needed goals. Based on this, the student crafts a set of personal, professional and academic goals along with a statement of purpose for the program. These goals and purpose are then compared with the MAGL learning outcomes to identify areas which the student has already "covered" and areas where more work would be helpful. The plan then continues by having the student address the needs for a required mentoring experience along with time management and resource issues. Finally, the student creates a personal "rule of life" or a commitment to certain spiritual practices or priorities to be followed during the program and works collaboratively with the entire cohort to create a community rule of practice. This learning plan becomes a working document that is updated regularly throughout the program as circumstances change.

Cohort Learning Community

The Master of Arts in Global Leadership is an 18-course program that combines aspects of intensive residential and distance education. It seeks to serve people engaged in culturally diverse ministries while they remain in their ministry context.

Students selected to enter this program must meet the general standards for admission to the Seminary, must have at least four years of ministry experience, and must be actively engaged in a leadership role (significant professional or lay responsibility in a church, parachurch, or agency of at least 10 hours per week). They must also submit a letter of recommendation from the ministry in which they are serving. The program is designed to be completed over five years rather than the standard two years of full-time study. Students entering the program are assigned to a cohort of approximately 25 students who will take 9 courses (equivalent of one year in residence) together. The remaining 9 courses may be taken with a combination of Pasadena, extension or distance learning courses.

Cohorts members are admitted competitively with a view toward creating the best possible diverse mix of in-ministry leaders. As an example, in the fall of 2006, the MAGL admitted its 11th cohort composed of 27 leaders serving in 7 countries around the world. Countries of service include Indonesia, Costa Rica, Japan, India, Ecuador and Canada, as well as the majority (21) from the U.S. Like their predecessors, these leaders bring a wealth of experience, having an average age of 40 (ranging from 24 to 60) with an average of 11 years in ministry (ranging from 4 to 27). These 8 women and 19 men serve in 18 denominations as pastors (11), missionaries (5), business managers (2), business CEOs (2), ministry program directors (3), evangelist (1), fund raiser (1), Salvation Army officer (1) and denomination executive (1).

Curriculum of Core Courses

As adult leaders in diverse situations, students' learning needs will also be very diverse. The curriculum therefore has been designed to provide flexibility to each student in fulfilling the 9 courses outside of the cohort sequence. The flexibility of one half of the course offerings allows students to strengthen areas of weakness, while the core global leadership focus brings each cohort to a clearer understanding of mission and leadership in their respective ministries. A central theme of the core courses is missional leadership.

Illustrative Time Frame

Quarter 1	Admitted to program, purchase books and set up computers
	Take online *Developing Your Learning Plan*
Quarter 2	Assigned readings and complete reports for intensive #1
	Attend 2 Intensive Courses in Pasadena
Quarter 3	*Character, Community and Leadership*
	Biblical Foundations of Mission
	Complete assignments for above
Quarter 4	Take online *Lifelong Development*
Quarter 5	Take online *Mentoring*
Quarter 6	Take online *Contemporary Culture in Missiological Perspective*
Quarter 7	Take online *Becoming a Missional Church*
	Prepare readings for intensive #2
Quarter 8	Attend 2 Intensive Courses in Pasadena
	Understanding Organizational Dynamics
	Global Leadership: Implications for Ministry
Quarter 9	Complete assignments for above
Quarter 10-20	Finish the remaining 9 courses via Pasadena, extension, online or Individualized Distance Learning

Technology & Online Course Quality

One of the major challenges in developing the MAGL was the issue of how to fund the hardware and software technology necessary for a quality online program. This required that Fuller provide a "public side" web site that offered prospective and current students all of the services normally offered on-campus and a "private side" site where the latest course delivery technology and 24/7 help desk for a global student body would be available. An in-house solution would have required a large upfront investment, which was not available. Consequently, Fuller chose to work with eCollege (www.eCollege.com) which provided all of this for a per user fee.

The public side site at http://fulleronline.org/ provides students with links to information about Fuller, how to apply and register, course information, and student services such as academic advising, library, bookstore, and financial aid. Also included is technical information and a browser test to help students know what hardware and software are needed to participate. Finally, the public side has a short quiz, "Is online learning right for you?" and a demo course.

The private side offers the latest in course delivery technology to display and interact with course materials. This includes an online grade book to give feedback, email and chat functions, document sharing, webliography and asynchronous threaded discussion boards. Course material can be presented as text, audio or video, although, in order to insure that students with low bandwidth connections can participate, video is seldom used.

In order to have outside benchmarks to insure quality of our online courses, Fuller has regularly submitted courses to the Association of Continuing Education Schools and Seminaries (ACCESS) yearly course of the year contest to have them assessed by an outside expert. Their feedback has been very positive. In addition, the MAGL will use the following rubric (see the next page) created by http://www.QualityMatters.org, a consortium of 19 Maryland community colleges, as a way to review our courses (MarylandOnline 2006).

Quality Matters Rubric for Online Courses

		Standard	Points
Course Overview and Introduction	I.1	Navigational instructions make the organization of the course easy to understand	3
	I.2	A statement introduces the student to the course and to the structure of the student learning and, in the case of a hybrid course, clarifies the relationship between the face-to-face and online components	3
	I.3	Etiquette expectations with regard to discussions, email, and other forms of communication are stated clearly	2
	I.4	The self-introduction by the instructor is appropriate and available online	1
	I.5	Students are requested to introduce themselves to the class	1
	I.6	Minimum technology requirements, minimum student skills, and, if applicable, prerequisite knowledge in the discipline are clearly stated	1
Learning Objectives	II.1	The course learning objectives describe outcomes that are measurable	3
	II.2	The module/unit learning objectives describe outcomes that are measurable and consistent with the course-level objectives	3
	II.3	The learning objectives are stated clearly and written from the students' perspective	2
	II.4	Instructions to students on how to meet the learning objectives are adequate and stated clearly	2
	II.5	The learning objectives address content mastery, critical thinking skills, and core learning skills	2
Assessment and Measurement	III.1	The types of assessments selected measure the stated learning objectives and are consistent with course activities and resources	3
	III.2	The course grading policy is stated clearly	3
	III.3	Specific and descriptive criteria are provided for the evaluation of students' work and participation	3
	III.4	The assessment instruments selected are sequenced, varied, and appropriate to the content being assessed	2
	III.5	"Self-check" or practice types of assignments are provided for timely student feedback	1
Resources and Materials	IV.1	The instructional materials support the stated learning objectives	3
	IV.2	The instructional materials have sufficient breadth, depth, and currency for the student to learn the subject	3
	IV.3	The purpose of each course element is explained	2
	IV.4	The instructional materials are logically sequenced and integrated	1
	IV.5	All resources and materials used in the course are appropriately cited	1

cont. on next page

Learner Engagement	V.1	The learning activities promote the achievement of stated learning objectives	3
	V.2	Learning activities foster instructor-student, content-student, and if appropriate to this course, student-student interaction	3
	V.3	Clear standards are set for instructor response and availability (turn-around time for email, grade posting, etc.)	3
	V.4	The requirements for course interaction are clearly articulated	2
	V.5	The course design prompts the instructor to be active and engaged with the students	2
Course Technology	VI.1	The tools and media support the learning objectives, and are appropriately chosen to deliver the content of the course	3
	VI.2	The tools and media enhance student interactivity and guide the student to become a more active learner	2
	VI.3	Technologies required for this course are either provided or easily downloadable	2
	VI.4	The course components are compatible with existing standards of delivery modes	1
	VI.5	Instructions on how to access resources at a distance are sufficient and easy to understand	1
	VI.6	The course design takes full advantage of available tools and media	1
Learner Support	VII.1	The course instructions articulate or link to a clear description of the technical support offered	2
	VII.2	Course instructions articulate or link to an explanation of how the institution's academic support system can assist the student in effectively using the resources provided	2
	VII.3	Course instructions articulate or link to an explanation of how the institution's student support services can assist the student in effectively using the resources provided	1
	VII.4	Course instructions articulate or link to tutorials and resources that answer basic questions related to research, writing, technology, etc.	1
Accessibility	VIII.1	The course acknowledges the importance of ADA requirements	3
	VIII.2	Course pages and course materials provide equivalent alternatives to auditory and visual content	1
	VIII.3	Course pages have links that are self-describing and meaningful	1
	VIII.4	The course demonstrates sensitivity to readability issues	1

To meet Quality Matters review expectations a course must: Answer 'Yes' to all 3-point Essential Standards: I.1, I.2, II.1, II.2, III.1, III.2, III.3, IV.1, IV.2, V.1, V.2, V.3, VI.1, VIII.1 **AND** Earn 68 or more points

OBSERVATIONS

The primary feedback about the program to date has been from student response and from one peer review visit by a team from the Association of Theological Schools. Since the peer review report addressed the student response, it will be summarized below.

ATS Visit Team Response

In the fall of 2003 the ATS sent a visiting team to conduct interviews with members of the senior administrative team, faculty and students in the program, to review materials and to assess the program. The team (Bourgond, Williams et al. 2003) listed the following strengths of the program:

- Strong administrative team with a convergence of mission, vision and values

- Resident and adjunct faculty trained to provide technology mediated delivery

- Time frame of the degree reasonable for students engaged in ministry

- Degree design provides flexibility based on needs, values and calling of students

- Cohort phase of shared learning and community building

- Initial online technology check and learning style quiz

- Developing a learning plan requires students to take responsibility for their learning

- Good diversity of student population

- Several course delivery options

- Fuller online courses rival the best in the field

- Student feedback is overwhelmingly positive

- Leadership emergence theory is the backbone of the degree

- Very comprehensive set of evaluation criteria

- Strong technological and student support systems

- Team teaching arrangements with teaching assistants

- Mentoring requirement

- Library support

The team listed the following concerns of the program (and Fuller's response to date is shown in parenthesis):

- Community after the cohort part of the program (will be developing an ongoing community of practice using blogs and eportfolios, see opportunities below).

- Student attrition (provided for short term leaves of absence and have increased the size of entering cohorts to account for attrition which is to be expected with in-service leaders).

- Technological resource funding (still a problem despite generous gifts from one Trustee).

- Development and training of faculty (twice yearly development retreats).

- Too much use of IDL courses (now limited to 4).

- Little material on character development (developed the course *Character, Community and Leadership*).

- How will learning outcomes be assessed in courses (course alignment process created)?

- Students desire more interaction with professors in online courses (still a problem in some courses).

- How will formation be assessed (character assessment paper due in *Character, Community and Leadership*)?

- How are findings from evaluation implemented (program assessment process with evidence created)?

- Plans for reentry of inactive students (advisors have created petitions for students to change cohorts).

Challenges and Opportunities for the MAGL

Affordability, recruitment and retention remain challenges for the MAGL. Of course all three of these are closely linked. The current cost of just one course in the MAGL is $1120. This has resulted in only 67 (25%) of the matriculated students being "international," and most of those are western missionaries serving internationally. Few international leaders can afford to pay Fuller's tuition rate, and the MAGL has very limited financial aid resources. Women are still underrepresented (59 or 22%) in the program, although this is probably due to their being underrepresented in ministry leadership. Retention is always a problem for in-service leaders as the demands of leadership and family regularly compete with time for study. However, appropriate admissions criteria and cohort community have so far helped to keep attrition to a reasonable level. Between the beginning of the program in fall 2002 and the fall of 2006, 266 leaders have matriculated into the program in 11 cohorts. Of these, 30 have graduated, 39 (15%) have withdrawn, and 7 are on an extended leave of absence.

A great opportunity exists for the MAGL to create an on-going, global community from students and graduates of the program using internet tools. Students have expressed an interest in staying "connected" as a community of practice which shares resources through such electronic avenues as blogs (an electronic journal) and eportfolios (an electronic repository of resources). Development of such a community will begin in summer 2007 and offers the potential of encouraging the on-going development of these leaders.

IMPLICATIONS FOR THE FUTURE OF TEE

The primary building blocks of the MAGL have promise to help TEE overcome some of its previous limitations. The problems of high dropout rates are helped by admissions requirements that insure that the right people are admitted to the program. A high level of community encourages students to continue, and with today's Internet technologies community can now happen anyplace, anytime. The Internet provides the convergence of multiple technologies so that we can transform not just where and when we educate leaders but also how and why we educate them. Finally, the field of adult education theory now provides a well accepted philosophy to undergird TEE, thus helping it fulfill its dream of more and better missional leaders.

Robert Freeman

rfreeman@fuller.edu

REFERENCES

Bible
> 1978 *The Holy Bible: New International Version.* Grand Rapids, Zondervan Bible Publishers.

Alan J. Roxburgh, F. R.
> 2006 *The Missional Leader.* San Francisco, CA, Jossey-Bass.

Banks, R.
> 1999 *Reenvisioning Theological Education: Exploring a Missional Alternative to Current Models.* Grand Rapids, MI, William B. Eerdmans Publishing Company.

Bourgond, G. W., D. E. Williams, et al.
> 2003 Report of a focussed visit, Association of Theological Schools.

Carroll, J. W. W., Barbara G.; Aleshire, Daniel O.; Marler, Penny Long
   1997 *Being There: Culture and Formation in Two Theological Schools*. New York, NY, Oxford University Press, Inc.

Carter, S. L.
   1993 *The Culture of Disbelief*. New York, N.Y., Basic Books/Harper Collins Publishers.

Communicorp
   1996 "CEE student survey: responses to open-ended questions."

Connick, G. P. and J. A. Russo
   1994 "Higher Education in the Age of Information." *Connection*. IX: 14-16.

Elliston, E. J.
   1997 *Developing Leaders at a Distance: Do We Need a New Paradigm?* Inagural address, Fuller Theological Seminary.

Guder, D. L.
   1998 *Missional Church: A Vision for the Sending of the Church in North America*. Grand Rapids, Mi, William B. Eerdmans Publishing Company.

Hill, L. D.
   1974 *Designing a Theological Education by Extension Program: A Philippine case study*. Pasadena, CA, William Carey Library.

Kinsler, F. R.
   1978 *The Extension Movement in Theological Education*. Pasadena, CA, William Carey Library.

Kraft, C.
   2005 *SWM/SIS at Forty*. Pasadena, William Carey Library.

MarylandOnline
   2006 Quality Matters Rubric.

Mead, L. B.
   1991 *The Once and Future Church: Reinventing the Congregation for a New Frontier*. Washington, D.C., Alban Institute.

Ogden, G.
   1988 "Pastoring between the Paradigms." *The Pastor's Update*. Pasadena, Fuller Theological Seminary.

   1990 *The New Reformation: Returning the Ministry to the People of God*. Grand Rapids, MI, Zondervan Publishing House.

Palloff, R. M. and K. Pratt
   1999 *Building Learning Communities in Cyberspace*. San Francisco, CA, Jossey-Bass Inc., Publishers.

Shaffer, C. and K. Anundsen
   1993 *Creating Community Anywhere*. New York, N.Y., Tarcher/Putnum.

Wagner, C. P.
> 1974 "Seminaries ought to be asking who as well as how." *Theological Education* 10(4).

Wakeman, W.
> 2006 Fuller Seminary Fall Enrollment Report. R. Freeman. Pasadena, Fuller Theological Seminary.

Willard, D.
> 2002 *Renovation of the Heart: Putting on the Character of Christ*. Colorado Springs, CO, NavPress.

Winter, R., Ed.
> 1969 *Theological Education by Extension*. South Pasadena, CA, William Carey Library.

QUESTIONS FOR REFLECTION AND DISCUSSION

1. *What does the collapse of Christendom mean for the purpose and orientation of theological education? What is missional theological education, according to this case study?*

2. *What is the place and understanding of leadership in this case study? What does this understanding indicate about the where, the how, and the why of theological education?*

3. *What are the learning and formational advantages and disadvantages of centralized, residential theological education, according to this case study? What are the advantages and disadvantages of distance or extension theological education?*

4. *What are the educational components of Fuller's Master of Arts in Global Leadership?*

5. *What are the missional goals of Fuller's Master of Arts in Global Leadership? Does your program of theological education include similar goals?*

The Open Russian Theological Academy

by Michael Huggins

I am very interested in the goals of the ORTA-SEAN training program. I am very concerned about the gap between church and society with its serious problems of marriage breakdowns, high divorce rate, abortion, drugs, alcohol and the problem of homeless children. I strongly believe that the church has a duty to bridge the gap, and, if necessary, pay the price that may be required to heal the sick, aid the poor and help those in prison. The church can too easily be distracted by the latest movement. We should concentrate on "train and penetrate" rather than just fill churches.

Gennady Ivkov
Baptist Bishop of the Primor'ye Region
Far East Russia

The Open Russian Theological Academy, ORTA, was founded in 2004. The mission of ORTA is to bring effective discipleship training through a Theological Education by Extension (TEE) programme based on the Latin American SEAN programme. ORTA materials are especially valuable for those churches which are situated in remote places. There are many of them in Russia, taking into consideration the vastness of the country. There is a very limited number of Bible colleges or training centres in Russia, and many of them are under a constant threat of being closed by governmental authorities. At the same time, the need for good theological training at this particular stage is much greater in Russia and other former USSR countries than can be met by the existing Bible education institutions. Also the majority of potential or actual Christian leaders cannot leave their families and churches and study full-time.

Considering these factors, TEE materials which provide solid Bible education within the church are especially valuable and can be used by churches as long-term educational programmes to train, equip and mobilise all God's people into service, and for some, into leadership.

ORTA works with and through the churches. Our TEE courses are Bible based and non-denominational. They are relevant and affordable. They provide an effective on-the-job training. They are not academically exclusive. Their educational technology is designed around busy working people, people with family responsibilities, people who rub shoulders with the outside world at work. Our core curriculum requires the student to do two foundational courses on the Christian faith and the Bible, then undertake a three-year discipleship programme that centres on the Life of Christ. It requires the student to seriously commit around three hours a week for home study for two semesters each year, plus a further two hours for group work, plus a willingness to undertake the practical ministry assignments linked to the study and local church needs. ORTA also provides special tutor-training seminar training for potential group leaders.

The Russian Federation—an Overview

The Russian Federation is the largest country in the world. Continental in size, it covers seven million sq. km. (6.6 million sq. miles). It is geographically about the same size as South America. It stretches for 11000 km., 11 time zones, across the continents of Europe and Asia. Its climate brings warm summers and long cold winters when temperatures can drop below –50 C.

The population of Russia numbers some 141.5 million today, having shrunk from 154 million in 1992. 127 people groups are represented, the majority Slavic. During the time of the former Soviet Union there were 80 different spoken languages, but Russian was used as the universal bridging and trade language; so in today's world over 250 million people speak Russian, 167 million as their mother tongue.

Russia possesses vast natural resources in timber, minerals, oil and gas. It has a nuclear stockpile greater than those of all other countries added together. Cities like Moscow, St. Petersburg, Khabarovsk, Nizhny Novgorod and Kalingrad have within them some outstandingly beautiful architecture. The standard of education in Russia's state schools, technical institutes and universities is usually very high.

However, Russia's greatest resource is its people. Their culture has given the world priceless treasures through its most engaging literature, outstanding art and immensely beautiful music and song. World-famous names quickly come to mind, such as Akhmatova, Borodin, Chekhov, Dostoyevsky, Gogol, Lermontov, Pasternak, Pushkin, Rimsky-Korsakov, Stravinsky, Tchaikovsky, Tolstoy, Turgenev, and Zhukovsky. Russia's ballet, with its inspired choreography and timeless performers such as Ulánova, Pavlova and Nijinsky, is agreed to be in a league of its own—as are the Russian chess players.

What we see from the West is but part of the background of a traditional and endearing culture of music and song that still pervades towns and villages, not just in their cultural centres but in the very hospitality within the homes of a people who are naturally affectionate. For example, what other language has such endearing words as *babushka* for a grandmother, *kapoosta* for a cabbage, or at least 11 different words for cat? Russians will provide you with the warmest and most generous of friendships—yet they are a people who have been manipulated, scarred, confused and continually betrayed within an unbelievably tragic and cruel history. As the largest republic within the former Soviet Union, Russia has suffered the most severe and sustained persecution of any nation in recent history.

Apart from the persecution of dissidents under the Tsars, deaths in gulags through Stalin's purges are believed to have been more than 20 million with a further 16 million perishing en-route. Scientists, writers, artists, musicians, engineers as well as some 200 of the top military commanders were exiled to these labour camps. Many were Christians. Many were in leadership. A further 20-30 million Soviet citizens were killed in World War II. Even during the post-Stalin years Christians were imprisoned, discriminated against and their children denied educational opportunities.

The Economic Climate
Political/Economic Changes
The Soviet economy and society stagnated in the post Stalin years, haemorrhaged by the demands of the Cold War, until General Secretary Mikhail Gorbachev (1985-91) introduced glasnost (openness) and perestroika (restructuring) in an attempt to modernize communism, but his initiatives led to the USSR breaking up into 15 independent republics. Since then, Russia has struggled in its efforts to build a democratic political system and market economy to replace the strict social, political, and economic controls of the communist period.

The Power of the Wealthy and the Vulnerability of the Poor
Glasnost and Perestroika were not, however, the answer to Russia's deep-rooted problems. Russia has emerged from 70 years of communism only to

find itself weighed down by new imperialisms that intensify the vulnerability of the poor.

Russia's natural resources include vast oil fields and the world's largest proven natural gas reserves. However, world oil prices are a key factor in determining economic strength. On the surface it would appear that the Russian economy has grown sharply in recent years, boosted by high world oil and gas prices. But the benefits haven't trickled down to the general population. Recent figures indicate that an estimated 22 million Russians, 15% of the population, live on less than £78 ($150) a month. According to the government figures, only 10% of Russians can be classified as middle class (or above), which is defined as owning their own home and having a monthly salary of at least £286 ($550).

Today the differentiation in Russia in terms of income and quality of life has reached extremes that threaten social stability. At a time when an estimated one quarter of the population does not even have the minimal means to survive, a 3% section of very rich people has emerged in Russia, defined as those who own prime residences, country houses and expensive cars and whose monthly income can be equal to US$5000-$8000 for just one member of the family. Furthermore, within this there is an additional thin stratum of super-rich who control about 40% of Russia's gross national product, its natural resources and enormous companies and enterprises.

The hope that reforms would have benefited all who want to work honestly and loyally has proved to be forlorn as the rich have become richer and the poor seem confined to never-ending poverty. With such affluence comes power; the rich have their own agenda, and dangerous situations are now brewing, including unconstrained control for *the oligarchs*. Moreover, all population groups have been effected by the current socio-economic climate; not just workers, teachers, pensioners, but also many company managers in charge of small and medium-sized businesses are finding themselves on the edge of bankruptcy.

It would also appear that the rich also do not trust the government that made them so wealthy. It is not just coincidence that they hide their capital abroad. Six years ago Dr. Anatoliy Ovannnikov, of the Russian Academy Socio-Economic Research of the Population Unit, Moscow, estimated that between 50 to 60 billion US dollars were being transferred abroad every year. Sadly, many of the rich do not intend to link their futures with Russia, the country that made them rich; they remain in Russia temporarily while they can still have a career.

The Effect of Global Free Trade

As well as a noticeable increase in the cost of living, the economy is being plundered through the increasing domination of global free-trade. Cheap undercutting imports from vehicles to an abundance of domestic appliances, toys and clothes, especially from China, are resulting in the closing down of many factories within Russia. Then there is the increasing exportation of Russia's raw materials like oil and natural gas, metals and wood and wood products; unbelievably long train loads of timber are witnessed in the Russian far east destined for countries like Japan. The concern is, if all this continues, what will be Russia's socio-economic position in the next five years or ten years?

The Russian Mafia Effect

The Russian Mafia, or "Red Mafia", is a name given abroad to groups of *organized criminals* of various ethnicity which arose from the *Soviet Union* after its disintegration. During recent years they have become responsible for the fast growth in organized crime with its consequential detrimental effect on the Russia economy. The Mafia control 70-80% of all private business and 40% of the nation's wealth. Apart from traditional protection rackets, foreign companies pay up to 20% of their profits to the Mafia as the on-going price of doing business in Russia. The Mafia target commercial centres of power, especially the nation's fragile banking system. Russian gangsters have murdered ninety-five bankers in the last five years.

SOCIAL CONCERNS

Population Shrinkage

Over the last centuries there have been several strong waves of emigration from Russia that have enhanced the economic and cultural life of the receiving nations. The most recent wave began in the 1990s and is still continuing. Since Glasnost an average of 100,000 people have been leaving Russia every year. By 1998, according to the records of the various embassies concerned, already no less than two million people had left Russia during the previous 15 years, a high proportion being highly qualified specialists, the majority (97%) emigrating to Germany, Israel, USA and Greece. By 1998 around 1 million Jews had left Russia and the former USSR—700,000 of whom have moved to Israel.

The reasons for such immigration included concern over the future of their children, dissatisfaction with living and working conditions and a *Cinderella syndrome*, a fatalistic belief that the clock would suddenly strike 12 and Russia would return to previous regimes.

Emigration and the Churches

There has been a haemorrhage of Russian church leaders to countries such as the USA and Germany, including those who have gone initially there to study. Operation Mobilisation recently reported the problem with Christians leaving Novosibirsk and their churches for a more comfortable life, usually in Germany or the USA.

Although the general population of the city has not been reduced by this phenomenon, the number of Christians has significantly fallen by as much as 50% in some churches. But it is not only the sheer number of Christians leaving over the last fifteen years that has caused such a problem, but the kind of people who have left. Typically those able to emigrate were well organised, motivated, middle aged, married couples with children. In other words, those whom you would normally expect to take leadership roles in their churches.

The Russian Baptist churches these emigrants have founded in Germany and the USA have too many leaders, but hardly any followers. In Novosibirsk there are many followers left, but few leaders to lead them. For instance, in one city centre church today with a membership of about 200, around 150 of these members are pensioners. The others are mainly young unmarried people. The church has no facilities for babies or very young children because there aren't any young couples with small children. Virtually everyone of middle age has left.

Changes in Birth and Death Rates

The population of Russia did experience a natural increase of nearly one million annually during 1986-87. This was accounted for by a combination of prenatal policies and the anti-alcohol campaign of the 1980s, However, since the collapse of the Soviet Union, birth-rates and male life expectancy have suffered sharp declines. From a fairly standard 10.7 per 1,000 in 1988, the Russian death rate has risen to a disturbing 16.3 per 1,000 in 2002. The number of deaths has increased by 720,000 annually, while the number of births has declined by close to 1.2 million.

While the high increases in deaths among middle-aged men from cardiovascular disease and such external causes as murder, suicide, accidents, and poisoning has received the greatest media attention, it is the decline in the birth rate that has had the greatest impact on population size. We are told that for a country to maintain its population a birth rate is needed of about 2.4 babies per woman. Russia's fertility rate plunged from 2.08 in 1990 to just 1.17 in 2004. Abortions now outstrip live births; in 2004 at least 1.6 million women had an abortion (a fifth of them under the age of 18), and about 1.5 million gave birth. Rural populations have been dying off or moving to towns and cities. Many villages are reported to have been abandoned altogether.

Prison Population Size and Problems

Most countries in the world have prison population rates of less than 150 per 100,000 citizens, with western European countries mostly in the range of 60-

100 and central European countries around 150-225. With an estimated 680 per 100,000, Russia is second only to the United States' 690 per 100,000.

Russian prisons are often overcrowded, with many jail cells far below internationally accepted standards. Some two thirds of prisoners in Russian jails are ill. The chief of the penal directorate, Vladimir Yalunin, reported that about 500,000 prisoners suffered from a range of complaints from mental illness to AIDS. Russia's justice minister, Yury Chaika, recently discussed the problems of the prison system with President Vladimir Putin, noting that 97,000 inmates have tuberculosis. Chaika also reported that one third of Russians with TB are either in a penal colony or a pre-trial cell.

Other Linked Social Concerns

One major concern is the loss of family cohesion; some eight out of ten marriages end in divorce. There is the growing problem of the homeless, including street children. UNICEF reports that statistics regarding street children are extremely contradictory, and estimates range from 50,000 to 150,000 in the Russian Federation. Many children who live on the streets do have living parents and potential housing.

There has been an increase in drug abuse and alcoholism. Russians are estimated to drink four billion litres of vodka a year—if correct, that adds up to more than half a litre per week for every man, woman and child. Experts estimate the number of drug addicts in Russia to be nearing 4 million people; but only a small percentage are officially registered in hospitals. In Feb 2004 *Pravda*, quoting Alexander Mikhailov, Vice-Chairman of the government's drug control, reported that the number of drug addicts in Russia had increased by 9 times in recent years and nearly 70,000 people were dying of drug use in the country each year.

The growing disillusionment within society was highlighted through a recent survey; only 4% trust politicians, 3% the businessmen, 13% the intelligencia, 31% the priests, 36% the teachers and 1% the police. Russia's suicide rate almost doubled between 1990 and 2003 to 40 per 100,000, twice the world average.

Whereas HIV/AIDS has so far not had a dramatic impact on the burden of disease or mortality levels in the country, the officially registered number of HIV/AIDS cases appears to be increasing at a fast rate, with 100,000 of the 180,000 cases in 2001 alone. Unofficial estimates place these numbers well below the actual figures.

During the Communist era there were a series of organisations linked to the communist party that sought to give controlled purpose and direction to the young, namely the *Little Octobrists* or *Octiabriata* (7–9), *the Young Pioneers*

10–15 (a Scout-like organisation which had an estimated membership of 25 million in 1974), *the Komsomol* 16–18 (around two-thirds of the present adult population of Russia is believed to have once been a member) and then the Communist Party itself. These organisations no longer exist, leaving a void and lack of purpose for many. Meanwhile more and more Western videos and films with their unprincipled and unrestricted exploitation of sex and violence appear on Russian television.

There is still a great spiritual hunger within the Russian soul, a hunger that Satan will try to dull through the counterfeit. There is much work for the people of the Russian churches to undertake to change Russia through the love and compassion of Jesus.

The Russian Orthodox Church

The Russian Orthodox Church, also known as the Orthodox Catholic Church of Russia, is the largest of the Eastern Orthodox Churches in the world. The Church has over 23,000 parishes, 154 bishops, 635 monasteries, and 102 clerical schools in the territory of the former Soviet Union and has a well-established presence in many other countries. It has historically been the dominant church of Russia representing the state religion. During the Communist years it experienced a demise of power; it underwent great persecution in 1922; then later it was infiltrated by Communist appointments. It is united under the Patriarch of Moscow, Alexius II, who in turn is in *communion* with the other *patriarchs* and *primates* of the Eastern Orthodox Church.

Celebrating its millennial anniversary in 1988, the Orthodox Church is now perceived as a major symbol of Russian identity. It has some 60 million professing adherents today, yet the reality is that only about 3% actually participate in church life. However, due to its deep cultural roots, various members of the Russian government are keen to display their respect for the Church; it is common for the President of Russia to publicly meet with the Patriarch on religious festivals, and many previously confiscated church buildings have been officially returned to the Church in recent years.

Generally the Orthodox Church is still reluctant to co-operate with any other denomination, while reclaiming what it considers to be its "heritage". Powerful elements within are using every possible means to regain its exclusive spiritual dominance. In 1997 the Church was involved in the instigation of the complex and ambiguous 1997 "Federal Law on Freedom of Religion", which discriminates against minor religious groups, including the Protestant churches, classified as *sects,* along with the Jehovah's Witnesses, Mormons, Hare Krishna and that ilk. There is nevertheless evidence that a number of open-minded priests within the Orthodox Church are willing to enter into a dialogue with other Christian denominations and even be critical of the existing Orthodox hierarchy.

The Orthodox church has vigorously resisted reformation throughout its history. There have, however, been a number of historic break-away groups, such as the Molokons (1659), who queried the Orthodox liturgy and accuracy of many of the Russian holy books and manuscripts.

THE RUSSIAN PROTESTANT CHURCHES
Historical Background

In an impressive eleven-article manifesto dated July 22, 1763 in the second year of her reign, Catherine the Great, aware of the untapped potential of the vast Russian lands, invited a number of foreign groups from Germany into Russia to develop agriculture and industries. Article 1 of this Manifesto granted such

> *… foreigners coming into Our Empire the free and unrestricted practice of their religion according to the precepts and usage of their Church. To those, however, who intend to settle not in cities but in colonies and villages or uninhabited lands, we grant the freedom to build churches and bell towers and to maintain the necessary number of priests and church servants, but not the construction of monasteries. On the other hand, everyone is hereby warned not to persuade or induce any of the Christian co-religionists living in Russia to accept or even assent to his faith or join his religious community, under pain of incurring the severest punishment of Our law. This prohibition does not apply to the various nationalities on the borders of Our Empire who are attached to the Mahometan faith. We permit and allow everyone to win them over and make them subject to the Christian religion in a decent way.*

These immigrants, mainly Mennonites with their pacifist beliefs and Lutherans, were guaranteed freedom of religion, lower taxes, exemption from armed service, and were given large grants of land. Lutheran congregations in Russia, however, began earlier in the 16th century through indigenous Lutheran Christians who came under tsarist rule when Peter the Great conquered the areas around the Baltic Sea. In the years leading up to World War II many Lutherans were deported to Soviet Republics in Central Asia and the Far East because they, as ethnic minorities, were seen as a threat to Soviet state security. The church survived, however, as underground faith communities led by lay leaders. It was only in 1988 that Lutheran churches of ethnic German heritage were able to begin officially to function again in Russia.

By the early nineteenth century Orthodox clergy were perceived to be very distant from the common people, and important pastoral needs were being ignored. Following the freedom of the serfs in 1861, the failure of formal Orthodoxy to give practical Biblical teaching led to break-away movements as hungry minds sought God's Word, like that of the peasant Stundism of Osnova. Although producing outwardly clean lives, they faced harsh persecutions, like the severe birchings of 1867.

Many of the educated classes were intensely religious but also unsatisfied with the detached formalism of the Orthodox Church. For example, by 1873 a strong evangelical movement had developed through the witness of an English visitor, Lord Radstock, who was happy to work with sincere Christians whatever their denomination. The movement drew in a number of the senior aristocrats of St. Petersburg, including Count Brobrinsky, Minster of the Interior, and Colonel Vasili Alexandrovich Pashkov of the Russian Imperial Guard.

Alarmed by any hint of change, the Russian aristocracy petitioned Tsar Alexander II to act firmly; furthermore, the wrath of the Orthodox Church had been aroused, and its leaders also joined the appeal to the Tsar. When in 1884 the United Evangelical Conference in St. Petersburg met in Princess Lieven's palace to organize a united fellowship of New Testament believers, police arrested converts, exiling some and jailing others. What might have become a reformation within the Church was forced to be a sect outside it. Harried, persecuted, imprisoned, exiled to Siberia, these Christians were treated as common criminals, suffering more than Lenin and the other later revolutionists did prior to coming to power. Yet they generated churches wherever they went. By 1891 over half the 41 Orthodox dioceses complained of being infected with evangelical growth.

In 1909, the All-Russian Union of Evangelical Christians was formed as a fellowship of autonomous congregations. Although persecuted as an heretical sect during the final decades of Tsarist Russia, the evangelicals received relative freedom immediately following the Communist Revolution, but after the introduction of Stalin's law on religion in 1929 they underwent a similar fate of severe repression as did Orthodox Christians.

In 1944 the northern "Evangelical Christians" and the southern Baptist group were united. They had held joint beliefs and worked with each other for a long time. The name "Baptist" is commonly used today, but the full name for this unified group is "Evangelical Christian / Baptist." At the close of *the Patriotic War* (World War II) the Communist government reorganized all evangelical groups under this one denominational label. All congregations were immediately required to register with the state, a step which granted believers a measure of religious tolerance providing they agreed to restrict their activities to passive worship. During Khrushchev's anti-religious campaign the pressures were stepped up and led to a split in 1961. The registered churches decided to try to work within the system, while the unregistered ones, in good conscience, could not register, attracting increased state opposition.

Pentecostalism was introduced to Russia and other Slavic nations by Ivan Voronaev, a Russian-born American who initiated a ministry in Odessa in 1920, the origin of the movement in the Slavic nations. He founded many congregations in Russia before being arrested by the Soviet police in 1929. He died in prison.

The Recent Past

Despite many problems, evangelicals continued to grow in the Republics of the former Soviet Union. Lifestyle contrasts between Christians and non-believers became an arena for witness to neighbours and fellow workers. Even with limited access to Bibles and discipleship materials they demonstrated a strong commitment to the Word of God and the Lordship of Jesus Christ, an example to the West of a purer church whose members were prepared to take risks to honour and obey their Saviour. This led to the support movement in the 1960s by some concerned Western churches in the form of sustained prayer and "Bible smuggling".

The Russian Bible

The Russian Biblical Society was established in 1813 at the command of Tsar Alexander I, who gave generously towards the work. Prince Golitsin became its first President. The aim of this society was to *enable the people of Russia to receive the Holy Scriptures in ethnic languages at a low price range*. The work was very effective. In the following years the Society was able to print 876,106 copies of the Bible and its separate books in 26 languages and dialects. The Old Slavonic Russian version, only vaguely understandable by anyone but clergy, was superseded by the Synodal version, its translation being completed by the Russian Orthodox Church in 1876. This translation blessed by the Holy Synod remains the first and the only Russian translation of the Bible recognized universally by all Christian denominations. As the standard translation used throughout Russia, it is a good translation, though some of the words are rather archaic and thus unfamiliar to those new to Christianity.

Post-Glasnost Protestant Leadership Training

The 70 years of Communist rule held back formal Protestant scholarship; a high proportion of Russian Protestant leaders were, compared to their Orthodox counterparts, men of limited theological education. During the

1980s the Russo-German missionary organization, LOGOS International, developed a program of Theological Education by Extension (TEE) in some of the cities of the Former Soviet Union, spearheaded by the Kazakhstan-born Dr. Peter Penner. A residential Bible School was established in 1990 with 45 students in the Krasnodar region of Southern Russia, being the first Russian Protestant Bible College to be opened for 70 years. The following year it moved north to become the St. Petersburg Christian University (SPCU) with Dr. Penner serving as the University's first Rector.

Dr. Penner, together with his wife, Katharina, perceived two important needs for the Russian churches:

- That of establishing sound evangelical scholarship, drawing in the selfless servant-hearted services of international scholars such as Dwight Acomb (USA), Hannes and Annamarie Further (South Africa), Johannes Lange (Germany) and many others.

- The need to establish effective distant learning levels for leadership training and effective discipleship to meet the needs of the majority distant and poor churches, seeking to adapt the South American SEAN TEE programme for the latter.

The Penners hoped that SPCU could serve as a centre for both educational thrusts and that TEE skills could become part of the curriculum for the resident students. However, the difficult financial demands of maintaining a residential university within a Russian economy needed Western support linked to the requirements for international accreditation, so SPCU had to pass the SEAN TEE development work to their associates in Oxen Ministries.

During the 1990s serious investment has been made to train their leaders, teachers and workers through the foundation of further "Western style" Bible colleges. Many valuable workers and leaders have already been trained through such institutions.

As well as the risk of producing young inexperienced and spiritually immature leaders, elite residential training systems cannot meet the enormous leadership and training needs of the wider and majority poorer communities of Russia. The diploma level Bible Education by Extension distant learning programme has sought to address this problem by enabling many leaders to study and train on the job. BEE perceived that the established churches are 80% women, which makes it difficult to raise up men leaders and that the main hindrance to the Gospel in Russia is that people have little or no Christian influence or background. They saw how small, home-based Bible studies provide solid education and positive exposure to the love and teachings of Christ.

Other effective distant learning initiatives developed, like Peter Dyneka's Russian Ministries (founded in 1991), dedicated to church-planting and church growth through providing the resources and training to equip the next generation of church leaders.

Concerns

The percentage of evangelical Christians is still below 3% of the Russian population. The most recent edition of *Operation World* records that the hopes of spiritual revival of the early 1990s were dashed by failures of both political and church leadership. Russian church growth failed to reach 1990s expectations through inappropriate evangelism and lack of effective discipleship.

The majority of the people who claim to be Christian remain untaught. Their poverty and their hopelessness have stimulated crime, drug abuse, alcoholism, emigration, family breakdown, and suicide to alarming heights. Many people live for months without receiving the wages due to them. Young people have often been neglected by the churches. There has been a growing incidence of teenage pregnancies, whilst the main method of contraception has been that of abortion. Crime is on the increase, and powerful networks like the Mafia make mockery of justice.

Many national evangelical Christians still isolate themselves from society because of the previous decades of persecution. It is very hard for them to accept new Christians because of the vast difference between the Christian sub-culture and overall society. However, there is also a concern that Western church example is far too compromising and, furthermore, that a number of Western attitudes are now being paralleled in these Russian churches, especially Biblically incorrect expectations of the role of pastor.

There is the problem of emigration, mentioned earlier. Very many theologically trained pastors with access to the West have left Russia these last ten years, or did not return to their home towns or villages—an ecclesiastical echo of the words of the American 1918 song: *"How ya gonna keep 'em down on the farm after they've seen Paree?"*

There is a great need for men mentors in the churches. So much of the church work seems to be held together, as with families, by the women. Too often men either fail to see a male role within the body of the church or become confused as to their role and responsibility, including that of seeking leadership for the wrong reasons and the wrong perception of the leadership role, drifting towards an autocratic or "Tsar" type, with associated problems of petty legalism, unquestioned authority and theological fads.

There is traditionally much superstition across Russia. Sadly, the Russian Orthodox Church has given very little Biblical teaching to the masses, relying instead on formal liturgy. An Itar-Tass News Wire of June 2, 2001 estimated five million Russian nationals to be involved in sects, claiming that most of the sects are Protestant, pseudo-Buddhist or neo-pagan with more than 5,000 groups functioning in Moscow alone. The agency spokesman warned that almost all these sects act under the disguise of public organizations and stealthily mesmerize people. However, although Protestants are treated as *sects*, there has nonetheless been a steady infiltration into Russia of groups such as the Jehovah Witnesses, Mormons, Hare Krishna, Unification Church (Moonies), Scientology and White Brotherhood. Sergei Torop, known to his followers as Vissarion, claims to be the Christ returned to earth to complete his work. Already he has a growing following of several thousand in Siberia.

Popular-Level TEE Leading to the Birth of ORTA

With the encouragement of SPCU, Oxen Ministries continued the work of formatting a *popular-level* TEE programme. They recognised that the purposes of God go beyond evangelism and that it is important that the churches have access to discipleship training materials that would help all believers understand the central truths of the Bible, so that they could grow into strong disciples of Christ and avoid false teaching and error.

An additional valuable tool to this TEE programme was the availability of Focus Radio's 125 radio broadcasts in Russian of the SEAN courses: *Abundant Life* (for new believers), *The Light of the Bible* (an overview of the Bible), *Spirit World* (recognising and dealing with the occult and superstition) and *Work for All* (the Biblical teaching on work). These were produced at an extremely high professional standard by Tatiana Satsuk, a graduate of SPCU, who was recommended by Dr. Penner for the task and enabled by the generous support of Focus Radio through its Director, David Couchman.

The vision of Oxen Ministries centres on the command of Matthew 9:35-38 and the vision of commitment within 1 Chronicles 13:23-38. Oxen were concerned that the emerging Russian churches should avoid creating elitist structures within the churches that disqualify the very type of people that Jesus chose to be His disciples from doing the very ministry that Jesus taught his people to do.

Today's socio-economic problems in Russia demonstrate that changing political systems does not change people's hearts. There is urgent work for the churches, and every member is needed. Why cannot at least an equal investment in thought, research, planning, prayer and finance that goes into training and equipping leadership be put into training and mobilising the masses—God's tent makers, God's ants, God's partisans, God's labourers—rather than God's loiterers, all envisioned and equipped to change society for Jesus? Christians are represented by school teachers, taxi drivers, policemen, shop assistants, soldiers, university lecturers, students, scientists, street cleaners, media personalities, doctors, bus drivers, artists, musicians, writers, politicians, busy working folk with *dacha* responsibilities, people understandably allergic to print at the close of a long working day, yet people who daily rub shoulders with all sorts and conditions of men and women. Up to 70% of the families living in cities and towns in the far eastern regions of Russia have plots of land known as *dachas*, often several kilometres out of the town, where they grow a high percentage of their family's requirements of vegetables and fruit.

Oxen firmly believes that church leadership requires clear accountable goals for each stage of a believer's growth and service. In Chile, for example, Alfredo Cooper had already demonstrated in his *PROGROMIN* programme that when popular level TEE is properly incorporated as a disciplined and integral part of church life, the spiritual gifting of each member becomes apparent, so that the potential leaders, evangelists, administrators, children's ministries, youth workers, teachers, helpers, worship leaders, TEE tutors, those with pastoral hearts can be recognised and their gifting encouraged, developed and proven within the church, leading in the process to the formation of church planting teams.

Oxen Ministries' Strategy

- to translate the SEAN core curriculum and associated courses,

- to make strategic contacts to field-test the material in Russian churches,

- to seek out or form some national organisation to take responsibility for the work,

- to seek "bridgehead" cities that could develop "strawberry runners" into the surrounding towns and villages.

Much of this was undertaken for Oxen through the tireless work of Vadim Poddubsky, a generous-hearted and mature graduate of SPCU. Hard-pressed donor agencies like Timothy Ministries, Feed the Minds, Hilfe fuer Bruder did much to encourage this work through grants, especially for printing, but it proved very difficult to interest Western churches, which themselves rarely have discipleship programmes and have little or no understanding of TEE, to give on-going support to such a concept. Although the work slowly progressed, funds were never sufficient to employ full-time translators. Eventually the long journeys proved damaging to Vadim's health, and he had to step down, but not before he made a major breakthrough by introducing

Oxen to important contacts in key cities in the Russian far east, Magadan and Vladivostok.

The far east of Russia proved to be a major step forward, firstly through Olga Rybakova, the founder/director of the St. James Bible College in Magadan. Magadan region is a huge territory with many scattered little towns and villages. Olga immediately perceived how TEE could serve the vast areas around Magadan region and beyond into Chukotka, Kamchatka and the NE regions of Siberia for long-term discipleship tools, especially in the newly-planted churches; secondly through the immense generosity and trust of Manfred Brockmann, Dean of the Lutheran churches of Eastern Siberia and the Far East of Russia. Manfred opened up the Lutheran churches in Vladivostok, Chita, Khabarovsk, Ussurijsk, Arsenijv and Komsomolsk-on-Amur for field testing the various courses. The cooperation, hospitality and generous friendship of these Lutheran Christians has been profound, and, as well as opening up the need for further editing of the material, has led also to important contacts in other churches. From these experiences Oxen Ministries invested all their reserves in January 2004 in a bold UK-based training project.

"What winter!?" was the unforgettable Russian response when during the minibus drive though the countryside to Devon from London an apology was made for bringing them over to England during the middle of the English winter. Nine committed Russians had travelled some 6000 miles from Magadan and Vladivostok to Moscow without any guarantee of receiving a visa there to proceed to England. Then, from Moscow they travelled a further 1500 miles to London—all in the depths of their Russian winter, where temperatures can drop to below –40 C, hence their dry comment "What winter!?" Nearly all of those who came had never been outside the former Soviet Union.

The delegates were carefully selected from those recommended by the two team leaders, Dr. Anneta Vyssotskaia, from Vladivostok and Olga Rybalova from Magadan. The two teams were as follows:

- From Vladivostok: Dr. Anneta Vyssotskaia, a church leader immensely respected across the Christian denominations within the Primor'ye Krai region and beyond, especially for her initiative and ability to get different churches to work together, Vladimir Vysotskiy, a graduate of the Faith Bible College in New Zealand, and Vera Sapojnikova, the Chief Education Officer of the of the North Union of Evangelical Christian Churches' Department of Christian Education, that covers the Russian far East regions of Yakutia, Amur, Khabarovsk and Primor'ye.

- From Magadan: Olga Rybakova, Founder/Director of the St. James Bible College, Magadan, and pastor of the Revival Church of Magadan; Lyubov Fedorova, an experienced accountant and administrator, who also serves as a professional advisor on labour laws and accounting to a number of related Christian organizations in Magadan; Irina Krizhanovskaya, a university teacher of English and founder/editor of an interdenominational Christian women's magazine; Galina Gerkina, the social worker in the St. James Centre and already an experienced TEE tutor; Igor Nichkasov, a senior Pentecostal pastor; and Alla Vysokova, an extension student of the Evangelical Lutheran Seminary in St. Petersburg and leader of St. Mark Evangelical Lutheran Church, Magadan.

The Reasons for These Seminars

The conviction that "grass roots" TEE, especially that represented by the South American-born SEAN material, has a vitally important role to play in equipping the people of God for effective discipled ministry and service within the vast needs of Russia and the former Soviet Union.

Realization that, although much effort had been put into translating and introducing the SEAN TEE curriculum into Russian, it is not being used to anything like its true potential within the churches. The reasons were twofold:

- Lack of proper introduction to the educational methodology leading to confusion and misunderstanding regarding its goals and use. The absence of a proper TEE tutor training programme for the Russian churches.

- The need for a regional and/or national umbrella TEE organisation that is Russian-owned, Russian-financed and Russian-led, to take responsibility for this work.

Oxen set and followed seminar goals, that having undertaken these two weeks in England,

the delegates, as a team, would be competent to set up the necessary TEE organisation required to facilitate the running of TEE programmes on a local, regional and even national basis.

The delegates, as a team, would also be competent to train other people in the specific skills needed in the fields of education methodology, editing, administration and financial policies that are associated with a well run TEE programme.

Summary of the Seminar and Workshop Contents

- Educational principles—curriculum development
- Administrative structure and goals—national organisation
- Administrative structure and goals—regional organisations
- Administration structures—local TEE centres
- Administration—financial policies
- Administration—production and distribution of courses
- Administration—accountability
- Administration—accounting principles and systems
- Accreditation
- Tutor training—principles, content and practicalities
- Course development
- TEE and help ministries
- International examples of "Grass Roots" TEE

The Seminar Leaders

Jacqui Brown, Field Director, SEAN, U.K.

Zafar Ismail, former Director of the Open Theological Seminary, Lahore, Pakistan, which now has 3000 registered students

Peter Bisset, Founder/Director of ITEEN, Nepal, which reached 3000 students in 2006

Tanka Subedi, National Coordinator, ITEEN, Nepal

Rita Subedi, Programme Coordinator and Translator, ITEEN, Nepal

Richard Collins, FCA, partner of Collins Davies Chartered Accountants

Bernard Cocker, Founder/Director of the International Aid Trust

Michael Huggins, Field Director, Oxen Ministries

Jacqui Brown took the delegates step by step through the vision and goals of *Grass-Roots* TEE, with its educational principles, covering in thorough and practical detail the principles behind programmed learning, group tutoring and the value of practical ministry assignments. Jacqui also covered a number of important practicalities, attitudes and commitments that needed to be understood for effective use of TEE within the local church. Her PowerPoint presentation was skillfully adapted into Russian prior to each seminar through the dedication of Vladimir Vysotskiy, who often worked into the small hours of the morning to accomplish this service.

Zafar Ismail provided the delegates with both a scholarly and Biblical background to grass-roots level TEE within the context of the church as the local witnessing community, arguing that the natural seedbed, *seminarium,* for growth in Christian character is the local church. The equipping of God's people, therefore, should happen where they are. The group examined together how this local focus for theological education and mission can be served effectively through a relevant TEE programme and how and why, therefore, the training of local church-based TEE tutors is essential for this.

The Nepalese team (Tanka Subedi, Rita Subedi, Peter Bisset) explained why and how ITEEN (Nepal) was established, working all the time with and through the churches. The importance of establishing clear and acceptable educational discipline within the program was emphasised. A sound tutor-training programme linked to this should be the priority of any serious TEE system.

Richard Collins' contribution to these workshops was through the seminars he conducted on accountability procedures needed for a successful TEE programme. He introduced a series of workshop sessions in order to build the capacity of the delegates to manage financial resources more efficiently and effectively and to develop the confidence and financial skills of individuals to operate finance systems which enable accountability, transparency and integrity.

Bernard Cocker focused on the Biblical teaching regarding the church's sacred responsibility before God to demonstrate the love of Christ through the Gospel hand-in-hand with a determination to care for and meet the needs of the poor, the homeless and dispossessed, the fatherless, the widows. Discussions included the relevance of TEE within such an area of responsibility for the churches. TEE courses are expected to undertake assignments linked to the teaching with the advice and support of the church pastor. Many such projects would be connected to community concerns and needs.

As an on-going practical extension to this tutor-training, throughout the two weeks all the delegates worked their way through a SEAN TEE course. The delegates were divided into two tutorial groups. Each group member would do the home studies daily in his or her "spare" time, then attend the group tutorial from 9.00 to 10.30 a.m. The purpose of the exercise was to provide the delegates with a daily opportunity to improve their group leadership skills. Everyone had to have a turn at tutoring the group, though no-one would know before each group meeting who the tutor was to be for that day, so all had to be prepared.

The Immediate Results of the Seminars

ORTA. The decision of the delegates to form the Open Russian Theological Academy, with two Regional Committees, Magadan and Vladivostok, plus a National Committee, co-opting Michael Huggins of Oxen Ministries as a member.

Matheteuo. This Russian seminar experience had convinced those concerned of the advantage of drawing together TEE training teams from within a network representing many years of valuable TEE experience in a wide range of countries, economies and cultures to be able to serve in the same way in other venues around the world. Worldwide experience had demonstrated that the aspirations of TEE can be significantly advanced through:

- An increased understanding of TEE, including the vision and potential, the methodology and the practical application involved.

- Adequate foundational training for those wishing to establish TEE programmes.

- A clearer recognition of realistic levels of pump-priming funding needed to establish national programmes.

- The need to work towards indigenous ownership and funding of the programmes.

Since its inception in early 2004, ORTA has had to concentrate on four key areas: tutor-training seminars, translation, financial support, international responsibilities.

Following the 2004 seminars, the Vladivostok team was immediately strengthened by addition of three key people: Maria Boyko (now Vdovina), a gifted Bible teacher from the Union of Evangelical Christian Church and two colleagues from the Lutheran Church: Irina Barsegova, a skilled translator and administrator, and Eduard Mishenko, a book-keeper/accountant. In June 2006 Irina became the National Coordinator of ORTA.

The Vladivostok team led by Vera Sapozhnikova aimed to achieve 8 tutor-training seminars a year—centering on Vladivostok, a city of about one million people of 200 nationalities, and moving then to other towns like Ussurijsk, Blagovestchensk and then to distant villages like Chernigovka and Rettikhovka. At the same time they planned to make contacts so that this work could spread beyond the region into areas like Sakhalin and Amurskaya. These seminars are brilliantly conducted, drawing in the UK and Nepalese examples and adding a great deal of Russian sparkle and spice. A generous grant from the J.W. Laing trust has enabled a very effective use of PowerPoint equipment. In June 2006 Maria replaced Vera as Regional Controller as Vera had resigned to undertake overseas missionary work.

There have been many wonderful testimonies sent in from ORTA tutors and students. Oxana Polikina, both an ORTA tutor and volunteer member on the tutor training team, commenting recently on *Abundant Life*, SEAN's TEE course for new believers, pointed out that:

> *"Abundant Life" may seem simple at first, but its impact on the inner person is huge! Everyone who went through it in our church loved it. This is the sort of knowledge that transforms you but also forms a new person and changes your relationship to God. All those in the original group are in ministry now. Oleg is tutoring and taking responsibility in children's ministry, Ljudmilla is leading a group, Natalia helps serve people, and is now pregnant, so ORTA makes you fruitful in other ways! She has since started a home group using ORTA principles. All the students are very excited, for they now feel equipped to share their faith. ORTA provides a systematic educational tool for the church that develops a taste for continuous education.*

Vladivostok-Primor'ye Region—Prison Ministries TEE Project

There are 25 prisons in the Primorskii region with a prison population of over 20,000 people. Already a number of Primorskii churches are collaborating in different aspects of prison ministries, from evangelism to the care for the needs of the families of prisoners, especially the mothers, wives and children; and also the follow-up of prisoners after their release. The work is voluntary, and the churches involved tend to be poor, yet give sacrificially. As well as these important ministries there is a recognised need for Christian education and discipleship within the prisons. Some of the prisoners are serving long sentences and are eager to study.

There are many restrictions facing prison discipleship, from very limited prison amenities that do not permit the group dynamics of TEE to increasing official opposition. ORTA's printed SEAN courses have nonetheless been successfully used as correspondence courses in these circumstances; the Russian prison ministries have a very good opinion of the material. Currently there are about 80 students in prisons doing these courses.

Sergei Smirnov, former Director of the Russian Bible Society in the Far East, is pioneering a tape/CD ministry into many of these prisons and is keen to work with ORTA on a project using the Focus Radio broadcasting/cassette/CD adaptations of some of the SEAN courses as the backbone of this work. He believes it is ideal for prison work, providing access to the teaching to far more prisoners. The printed ORTA material will also continue to be used where possible.

The Magadan Division of ORTA

Founded in 1933, Magadan is a port on the Sea of Okhotsk. It is the administrative centre of the Magadan region and has a population of about

120,000. Magadan is very isolated. There is only one road in and out, and the nearest city is Yakutsk, 2200 km away.

As well as their own tutor-training programme, the Magadan team forged close links with the New Life Radio station, who undertook twice-weekly broadcasts of the Focus Radio's brilliant radio/CD adaptations of four of the SEAN courses over a three-year period, linking these broadcasts to the work of ORTA. However the station has been experiencing growing technical problems associated with old equipment; furthermore, they are currently having problems over their license renewal from the Ministry in Moscow.

As projects, ORTA Magadan are seeking ways to serve some 24 Christian fellowships along the Tracca. The Tracca is the infamous 1600 km "Road of Bones" of the former gulag. Under this highway lie the bodies of many of the Russians who died in the gulag work camps. Also ORTA hopes that TEE will be used to serve in a remarkable Pentecostal mission to the Koryak people that uses an old Russian army heavy-duty snow vehicle to take the Gospel to them; this work can only be undertaken in winter as the terrain is impassable once the snow and ice have melted.

TEE materials are used not only by evangelical churches. The Catholic priest Father Michael in Magadan said that 28 people from his church studied *Abundant Light* (Bible introduction), and he now wants to study another TEE book, *The Bible Encounter Manual,* with them. Incidentally this church has a special ministry to the elderly survivors of the gulag—"*their dignity was taken from them, we want to restore it in old age*".

Translation, Editing and Publishing

ORTA has made the editing of the existing Russian translations of SEAN books a priority. Some they are having to re-translate from more updated versions of the English. By 2006 *Abundant Life, The Light of the Bible* and Book 1 of the *Life of Christ* had been re-edited and re-published, and Anneta Vyssotskaya completed the draft translation of the *Bible Encounter Manual* and undertook the work on *Feed My Lambs* to serve children's ministries within the Russian church.

Although some much appreciated publishing grants have been received, ORTA still found it difficult to raise realistic financial support for this key translation work. Because of this each member of the team, Irina Barsegova, Anneta Vyssotskaia, and Maria Vdovina, undertook the work at very low rates and have had to support themselves through outside work. This has meant that the difficult and exacting work of translation and editing has had to be fitted into spare moments, usually at the close of a long and demanding working day.

Meanwhile the demand for the courses has out-stripped the speed of translation and the ability of ORTA to make the next courses available when needed. This demand not only comes from the Russian churches, but also from Russian-speaking countries in Central Asia, such as Uzbekistan, Kyrgyzstan and Kazakhstan, where Russian is both used as a bridging language and a source language for further translation.

At the National Committee in June 2006 it was agreed that the translation programme urgently needed to be advanced. A fourth member, Natalia Goncharova, was added to the translation and editing team. Like the others, Natalia has a very good university degree in English plus valuable experience in translating Christian material into Russian. By providing funds to advance the translations this project would allow two of the team to move more towards full-time translation work and also allow the other two to set aside more professional time to concentrate on the editing. The result would be that the whole of the core SEAN TEE curriculum would be available by the close of 2007 with further courses added the following year. ORTA have budgeted their total needs for this translation project to be US\$ 13,000 a year for three years—\$39,000 in total. This funding project includes all translation and editing costs but not printing.

The International Ministry of ORTA

As well as their commitment to Russia, ORTA is also being challenged by a growing international ministry. Anneta Vyssotskaia and her family moved to New Zealand in the summer of 2004, as husband, Dr. Mikhail Vyssotsky, had been seconded there to head up marine scientific research. However communication technology has enabled her ORTA work to continue and expand, both as an active member of the translation team but also as ORTA's International Director.

Not only is Russian spoken in FSU republics of Europe and Central Asia, but requests for access to the Russian SEAN translations are being made to ORTA for Russian speaking communities and immigrant workers in countries like the USA, Israel, Mongolia, Bahrain. Furthermore, the South Korea churches have a massive missionary presence across the Russian-speaking world, and the TEE Korea programme uses Korean versions of the same SEAN material as ORTA. All this requires special printing and publishing license agreements in association with the author body, SEAN. To avoid the incorrect use of their material and a multiplicity and confusion of Russian translations, ORTA are firstly insisting that groups outside Russia who want access to their material abide by the same rules applied within Russia. They should provide evidence of prior TEE tutor training, and secondly all the editing of the Russian SEAN material should be undertaken by ORTA, and any cultural changes within the Russian text should be made with the agreement of both ORTA and SEAN.

ORTA's Administration and Financial Policies

ORTA has two administrative bases, its main office in Vladivostok and an office in Magadan within the St. James Bible College. Annual budgets are carefully worked out within the regions and agreed with the National Committee. All funds are carefully accounted for and, if necessary, ring-fenced. Although the long-term aim of ORTA is to be financially independent, the work is still at that early stage of dependence on outside financial help. The budgets cover capital items and working expenditure both for the general administration of ORTA as well as the important associated projects such as tutor training, translation and prison ministries.

The annual ORTA salary budget should be at least US$40,000, if all salaries and associated taxes could realistically be covered, which they are not. US$20,000 are needed for administrative costs and tutor training, and US$24,500 is needed initially for the prison ministries work. These calculations do not include the annual travel costs into Russia by Anneta Vyssotskaia and Michael Huggins, who seek such travel funds outside the National ORTA budget, and have been helped by groups such as Timothy Ministries USA and the Swiss-based Matanav Foundation.

Growing Opposition

One disturbing trend is the strong evidence of the growing official opposition in the cities of Vladivostok, Magadan, and Khabarovsk to the increasing amount of social work initiatives being carried out by the Protestant churches—prison work, work among drug addicts, alcoholics, invalids and the destitute, especially street children. There are also the un-reached people groups. Sadly, much of this opposition has been instigated by the Russian Orthodox Church in its mounting resentment of the growth of Protestant churches, yet it does not seem to have alternative help ministries in place. This year we received news that the government plans to investigate all drug rehabilitation centres in the Vladivostok region, believing that Protestants were using them to spread the faith.

Olga Rybakova, reporting on the social work activities by Protestant churches in Magadan, says already the Sceptre of Truth Church's canteen for the poor has been stopped by officials. Olga stresses the importance now of drug and alcohol rehabilitation, yet there are still no rehabilitation centres in Magadan. Furthermore, many women and children are in misery because men abuse alcohol—whole families are suffering.

The application for the renewal of their broadcasting license by Magadan's New Life Radio Station has been refused, but the staff—André, Olga, Lilia and Lyuba—are waiting for their appeal to be heard. This is the same broadcasting station which has been so effectively broadcasting Focus Radio's adaptation of some SEAN courses in collaboration with ORTA.

Anneta Vyssotskaia, who also serves on the WEA Religious Liberty Commission, was the guest writer of this RLC release dated September 6th 2006:

NEW LAW IN RUSSIA WOULD IMPACT CHURCHES' OUTREACH

Religious bodies in Russia seem likely to be more restricted soon in their normal activities, especially missionary work and evangelism. In August the Ministry of Justice informed registered religious bodies of a draft law 'On the amendments to some federal laws aimed against illegal missionary activities'. The proposed law contravenes the Russian Constitution as well as international treaties guaranteeing people the right to share their religious views and act in accordance with them. Even humanitarian work in the name of Christ would be outlawed. The draft legislation is due to go to the Russian parliament before the end of this year. If enacted the law would especially threaten churches for whom outreach and evangelism is basic in their activities. Please pray that the advocacy of believers, lawyers and others will succeed in getting the oppressive nature of the proposed law changed.

ORTA's Future Development

As more and more tutors are trained for the various churches and registered student numbers grow (some 500 within these last two years), ORTA is seeking how the city of Khabarovsk, capital of the Khabarovsk region, could become a regional bridgehead.

ORTA value greatly the SEAN core curriculum, but do not plan to restrict their programme to SEAN. They are looking at additional material from other programmes, including material on relationships, marriage and family life. There is a possibility also of writing material of their own. As the basic level TEE curriculum becomes securely established, there is the prospect of adding diploma level material from other international programmes.

As Chairman of ORTA, I am immensely moved by the tenacity, imagination and sacrificial dedication of my Russian colleagues, including the many voluntary tutors, especially the way they see taking risks for Jesus part of their service, accepting that Christian service has its cost. It is an immense privilege to work with people with such a capacity to understand, accept and forgive.

Much prayer is needed about the threatened religious laws, but even if they are implemented I do not believe they will succeed in stopping the ministry of

ORTA. The greater threat is that of financial starvation. My colleague, Anneta Vyssotskaia, best summed up this in her 2005 ORTA report:

All the people who are now involved in this (ORTA) work both in Vladivostok and Magadan are committed Christians and have been serving for a long time in Russian churches of different denominations (Evangelical, Lutheran, Pentecostal, Baptist, etc.) in a leadership role.

There are pastors, pastor assistants, Bible teachers, missionary workers, church administrators, Christian writers and editors, etc., in our team. In addition to this the people who are involved are also professional university lecturers, school teachers, translators, social workers, accountants, etc. It is a highly professional and at the same time very spiritual group of people. They also have a good reputation in the churches. A better team cannot be even imagined or desired.

However, as International Director of ORTA work, I express my deep personal concern about the continuation of this work. After our recent visit with brother Michael Huggins to Russia, I saw again the hard work of ORTA teams in Vladivostok and Magadan, which however is not financially supported in the way it should be. The people have to work on the edge of their strength because they also have to work very hard to provide for their families.

At present most ORTA workers are women: two of them are single women; two have unemployed husbands; some of them still have small children to care for. They have shown their sacrificial commitment for this work for a long period of time. They are all financially very unprotected. This is the actual situation that must be taken into account when we speak about long-term work. In my opinion, the financial support of the workers is number one priority in this particular situation.

Michael Huggins, ORTA Chairman

michael@oxenministries.fsnet.co.uk

Contacts outside the Russian Federation: mvvysot@xtra.co.nz

Within the Russian Federation: irinabarsegova@mail.primorye.ru

QUESTIONS FOR REFLECTION AND DISCUSSION

1. *Summarize the socio-economic and spiritual context described in this case study.*

2. *What is the mission of the Protestant churches and the role of TEE in this context?*

3. *What have been the critical steps in the development of this "grass roots" program of discipleship and leadership formation? What should be the critical steps in the development of any new "grass roots" TEE program?*

4. *Explain the role of the U.K.-based seminars in the formation of ORTA in the far east of Russia. Explain the role of SEAN.*

5. *What are the prospects for the future of this TEE program in the face of scarce funding and legal threats? Can such a program continue without paid staff and outside funding?*

LIST OF CONTRIBUTORS

Peter Bisset is the Director of the Institute for Theological Education by Extension in Nepal.

Judith Castañeda is the General Coordinator of the Centro Evangélico de Estudios Pastorales en Centroamérica, which is based in Guatemala, Guatemala.

José Duque is Professor of Missiology and former President of the Universidad Bíblica Latinoamericana, which is based at San José, Costa Rica. He is also Latin America Coordinator for Ecumenical Theological Education of the World Council of Churches.

Robert Freeman is Associate Provost for the Horner Center for Lifelong Learning at Fuller Theological Seminary, Pasadena, California, USA.

Roger Gaikwad is the Director of the Senate Center for Extension and Pastoral Theological Research of the Senate of Serampore College, which is the accrediting body for theological education throughout India and other South Asian countries. SCEPTRE is based at Kolkata (Calcutta), India.

Helena Hooper is the Coordinator of Theological Education by Extension programming for the Organization of African Instituted Churches and also for the Ghana Association of Theological Education by Extension.

Michael Huggins is Chairperson of the Open Russian Theological Academy and a member of The Executive Team of Matheteuo, which offers seminars and workshops and resources for Theological Education by Extension in various countries. He lives in England.

Kangwa Mabuluki is the Director of Theological Education by Extension in Zambia, which is based at Kitwe, and Secretary of the All Africa Theological Education by Extension Association.

John A. MacKenzie was for many years the Director of the Center for Theological Education by Extension in Terrace, British Colombia and Director of the Native Ministries Program at Vancouver School of Theology in coordination with the Anglican Church of Canada, the United Church of Canada, and the Native Ministries Consortium.

Tony Moodie is the Principal of The Theological Education by Extension College of Southern Africa, which is based in Johannesburg, South Africa.

Stephen Pickard was until recently the Director of St. Mark's National Theological Center and Head of the School of Theology of Charles Sturz University, Canberra, Australia.

Norberto Saracco is a pastor of the Church of God Association and the Director of La Facultad Internacional de Educación Teológica, based in Buenos Aires, Argentina.

Charles Van Engen lives in Southern California and teaches at the Institute for Intercultural Studies of Fuller Theological Seminary. He is the Dean of El Programa Doctoral Latinoamericano and the President of Latin American Christian Ministries, which undergirds PRODOLA.